# THE CASE AGAINST FREE SPEECH

P. E. MOSKOWITZ

# THE CASE AGAINST FREE SPEECH

## The First Amendment, Fascism, *and the* Future *of* Dissent

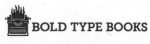

BOLD TYPE BOOKS

New York

Bold Type Books
116 East 16th Street, 8th Floor, New York, NY 10003
www.boldtypebooks.org
@BoldTypeBooks

Printed in the United States of America

First Edition: August 2019

Published by Bold Type Books, an imprint of Perseus Books, LLC, a subsidiary of Hachette Book Group, Inc. Bold Type Books is a copublishing venture of the Type Media Center and Perseus Books.

The Hachette Speakers Bureau provides a wide range of authors for speaking events. To find out more, go to www.hachettespeakersbureau.com or call (866) 376-6591.

The publisher is not responsible for websites (or their content) that are not owned by the publisher.

Print book interior design by Amy Quinn.

Library of Congress Control Number: 2019937311

ISBNs: 978-1-56858-864-3 (hardcover), 978-1-56858-866-7 (e-book)

LSC-C

10 9 8 7 6 5 4 3 2 1

*In memory of Heather Heyer*

# CONTENTS

# introduction

THIS BOOK IS NOT ANTI-FREE-SPEECH. IT IS ANTI-THE-CONCEPT-OF-free-speech. It's an important distinction. Everyone should have the right to say what they want. I will not argue otherwise. I am not an authoritarian.

In this book I will not argue that the United States should adopt laws banning racist speech like the ones that have proliferated throughout Europe, for example. I think those laws are often counterproductive and end up being used against leftists instead of racists. I won't argue that Nazi speech should be outlawed, as it is in Germany. I won't argue that the First Amendment should be reformed, nor more firmly upheld.

This book is not about whether the First Amendment is good or bad. This book is about why the First Amendment is nearly irrelevant, except in its power as a propaganda tool.

In the following chapters I will argue that free speech, as a concept, is meaningless; that it is a dialectical smokescreen more than an ideal to be upheld; that in a grossly unequal society, in which a few corporations control the means of media dissemination and a small group of the ultrawealthy bankroll entire political movements, there can be no meaningful definition of free speech. On paper, I am as free to speak as a billionaire, yet I do not have the power to change laws through political donations, to influence college curricula, or to quash entire movements for economic liberation. And still I hold more speech power than most: I am a published author, and my speech is sanctified by the gatekeepers of my publishing house. Therefore, the path to free speech, I will argue, has less to do with a law about speech, or many laws, than with ending racism and inequality.

Throughout US history, disparate groups have claimed to cherish free speech more than their enemies—unionists in the 1920s saw free speech as synonymous with striking and, ultimately, class revolution. Today, conservatives are the group to most often shroud their politics in free speech, arguing that any silencing or protesting of their speech runs counter to US values of freedom and liberty for all.

But as I hope to prove in this book, free speech has never really existed because freedom and liberty have never really existed for the vast majority of Americans. Instead, the US has systematically acted against those values, suppressing the opportunities, speech, movements, and actions of the masses, especially people of color and anticapitalists, in order to favor the free flow of capital to the owning class. This oppression and suppression have been constant since the founding of this country, and therefore free speech is a hollow signifier—pointing to a past that never existed.

The funny thing about free speech is that it has been used to fight for and against these liberties: both as a guise for the wealthy and powerful to oppress the poor, like the Koch brothers and their supporters using free speech to push through antidemocratic legislation and rip apart campaign finance laws, and as a rhetorical tool for the working class to further their cause, as happened in the early 1900s when leftists argued that free speech includes the freedom to riot and the ACLU argued that it was the only way to prevent a violent revolution. I don't argue that one definition of free speech is more legitimate than the other, but that they are all relatively empty signifiers, hiding more tangible structures of power and ideas underneath them.

So why write a book on free speech if I think the term is essentially meaningless? Because the concept holds so much weight in our country.

We argue endlessly about whether it is being trampled on, whether college students hate it, whether the government is adequately upholding it. But we rarely ask what free speech *is* or how we got to the free speech crisis we supposedly face today. When you scratch the surface of conversations over free speech, you find more difficult issues underneath. It is much easier to talk about the ability of conservatives to speak on college campuses than about the systemic racism, sexism, and transphobia college students experience—and those are the things that the students who protest campus visits by right-wing conservatives are fighting against. It's easier to fantasize about a country that values free speech than to grapple with the fact that we place so much emphasis on free speech while jailing dissidents and allowing tens of millions to live in poverty. What is free speech to someone who works sixty hours a week and has no time, nor a platform, to use their supposed right?

There is relatively little literature and philosophy on free speech, despite the fact that it has been in constant contention since the founding of this country. Even the legal history of the First Amendment is sparse for something so foundational to the values of this country. A few have seriously grappled with ideas of what free speech does and does not mean, most notably literary theorist Stanley Fish, who has argued that the term does not mean much at all. Leftists like Noam Chomsky have written about free speech tangentially in their explorations of media as a propaganda tool. Most history books on speech are written as hagiographies, unquestioning of the intent of the Founding Fathers and their morals (with a few notable exceptions, such as Laura Weinrib's *The Taming of Free Speech*). I don't intend to fill the yawning gap of research, history, and philosophy. This is not a definitive account of free speech, but a necessary intervention, prodding us to be more critical of the term, and maybe along with it many of the other lofty concepts we hold near and dear (democracy, freedom, etc.).

I focus on the United States in this book for two reasons. First, I live here; it is the country I am most experientially familiar with, and therefore the country I feel most comfortable writing about. Second, it is only in the US that the concept of free speech holds so much power over daily discourse. We are taught from a very early age that the First Amendment is one of the most important things that separates us from most other countries, that it not only separates us but makes us better, morally superior, and more high-minded than every other nation on earth (despite our high levels of poverty, infant mortality, and air pollution). It's important that we poke some holes in that theory.

This book primarily deals with freedom of speech and freedom of assembly, because that's where I see the most contentious fights happening. Religious freedom and freedom of the press are touched on, but I believe the lessons learned from our current speech and protest debates can apply equally to them.

I think if we start to interrogate the meaning of free speech, we will get to some messier questions about our country, and that's a large part of why I wanted to write this book: to encourage people to pick apart the rhetoric we encounter daily, go beyond headlines and opinion pieces, and ask of free speech the same questions we ask of other political tools—who benefits from them, and who doesn't?

This book is divided into two sections. The first deals with our current discourse surrounding free speech and how we arrived at it. Chapter One is about my experience during the 2017 "Unite the Right" rally in Charlottesville, Virginia, and how free speech became central to the fight between far-right and leftist groups in this country. Critical to legal and philosophical arguments about free speech is defining the line that separates speech from (illegal) action. Charlottesville suggests there's no real way to define that line. I then delve into the history of free speech in Chapter Two, exploring how we developed our current conceptualization of free speech and asking whether free speech ever really existed in this country. Chapters Three and Four are about college campus fights. Although free speech fights extend well beyond college campuses, the majority of our current free speech discourse has been centered on college protests. In those chapters, you'll meet some of the figures central to those fights, and hopefully gain perspective about what these fights are really about. Chapter Five explores alternative conceptualizations of free speech in this country, including those developed at points in our history when there were movements to limit it and movements to turn it into a rallying cry for leftist causes.

The second section imagines where free speech, and especially political dissent, is headed in this country. Chapter Six returns to the campus, this time to reveal that powerful outside forces like billionaire Republicans are behind the instigators of campus free speech battles. Chapters Seven and Eight delve into the repression of protest in this country, both current and past, elucidating how the powerful have tried repeatedly to suppress speech when it threatens US capitalism. And the final chapter considers how corporate control, especially on the internet, threatens our collective ability to change the world, specifically by limiting our speech.

I hope this book is an invitation to conversation. I write about topics that are presented in the media and our mainstream discourse as clear-cut but that, I suspect, are much more complex than they appear. My previous book, on gentrification, came from the same desire: to unravel the rhetoric we had been taught and identify the systems, power players, and solutions to a massive problem. I view this book similarly: I wanted to move beyond headlines and get a real understanding of what free speech means in this country. In the process, I learned more than I could have imagined, not only about speech but about race, class, and the history of oppression in the United States.

This is not an optimistic book, but hopefully it is a fun one (at least I had some fun writing it). I did not want to be prescriptive, but exploratory. Our understanding of free speech has been so limited, and I don't think my book alone can solve that. This book is also not unbiased—I am an anticapitalist, and my views on free speech emanate from a materialist understanding of the world. I believe in what some have called "positive liberty," the idea that people are free only when their material conditions are equal (as opposed to "negative liberty," in which freedom is defined as a lack of formal obstacles to achieving one's goals).[1]

I believe the more we all interrogate what we have been taught as fact—that we have free speech, that we live in a democracy, that the US is some kind of arbiter of freedom—the more truth we will unveil about who controls our politics and why our society remains so unequal. If we can get beyond rhetoric to address those scarier questions, we can get closer to true equality in this country. This book is one small step in that interrogation. I hope you find it a worthy one.

◇◇◇ PART 1 ◇◇◇

# WHERE WE ARE NOW

## chapter one

# THE LINE

THE VIOLENCE OF AUGUST 12, 2017, IN CHARLOTTESVILLE, VIRGINIA, which we've come to call just Charlottesville—the white nationalist rally that ended with leftist organizer Heather Heyer dead, run over by James Alex Fields Jr. in his gray Dodge Challenger, and dozens injured—allowed us to forget what the rally was originally about: free speech. That's how members of the alt-right and neo-Nazi groups that had organized the march billed it. In many of the promotional materials before the event, the rally was referred to as the "Unite the Right Free Speech March," or a "free speech rally." And the now-infamous rally was actually the third in a series staged by different white nationalist groups, though the first two brought out fewer people and drew less media attention. Three months earlier about one hundred opponents of a plan to remove a statue of Robert E. Lee from a public park at the center of Charlottesville gathered at the statue to protest. Then, in July, about fifty members of the Ku Klux Klan held another rally at the statue. Scuffles between them and approximately 1,000 counterprotesters led to two dozen arrests.[1] At each rally the vast majority of protesters were from far-right and blatantly white supremacist groups, though until August 12 most insisted they had come to protect free speech. If the government could remove a statue of Robert E. Lee, they argued, what else could it do?

"In response to the Alt-Right's peaceful demonstration in support of the Lee Monument on May 13th, the City of Charlottesville and roving mobs of antifa have cracked down on the First Amendment rights of conservatives and right wing activists," one flyer for the August 12 rally read, playing up the idea that their free speech was being impinged.[2] "They have threatened our families, harassed our employers and tried to drive us from public spaces with threats of intimidation. We are not afraid. You will not divide us."

By the time I arrived in Charlottesville, at around 8:30 a.m. on August 12, the organizers seemed to have dropped all pretense that they cared about free speech. They were ready for battle. There were no free speech flyers to be found. The messaging had switched from protecting free speech and not erasing US history to blatant racism and xenophobia. Hundreds of neo-Nazis carrying shields, militiamen armed with semi-automatic rifles, and neatly dressed members of more "respectable" far-right groups like the Proud Boys stood ready to fight. And thousands of counterprotesters were there either to drown them out or run them out of town. By the end of the rally, after I and hundreds of others ran from that gray Dodge Challenger, after I saw Heather Heyer's lifeless body being lifted into an ambulance and sat in shock, smoking a cigarette with a friend on a curb as police in armored vehicles rushed past us, I thought, How could we have been so naïve? The violence, in retrospect, seemed inevitable. How could it not end like this?

Charlottesville, it turned out, was a real-time exercise in free speech politics. For decades, we as a nation have debated the merits of allowing even the most heinous of opinions to be voiced freely. This has been the extent of our free speech debate—whether Nazis, and whoever else the general public finds detestable at the time, should be able to say what they want, without consequence. But the question of whether a neo-Nazi in Charlottesville should be able to chant, "Jews will not replace us" and tell black people that they do not belong in this country is superficial. It ignores everything that got us to that point. Why was a Nazi there in the first place? Why does he hate Jews and black people so much? Why are the police and courts willing to protect him? Those, I learned in the course of reporting this book, are more important questions that are much harder to answer. What got us to Charlottesville is the entire history of racism and organized right-wing political terrorism in this country. It is what, over the course of hundreds of years, we have decided is acceptable or unacceptable as speech, or protest, or art. What we deem worthy of protection, and what we are willing to override to protect other rights.

The history of free speech in this country can also be thought of as a history of how we define action, and particularly how we define violence. Where we put those lines—between speech and acceptable action, acceptable action and violence—depends completely on political context. Until Charlottesville (and perhaps afterward too), many understood that the line falls at something like: anything up until actual physical bodily harm is not violence but protected speech, and anything after that is. But that line is too uncomplicated because it ignores power and defines violence too narrowly. Something I write on a piece of paper does not become law, though the same action performed by a lawmaker can affect the lives of millions—a bill stripping health care from millions, for example, is an example of violence that we currently consider acceptable in our democracy. When you add a racial, gender, and economic analysis to that line, you get a different conceptualization of free speech, suggesting not that speech is bad, but that the line is defined unevenly.

The ability to speak without consequence is significantly more limited for someone living in poverty and at risk of police brutality than for someone who can broadcast their speech on television and radio, or from a podium on college campuses. What we've seen in the past few years is leftists trying to push the line. If a conservative with a large media platform—say, Milo Yiannopoulos in his heyday—is speaking at a college campus, shutting him down is not a violation of free speech in many students' view but an evening of the playing field, allowing those with much less power than Yiannopoulos (trans students and students of color, for example), an equal say. The same was true in Charlottesville: for leftists there, limiting the speech of Nazis was not understood as silencing them because historically racists have had a much larger platform to speak from than oppressed peoples have.

For free speech absolutists, this argument will fall flat because they believe free speech should be completely unrestrained no matter what. But what we rarely acknowledge is that in every case concerning free speech, we are already starting from a severely restricted baseline. There are countless legal limits on free speech that we rarely debate.

For example, we ask, "Should a Nazi be able to speak?" But we rarely question *where* a Nazi should be able to speak because we've already concluded that free speech rights normally do not exist on someone's private property (if a Nazi broke into my house to lecture me, he would not only *not* have First Amendment rights; in many states, I could legally kill him). We have decided that many actions are indeed speech, even though they are blatantly not *just* speech: writing, protest, and art, for example, all involve actions that go far beyond speaking, and are generally allowed. But we've decided that other actions, even those involving the same processes, go beyond speech: writing that advocates killing the president, or a protest that blocks the flow of vital emergency services, for example. You cannot harm someone without their permission for the sake of art. The First Amendment already has many inborn limits.

Those are perhaps some obvious limits, but they prove that what we think of as free speech is already free-*ish* speech. It's free speech that we have decided does not trump other things we think are more important (the right to private property, or the right not to be murdered). We take these limitations with apparent ease—they do not light up the opinion columns of many newspapers.

When we debate free speech, we are not debating whether we like free speech, because we've never really had free speech. We're debating where the line is, and who gets to hold the line in place or move it. We've settled, for now, on some limits to free speech, but we haven't yet decided that, for example, the right to walk down the street without being yelled at by a Nazi is as important as the right to private property. That line is in constant flux. Not only flux; it's constantly embattled: millions of dollars get spent defining that line each year by super PACs and other political groups and by nonprofits like the ACLU. Millions more get spent by corporations to keep the definition of free speech from encroaching on intellectual property (if your free speech meant you could set up a company called Google, that would be a problem for Google). Countless hours and huge sums of money go into defining and protecting the currently accepted lines of free speech.

With fewer column inches dedicated to it than to the hemming and hawing over one rally at a college campus, the Supreme Court decided one of the largest free speech fights of the last few decades in 2018, when it ruled that public sector unions couldn't force those who didn't want to join the union to pay fees the union uses to bargain for employees' contracts. *Janus v. AFSCME* was a huge blow to unions, which will now have to convince each and every member to pay "agency fees" instead of collecting them automatically. And the case was decided on free speech grounds. Justice Samuel Alito said in his opinion that "fundamental free speech rights are at stake," and that no interest of unions outweighs "the perpetuation of the free speech violations."[3] In other words, being compelled to pay fees by a union is the same thing as forced speech. But forty years earlier, in *Abood v. Detroit Board of Education*, the Supreme Court had *unanimously* decided the opposite when a public employee came to the court with the same argument.[4] It would be unfathomable to imagine the Court deciding something similar in regards to private property ("No interest of homeownership outweighs the right of someone to come into your house and yell at you"), yet in four decades the Court, reflecting our politics and culture, had shifted so vastly that free speech now outweighed the financial security of workers. And that did not happen naturally or inevitably, but because conservative billionaires had poured large sums of money into an anti-union fight to define free speech in such a way.

We've been arguing about free speech, but we haven't been minding the line, or paying attention to who is influencing it. *Janus* was just a particularly obvious example of what *all* free speech fights are about: who has the power, the money, the influence to control that line, and who does not.

◇◇◇

Charlottesville too was an exercise in line-pushing. Though they were largely represented by the media as a group of fringe right-wingers, a case of bad apples in an otherwise relatively placid America, the alt-right, a loosely-affiliated group of white nationalists who attempt to present themselves as more mainstream and less violent than their predecessors, and their more openly white nationalist counterparts were part of a long history of the white supremacist right being protected by the US government for what they believe. For all of US history, free speech has been defined to favor white people. People have, of course, always pushed back against this, as they did when they advocated taking down Confederate monuments across the country. Charlottesville was the alt-right trying to push back, hold the line at its racist past and present.

On the drive down to Charlottesville from Philadelphia, where I live, a friend who has lived outside the US for most of his life said the difference between this country and many others is that after a war elsewhere, there's often something like South Africa's Truth and Reconciliation Commission. People are tried in court, and the government makes an official vow not to repeat its crimes. After World War II, Germany banned not only Nazi gatherings, but all forms of Nazi propaganda, the swastika, and the "incitement of hatred" against any group of people—which carries up to a five-year prison sentence.[5]

That never happened in the United States. There was only one war crimes trial after the Civil War.[6] There were no reparations (I remember as a kid the checks my grandma, a Holocaust survivor, would get in the mail from Germany. That never happened here for African Americans). Confederate flags are still legal; they still fly, even outside government buildings. My friends and I passed a few of them, waving in people's yards, as we drove into Virginia.

The Civil War, my friend in the car said, had never really ended. We had never decided, as a country, what was officially not okay—where the line was drawn. But until the chaos of 2017, to many, including me, the line seemed to be headed in the right direction. Yes, there were people arguing for white supremacy back in 2016, too. People of color were being killed, arrested, and oppressed in the same ways they are today. But now Donald Trump was president and the alt-right, the loosely affiliated groups of white nationalists who are united by their love of memes and racism, had a direct line to the White House in the form of Steve Bannon.[7] They had become emboldened, angrier, and more militant.

The rally seemed to make it clear that the alt-right was not just a conservative meme factory, but an armed and dangerous nationalist group with a specific (though usually unstated) definition of free speech that allowed for white supremacy and framed any opposition to it as anti-free-speech. More than that, they knew they had power on their side—not only grassroots power, but the power to define themselves in favorable terms, as inherently American as the First Amendment. Ralliers knew that if they went to Charlottesville they would be protected by police, protected by courts (unless they committed violence), and rhetorically protected by the mainstream media. They had every reason to believe this because by and large they have been protected: The Supreme Court has repeatedly upheld the right of white supremacists to rally, the federal government has repeatedly refused to classify violent white supremacists as terrorists (while applying the word, with its political and policing ramifications, to large swaths of US Muslims), and the US media in the 2010s seemed as ready as ever to defend their actions.[8] The closest precedent to Charlottesville was a planned Nazi rally in the Chicago suburb of Skokie in the late 1970s, which drew thousands of protesters. If anything, the political and media support system for Nazis and white supremacists has only grown since then. The Skokie march was declared legal by state courts, but the media largely lambasted the idea, and many politicians did everything in their power to stop the march from happening (Skokie was majority-Jewish at the time, and many residents were Holocaust survivors). Amid fierce public opposition, the march never happened in Skokie.

Leftists have seen this line shift over the last few decades and have decided to act with their own force. Knowing that the courts, cops, and media would not necessarily protect them, they've increasingly organized into their own groups to push that line back, or at least hold it in place against the Nazis. Even those committed to nonviolence accepted that their side had to have an adequate response. Cornel West told the *Washington Post* after the Charlottesville rally that "the police didn't do anything" to protect the counterprotesters. "If it hadn't been for the antifascists protecting us from the neo-fascists," he said, "we would have been crushed like cockroaches."[9]

Weeks before the event, antiracist organizers in Charlottesville had been gearing up, meeting with different factions of the left, and gathering intel on their adversaries. I was told by activists on the ground that a team of volunteers in the city was dedicated to infiltrating online alt-right groups and putting faces to names so they'd know whom to look out for at the rally. One organizer said they'd assembled a dossier more comprehensive than the cops' file.

The activists saw self-defense—gearing up in black masks and baseball bats—as a last resort. For months they'd tried to get cops and city officials to prevent the white nationalist gathering from taking place, sending them screenshots of Facebook posts and information about known violent fascists who planned to come to town. But they believed from past experience that the state would protect the white nationalists' right to free expression—police had worked hand in hand with white supremacists in 2016 in California, hired an officer with a white supremacist background in Oklahoma, and regularly protected white supremacists at rallies before Charlottesville. In a leaked chat from a white supremacist message board, several white nationalists voiced their belief that the police were on their side. Only after Charlottesville activists' requests and warnings were ignored by authorities did they decide they'd have to take things into their own hands.[10]

"We knew there were really specific plans for violence," one organizer told me. "We engaged with the police, we engaged with the state, and we got no response. What are you supposed to do?" The organizer had spent the last few weeks in the lead-up to the rally coordinating with other activists and gathering social media posts from known white nationalists who promised to "crush," "stomp," and "get rid of" antifa members, Black Lives Matter supporters, and others. There had been several memes before Charlottesville where members of the alt-right joked, or sometimes promised, to run over any protesters who got in their way. "All Lives Splatter," one meme read, with a drawing of a Jeep plowing into stick figures. (There's even an entire Tumblr dedicated to documenting how many memes and social media posts exist in which right-wingers fantasize about running over protesters). During James Alex Fields's trial, it was revealed that he shared some of these memes before enacting them in real life.[11]

On the day of the march, down another street in another small park, groups gathered and prepped, putting on their face masks and helmets, discussing strategy. Some carried batons. A leftist group called Redneck Revolt, a kind of armed version of what the media has termed "antifa," showed up with rifles.

Adding to the tension was the fact that the city had tried to move the rally from its original location, Emancipation Park—formerly Lee Park, where the statue of Robert E. Lee stood—to a larger park on the edge of the city, less than a week before the rally was scheduled to begin. The city cited safety concerns. But on Thursday evening, the ACLU of Virginia and the Rutherford Institute, a local civil liberties group, took the city to court, representing march leader and white nationalist Jason Kessler. The groups argued that because the city had allowed protests in Lee Park before Charlottesville, to limit them now would be a form of prior restraint against speech.

"The First Amendment guarantees political speech, including protest, the highest level of protection—and the right to speak out is the most robust in traditional public fora, including public parks and streets," the lawsuit said.[12] "Since the country's founding, people have taken to the parks, streets, and sidewalks to make their voices heard on matters of public concern."

The court agreed. The rally was moved back to Lee Park.

"I'm representing the First Amendment, the principles of constitutional governance," Claire Gastañaga, the executive director of the ACLU of Virginia, told me before the rally. After Charlottesville, the ACLU of Virginia and the national ACLU defended their representation of Kessler, arguing that failing to represent him would contribute to pushing hatred out of the sights of Americans but not actually eradicating it, and thus making it harder to fight.[13] The ACLU of Virginia did not return my follow-up requests for an interview after the rally.

A few days later, the ACLU announced it would no longer defend groups of protesters who carried guns. No mention was made of the fact that the violence that day had been carried out with a car, tear gas, and fists, not guns (though guns were present).[14]

And so, with legal backing secured, the rally took place in a park the size of a square block, surrounded by quaint residential streets and police barricades. Even though it was scheduled to start at noon, by 8 a.m. the white supremacists were arriving, eventually numbering in the hundreds, and counterprotesters had filled the streets, a line of riot police separating the two groups.

Down the block in another small park, a coalition of liberal and church groups had set up a prayer circle, a water distribution tent, and an eyewash station. There, Wes Bellamy, vice-mayor of Charlottesville, told a crowd of about 200 counterprotesters that this was Charlottesville's chance to "show the world that this is our community, our city."

"Nobody is running us off," he said. "Nobody is making us afraid. This is a celebration, not a funeral."

Back at Emancipation Park, two men with a group called Alt-Right Minnesota told me the rally was just about the statue of Robert E. Lee, and that they were not here for violence.

"It's part of white history, even though a lot of people think it's a sad part of history," said John, a man in his early twenties wearing the day's agreed-upon uniform of a white button-down and khakis. "We're not anti-anyone. We're just pro-us. But if anyone is anti-us, then we have a problem."

After that, approximately one hundred white nationalists, most from Vanguard America, a prominent white nationalist group that splintered after Charlottesville, marched into the park. They chanted, "Blood and soil! Blood and soil!"—a reference cribbed from German Nazis and used heavily during the rise of Hitler, that speaks to the belief that those born to families on a specific plot of land (e.g., the United States) have an inherent right to that land.[15]

One member gave a pep talk to those assembled. "If you don't racialize, if you don't tribalize, you will go extinct," he said. "We'll be a minority soon, and do you think we'll get a reservation? Do you think we'll get affirmative action? If we don't adopt an ethnocentric mindset, we're finished."

The group then kicked out press and people of color from the park—even those who identified with the alt-right. ("We have nothing against them, but this is a white identity rally," one leader said.) They closed the entrance with a barricade. A coordinated group of armed militiamen with semi-automatic weapons formed a line in front of the park's entrance, helping to block anyone who tried to get through. Progressive clergy, including Cornel West, formed a line in front of them and began reciting personal prayers, one by one.

"Forgive us for the sin of white supremacy," one said. The rest of her prayer was drowned out by chants of "White Sharia now!" emanating from the park and the sound of drums down the street, signaling the arrival of the antifascists, who came in a line, headed by a banner with "FUCK FASCISTS" spelled out in black duct tape.

Off to the side of the demonstrations, an alt-right YouTuber who goes by the name Johnny Cash Flow told me that the rally was going well. "There is no such thing as hate speech," he said. "They have a right to protest and say they are Nazis. They're not forcing violence. If a guy was told by someone to punch a journalist, it would still be up to the guy to act on that. There's still agency."

Then the tear gas and pepper spray started. Antifa groups had some, the white supremacists had more, and so the streets surrounding Emancipation Park slowly emptied as more and more people came into contact with the gas and spray. Volunteer medics down the block poured milk into dozens of protesters' eyes. This continued for two hours—a few people were punched, a few others were badly beaten, and the cops stood by, down the block, for all of it. Eventually, only those most willing to risk their safety were left in front of Emancipation Park.

Nic Smith, a twenty-one-year-old Waffle House waiter from Roanoke, Virginia, spilled his coffee on a white supremacist protester, got punched, and punched the protester back, knocking him to the ground. He felt there was no point in arguing over free speech when there were Nazis at his door.

"They want genocide," he said. "Is there a passive way to do that?"

I asked him if he had punched white supremacists before, and he said he couldn't comment on that, but his line of thinking was one I heard from most antifascists I interviewed that day: free speech didn't mean anything when the people they were battling were advocating genocide, and when the entire apparatus of the state seemed willing to take their side.

A few minutes before the scheduled start time of the rally, riot police showed up. And then, at noon—the official start time—the city declared the gathering an unlawful assembly (though what made it a lawful assembly before and an unlawful one after the police declaration was never clarified). People dispersed. Some white supremacists went back to a larger park they'd used as a staging ground earlier that day; others went home. Counterprotesters went back to the two smaller parks to strategize, drink water, and eat orange slices. A few took a brief moment to lazily swing on the park's swing set.

Half an hour later, after hearing that a rogue group of white supremacists had attacked a man named Dre Harris a few blocks away, groups of counterprotesters left the parks and converged on Charlottesville's streets, passing cars with horns honking in support, disinterested police, and a white family sitting on a porch eating brunch.

As the counterprotesters headed toward where Harris's attackers were last seen, they were met with another stream of hundreds of counterprotesters coming from another section of the city. Cheers erupted from the entire crowd as more and more took over the streets.

And then, while turning up a small side street downtown, a silver Dodge Challenger sped up and rammed into a crowd of counterprotesters, causing a tidal wave of bodies to fall back down the street. People ran. The driver, later identified as twenty-year-old James Alex Fields Jr., then backed up his car and sped into the crowd again. The uninjured protesters, including my friends and me, dispersed rapidly. Volunteer medics stayed behind, clearing the way for ambulances. A block away, a small contingent of protesters held a black antifa banner above the bodies of the wounded to protect them from the sun. Paramedics performed CPR on Heather Heyer, who would later die of her injuries, and loaded her into an ambulance.

The sense of calm and celebration quickly transformed into terror. The scene was chaotic, but it was clear almost immediately that the act was deliberate. In retrospect, it seemed obvious that something like it could happen. The rally, after all, was in support of a white America, an America based on genocide, a rally organized by people carrying semi-autos and shields, who said they'd resort to violence if necessary.

I know how harmful speech can be, because I've experienced its worst effects viscerally. I wrote a large part of this book while struggling with post-traumatic stress disorder. After a period of calm, which I've now come to realize was in fact numbed shock, I woke up about a month after Charlottesville shaking. My eyes and legs twitched. I couldn't keep things in focus. I was convinced that my brain was melting, which I believed could be the only explanation for the sudden onset of a terror so present that it literally blurred my eyesight.

I couldn't eat. I could barely speak. That little feeling of, "Oh, shit, did I leave the stove on?" (or, as described by journalist Andrew Solomon in his book *The Noonday Demon: An Atlas of Depression*, that feeling when you trip and think, "Oh, no, am I about to fall?") became an every-second-of-the-day thing. Panic exploded within me, infected my entire body, unearthing traumas I thought I had long ago processed and forgotten. I took several months off of full-time writing and reporting work. I could barely leave my house most days—the only thing that would get me out was walking my dog or seeing a trusted friend.

The car that had almost killed me and my friends, and had killed Heather Heyer, was all of a sudden a constant presence, there when I closed my eyes, around every corner. Excitement became anger and anxiety.

When you're always fearful, calmness can become depression—a nice night at home alone became a shadow-filled solitude I needed to escape from but had no clue how to. I thought constantly about how my grandparents could have survived the Holocaust and at least pretended to be normal once they'd arrived in America. Did they feel shadows lurking everywhere too? Did they think every event had the potential to turn deadly?

With therapy and drugs and kickboxing and acupuncture and friends and family, I slowly got better. Though as I write this, one-and-a-half years later, I'm not quite there yet. I still have so much anger. I can barely talk about Charlottesville. I remember stumbling onto a white nationalist forum on an unrelated reporting assignment a few months after Charlottesville and seeing people posting images of Heyer's body, and commenting on her size, speculating that she had a heart attack, not that she was murdered, as if she was somehow responsible for James Alex Fields's decision to ram his car into her. It made me want to vomit. It made me feel like a pit of tar had been placed at the bottom of my stomach. That feeling has faded, but it has never really left me.

Free speech, which I had decided to write about before Charlottesville, had become something tangible to me through Charlottesville. It was not a subject to be abstractly debated. It had life-and-death consequences. I doubled down on my conviction that people like the white supremacists I saw in Charlottesville needed to be dealt with, and quick, and that we needed to change the way we think of free speech—from the streets to the offices of the ACLU to the halls of the White House—or else the country would be in further trouble.

I kept asking myself: How was everything leading up to James Alex Fields's decision to kill Heather Heyer legal, protected, even encouraged as an expression of free speech—but the murder itself was somehow different? Where was that damn line? It seemed impossible to me to separate the two. Wasn't it clear that James Alex Fields would not have murdered Heather Heyer if white nationalist rhetoric was not allowed to grow unchecked on the internet? Wasn't it clear that he wouldn't have had the opportunity to be so close to us, surrounded by counterprotesters, as cops stood idly by, protecting their First Amendment right to assembly, if the

ACLU of Virginia had not ensured that the white nationalists had a safe and legal space to rally at the center of the city, protected by those cops? If chanting "Jews will not replace us" would land you in jail, as it would in France and Germany, for example, there would have been no opportunity for someone like Fields to strike.

The only *illegal* actions to take place in Charlottesville were the murder of Heather Heyer and the sporadic beatings doled out by the white nationalists and counterprotesters throughout the day. Everything else—the white nationalist chants encouraging the murder of Jews, Mexicans, and black people; the alt-right internet forums whose members encouraged one another to shoot leftists and run them over with their cars prior to August 12; the fact that many of the right-wing protesters were armed with semi-automatic weapons—that was all sanctioned. It wasn't only legal, it was grounds for police protection.

But we as a country questioned none of this. Charlottesville was unfortunate, we decided, but it couldn't be solvable. Policy analyst Sean McElwee found that Jonathan Chait, a *New York* magazine columnist and one of the most prominent writers on free speech, had dedicated more than 7,000 words of his column space to lambasting political correctness, mostly on college campuses, and zero words to the threat of white nationalist organizing.[16] The *New York Times* op-ed page regularly blasted out a different take from conservative writers Bari Weiss, Bret Stephens, and David Brooks on the dangers of college students shutting down campus-sponsored talks, or even the threat of making fun of conservative writers on Twitter. Though several also wrote about Charlottesville, based on the volume and fervor of their work on both subjects, it's clear they saw where the bigger threat lay: college students.

In a March 2018 column, Weiss called the protests at universities over right-wing speakers, and the disparaging tweets of leftists, a "concerted attempt to significantly redraw the bounds of acceptable thought and speech."[17]

The consensus seemed to be that Charlottesville was bad, but to do anything about it would be worse—it would threaten the liberties of everyone. But worse still would be allowing anyone else—leftists, campus organizers—the same power we'd given the alt-right to dictate the terms of the free speech debate. So, the overarching discourse in America in 2017 went, we must reluctantly support the Nazis and make sure they're allowed to speak anywhere they please, and lambaste the people who try to stop them, or else we risk silencing everyone.

But the solution after Charlottesville was a lot less clear to me. Getting the state involved in criminalizing speech, even Nazi speech, seemed dangerous—who's to say the state wouldn't use that power to prosecute anyone critical of the government? Lawmakers in Georgia, for example, have used a law meant to prevent the Ku Klux Klan from donning hoods to arrest masked leftist protesters.[18] And police have beaten up and jailed my leftist friends for protesting. How would you effectively monitor the internet for people like James Alex Fields and his encouragers without vastly increasing the surveillance state? How would you stop Nazis from protesting and deny them permits without worrying about the ability of governments to deny permits to anyone, especially people of color, fighting for radical change, whom history suggests governments will suppress in whatever way they can?

We have a lot of line-defining work to do. For something that is supposedly so deeply ingrained in our country's history (it's the First Amendment! Not Second or Third!), we have a remarkably terrible and vague definition of what free speech actually is, how it can be used, and why it is always in contention. The only other amendment to cause so much controversy is the Second, and yet we have debates about that one all the time. We have people trying to influence its meaning with heaps of money (the National Rifle Association, for example). We have activist groups opposed to it. The First Amendment, though it remains as integral to American values as the Second, gets a lot less scrutiny.

And yet it was clear as day after Charlottesville that the First Amendment, like the Second, is neither neutral nor without consequence. The First Amendment, like any law, picks winners and losers, and those in power get the deck stacked in their favor.

Charlottesville did not happen in a vacuum. Like the *Janus* court case, it was the culmination of several decades of work to ensure that certain people have the right to speak while others do not. Whether you come down on the side of the ACLU and believe that a platform for Nazis needs to be protected in order to ensure equality for all, or on the side of activists like those who participate in antifa, who believe that violent white nationalist rhetoric must be stopped at all costs, or somewhere in between, it's important to understand how we got here.

As the months wore on, the right and its supporters got back to couching their actions within the framework of free speech. Alt-right provocateur Milo Yiannopoulos and several other far-right leaders garnered sympathy from the liberal media as they were shut down on college campus after college campus. A report by media watchdog Fairness and Accuracy in Reporting (FAIR) found that in the month after Charlottesville, the *New York Times*, *USA Today*, the *Los Angeles Times*, and several other mainstream papers ran as many op-eds condemning antifascist organizers as they did op-eds condemning Nazis or asking politicians to condemn them.[19]

Charlottesville, it turns out, had not changed much. It had not redrawn the lines of politics; it had solidified them. There were those—including fascists, conservatives, and many liberals—who were going to support our current definition of free speech at all costs, and those—leftists and some liberals—who were going to try to expose that line and push it in a different direction.

In October 2017, two months after the white nationalist rally, the city of Charlottesville, along with local business groups, filed suit against the armed militia groups that had come to Charlottesville in an attempt to prevent them from ever returning. The lawsuit mostly focused on white supremacist groups, but it also named two leftist armed groups that were present—Redneck Revolt and the Socialist Rifle Association.[20] Many on the left, and even mainstream progressive groups like the National Lawyers Guild, came out against the lawsuit.[21]

"We're not opposed to free speech, we're opposed to violence, we're opposed to genocide," Emily Gorcenski, a prominent Charlottesville-based activist, told me. "This lawsuit runs a risk of making it impossible for community groups to defend their community from violence."

What else can we do? I asked Gorcenski. Where's the line between suing these groups and preventing them from rallying in the center of the city in the first place?

"I don't think we lose anything by restricting speech advocating hate or genocide," Gorcenski said. "We have already as a society and a culture litigated whether genocide is good, and we've decided it's not. So I don't think calls to genocide should be protected speech." She pointed to laws already on the books in many other countries criminalizing hate speech and speech advocating for genocide.

But she doesn't think criminalizing speech is a good idea—that could lead to more people, especially leftists, whom the government already targets, in prison. "I believe there should be limits to what the government will protect," she said. "We don't need to put more people in jail. But there should be no guaranteed police for something like a pro-genocide rally. If you wanna go say some Nazi shit in a park, go ahead, but there will be no police protection. There will be consequences."

In the dozens upon dozens of interviews I compiled for this book, I found that, contrary to media portrayals, leftists, college students protesting right-wing speakers, and others with less traditional views on American free speech have grappled with the nuances and possible fallout of silencing the most depraved among us. They have not come up with a definitive answer, but it's a question that must be taken seriously. How do we actually get to this place where free speech isn't just another word for the protection of white supremacists?

Back home in Philadelphia, I asked a young antifascist activist what she thought of Charlottesville, and what it foretold for the country. She warned that people would try to get away with violence again and again under the premise of free speech.

"We have to analyze how people are trying to manipulate us with certain language," she said. "'Free speech' is like 'terrorist'—who doesn't hate terrorism? Who doesn't love free speech?"

In other words, the constant focus on it as a term makes us all feel like we're fighting for a universal good, but it might obfuscate some harder truths. Charlottesville was proof: free speech is not just about speech, but about the history of white supremacy in our country, the politics of inequality and racism, and our failure to reckon with, and settle, our violent past and present.

chapter two

# ARE WE ALL SNOWFLAKES?

"THE DEFENSE OF FREE SPEECH HAS ALWAYS BEEN A BEDROCK BIPARTI-san principle," begins a 2018 *Boston Globe* article, excoriating liberals for siding with college students in campus fights over race, safe spaces, and trigger warnings.[1]

In our current free speech war, especially when we discuss free speech on private college campuses, we tend to lose sight of something important: we're not actually talking about violations of the First Amendment. Of course the First Amendment only applies to the *government's* ability (or lack thereof) to interfere with your speech. It has nothing to say about college curriculums or the merits of students interrupting conservative speakers. By and large, we are not debating the legality of the First Amendment, but the morality of it.

Sometimes, the free speech prognosticators admit this. "The government is not preventing anyone from speaking," Andrew Sullivan, a *New York* magazine columnist, wrote. Nonetheless he and others point to a battle over our country's founding ideals. "It is about the spirit of the First

Amendment," Sullivan argued, adding that campus politics and "politically correct" culture were threatening to erase every American's individual identity.

The First Amendment: It is invoked in nearly all our debates over free speech, it is the moral compass so many point to, and yet it has little to no bearing on the vast majority of free speech controversies. Still, our understanding of it—flawed as it is—remains the hidden influencer behind these fights, despite the fact that the First Amendment has rarely been enforced to protect speech, and the fact that our current conceptualization of free speech rights largely dates back not to the founding of this country but to a series of court cases that are barely fifty years old. In some ways it makes sense: free speech sounds like a lofty concept to uphold—who could really disagree with it? But its continued influence in nongovernmental matters also points to a conservative plot to frame everything that encroaches on conservatism in terms of free speech.

Without the First Amendment, we would likely have fewer people arguing that right-wing provocateurs or Nazis in Charlottesville have an inherent right to have their voices heard. We scream, "Freedom of speech!" at each other on college campuses and in the op-ed sections of our newspapers because most Americans believe that we have a right to say what we like, when we like, and where we like. And though this right is rarely interrogated, if you were to ask people why they think they have that right, the vast majority would likely say, "Because of the First Amendment."

The First Amendment holds as much rhetorical sway, if not more, than the Second. The Second is, after all, routinely debated. Entire political careers are made over support of the Second Amendment. And sometimes politicians even come out against the current understanding of it. It's hard to imagine a similar scenario involving the First. Who among us would disagree with the idea of free speech? What politician would win an election based on an anti–First Amendment platform?

There's a key difference between the two amendments, though: the Second is actually a legal sticking point in our current debate over gun rights. Nearly every argument for and against guns in the United States must come back to the Second Amendment: Does it allow further regulation, or should it be done away with in favor of something more re-strictive? That's just not true with the First Amendment. As Andrew Sullivan wrote, we are talking more about the *spirit* of the First Amendment than the actual legal definition of it. What other law is like that? What other law has that power?

As a result, the debate over free speech is not a debate with a definable center. It is largely a debate over how we should conceptualize and draw inspiration from the First Amendment, without actually modifying it and without it actually being legally applicable in most cases (remember, the First Amendment is by and large about government suppression of free speech, not private suppression). No other law holds such sway over our discussions without having actual *legalistic* consequences. The First Amendment, then, has become primarily a propaganda tool. The question then becomes: How did that happen? Why did we start caring about free speech so much?

There are other constitutional amendments that have been challenged, modified, or reinterpreted to the point of unrecognizability, but Americans get much less up-in-arms about them. For example, the Sixth Amendment's right to a speedy trial is rarely a cause for protest, even though almost 500,000 Americans at any given time are behind bars awaiting trial, often for months or years, and often because they can't pay paltry bail sums.[2] That may elicit anger, but not thousands of op-eds in a given year. The Fourth Amendment, which is supposed to protect against invasions of privacy, has received attention in recent years as journalists and whistleblowers like Edward Snowden revealed the extent to which the US government surveils its own citizens, but when was the last time you heard someone bring up the Fourth Amendment? It is not a rallying cry or a litmus test for elected officials the way the First and Second are.

Part of the reason for this is that the Fourth Amendment is much vaguer than the First ("The right of the people to be secure in their persons, houses, papers, and effects, against unreasonable searches and seizures"). The First Amendment, by contrast, seems more clear-cut, maybe even more clear-cut than the Second, which starts out by talking about militias and doesn't specify that it's about *private* gun rights at all. The First Amendment is very direct: "Congress shall make no law respecting an establishment of religion, or prohibiting the free exercise thereof; or abridging the freedom of speech, or of the press; or the right of the people peaceably to assemble, and to petition the government for a redress of grievances."

It's right there in the first word: *Congress*. It is the government that shall not interfere with free speech. Private citizens are, of course, free to interfere with it in any way they want. If you say, "Fuck you" to your boss, they're free to fire you. If you pen a letter to your wife saying you don't love her anymore, she is free to divorce you. The First Amendment is not meant to protect us from the consequences of anyone but the government infringing on our rights. In fact, for the vast majority of American history, virtually no one thought the First Amendment meant we had an unrestrained right to speech. That idea is very new.

Let's start with its inborn limitations: when the Constitution was crafted, no one but men who owned property could vote, which amounted to about 6 percent of the US population.[3] If you consider voting a bedrock of free speech, we can acknowledge that those who drafted the First Amendment were somewhat hypocritical right off the bat. The right to vote wasn't expanded to black men until the ratification of the Fifteenth Amendment in 1870, eighty years after the passage of the First Amendment. Women were given the right to vote with the Nineteenth Amendment in 1920, and Native Americans were able to vote starting in 1924. Whatever your views of free speech may be *today*, it seems important to point out that the same Founding Fathers who believed that free speech was important also thought one of its most important forms— voting—should be restricted to a tiny fraction of the US population (and, although it's an obvious point, it's always worth mentioning that those same people also believed in the legality of chattel slavery, so their opinions must be taken with a grain of salt).

But taking for granted, like so many Americans do, that the Founding Fathers were good men of moral purpose who wanted to create a society of rules and laws that would improve the human condition, even then, the purpose and scope of the First Amendment was unclear from its outset. As David Yassky, the former dean of Pace University's law school, has written, "Despite all the rhetoric in First Amendment cases about the Founders' intentions, contemporary free speech doctrine is thoroughly modern. Not until the 1930s did the courts begin to recognize anything close to a prohibition on censorship. To the contrary, throughout the first 150 years of the First Amendment, federal courts regularly enforced severe restrictions on citizens' ability to speak freely."[4]

The early consensus from the government on the First Amendment appears to have been that it in no way granted Americans the right to free speech. Some of the first laws following its passage were ones that, today, we'd consider to be in direct conflict with its meaning. Just a few years after the Bill of Rights was signed, Congress passed the Alien and Sedition Acts, a group of bills that, among other things, allowed the federal government to prosecute *anyone* critical of the government.[5] While the acts were ostensibly passed to strengthen the United States as it prepared for a possible war with France, the dozens of prosecutions carried out under the acts were against political enemies of the Federalist-controlled government. Vermont Representative Matthew Lyon, the first person to be prosecuted, was convicted for writing a letter to the editor of a local paper, as well as a poem, that were critical of John Adams and his government.

After Thomas Jefferson was elected president in 1800, most of the acts that could land you in prison for speaking out against the government were repealed or allowed to expire, but that didn't actually stop the government from persecuting citizens for exercising their supposed rights to free speech. In the early and mid-1800s, as abolitionists worked to persuade the country to end slavery, most southern states enacted laws that prevented the distribution of abolitionist literature. Virginia, for example, could prosecute anyone distributing material "calculated to incite" rebellion among slaves. The law carried a maximum sentence of death for black people.[6] Other southern states had similarly harsh laws on their books. But the flood of abolitionist literature, especially coming in from the North, did not stop, and so seven southern states petitioned the federal government to prevent the US Post Office from delivering any of it. As southern lawmakers pressured the White House, President Andrew Jackson proposed a bill that would ban *all* material discussing slavery from being shipped through the US mail. The bill looked slated to pass Congress. The only thing that stopped it: South Carolina Senator John C. Calhoun, who killed it in committee. Calhoun was an unlikely opponent of the bill: he was one of the leading promoters in the US government of chattel slavery. In a speech he gave against the bill, he alluded to freedom of the press, but he largely focused on states' rights, namely the right to keep slavery legal as momentum built across the country to end its legalization at the federal level.[7] His committee's report called the abolitionists' efforts to send literature through the US Post Office "evil and highly dangerous." But Calhoun reluctantly concluded that allowing the federal government to regulate speech could have the unfortunate effect of allowing it to dictate what states could do with regard to slavery.[8] Calhoun saved free speech to save slavery.

Except it really wasn't saved at all. To go over each and every instance in American history in which someone was silenced, de-platformed, or even jailed for their opinions would take several thousand pages, but here are a few that were not only deemed legal locally but upheld by the Supreme Court. In 1878, the Court ruled that the government could prevent anyone from shipping materials that discussed "lewd" subjects like getting an abortion.[9] In 1918, Eugene Debs, a socialist leader, was sentenced to ten years in prison for giving speeches critical of the country's involvement in World War I. In 1920, a socialist named Benjamin Gitlow was sentenced to five years in prison for publishing leftist literature. The Supreme Court upheld the conviction seven to two.[10]

One of our most oft-cited quotes about free speech today suggests that it protects you in saying anything short of shouting fire in a crowded theater—i.e., that you can say anything you want unless it incites panic or violence. This is one of the greatest misrememberings of American history for two reasons: The hundred-year-old case it's referencing no longer has any legal bearing on how free speech operates in the United States, and it wasn't even about fires, or panic, or violence. The fire referred to in the opinion was leftist antiwar politics (and the movie theater referred to America writ large). The Supreme Court was arguing not about fire safety codes, but about the government's right to jail anyone who might influence Americans against a war.

During World War I, Charles Schenck, secretary of the Socialist Party of America, distributed thousands of pamphlets in Philadelphia urging men to resist being drafted into the army. "LONG LIVE THE CONSTITUTION OF THE UNITED STATES; WAKE UP AMERICA! YOUR LIBERTIES ARE IN DANGER!" the pamphlet read in bold. The pamphlet argued that being drafted was a form of involuntary servitude, and therefore a violation of the Thirteenth Amendment, and critiqued powerful politicians and their Wall Street backers for preying on average Americans. Schenck did not advocate for any violence or civil disobedience, but he was nonetheless prosecuted under the Espionage Act. The case worked its way up to the Supreme Court, and that's where Oliver Wendell Holmes issued his famous . . . fiery words: "The most stringent protection of free speech would not protect a man in falsely shouting fire in a theatre and causing a panic. . . . The question in every case is whether the words are used in such circumstances and are of such a nature as to create a clear and present danger that they will bring about the substantive evils that Congress has a right to prevent."[11] The Court agreed that Schenck's advocacy against the draft was indeed a clear and present danger to the United States, despite the fact that Schenck was not advocating for any violence. His conviction was upheld unanimously.

What does it say about our understanding of free speech today that we believe our inherent right to it is so tied to this quote—and that the quote comes from a case where advocating for peaceful resistance was equated with overthrowing the country? At the very least, it means we've misunderstood our historical commitment to free speech as a country. Leftist and antiracist ideas have often been equated with danger in the United States—from the abolitionist movement, to the McCarthy era, to today, when leftist protesters are routinely arrested for peaceably assembling— and the prosecution of Americans espousing these "dangerous" ideas is often justified as a necessary exception to the First Amendment. Have we completely misunderstood the history of free speech in this country, or have we been successfully duped?

It wasn't until 1969, a mere fifty years ago, that the Supreme Court fundamentally challenged the idea that the government could or should have a deciding role in whether speech is too dangerous to allow. When it finally did reverse itself, in *Brandenburg v. Ohio*, it did so to protect the speech of a KKK leader. Just as was the case with Calhoun and slavery, the country finally agreed to stick up for free speech—in an attempt to defend the rights of virulent racists.

How, then, did something with such murky, morally conflictual beginnings become viewed as an inherent good, something we should strive for not only legally, but in every interaction, every protest? Free speech in the United States began as a right reserved only for property-holding white men and was gradually expanded over hundreds of years to include everyone, though some of its largest expansions came in defense of slaveholders, Nazis, and the KKK, while the largest exceptions to those expansions were (and, as we'll see in the second half of this book, still are) almost universally used against leftists, abolitionists, and antiracists. Even our most common conception about the limits of free speech—that we should stop speech only when it presents a clear and present danger—comes not from a case in which speech presented a clear and present danger, but from the US government prosecuting peaceful dissenters. This is the history, the bedrock principle, we are upholding. It seems at the very least op-ed columnists should acknowledge its deep, foundational flaws before making pronouncements about its universal good. Where did they get that idea in the first place?

The legal history of free speech goes back to the founding of the country, but pundits' and politicians' use of the term to signal changing political and cultural norms—i.e., college students shutting down speakers, or antifa protesters going against what our country stands for by shutting down Nazis—is more recent. Much more recent. Two hundred years of history shows that free speech was never legally guaranteed in the United States. Until the 1970s it was widely assumed that the government *could* regulate or punish the speech of dissenters (especially socialists and communists). So in the roughly fifty years between *Brandenburg v. Ohio* and now, what happened?

In short, the rich got richer: the tax cuts for the wealthiest Americans, passed by the Nixon and Reagan administrations, meant that by the 1980s, millionaires and billionaires had more access to capital than at any time since the Gilded Age. And they were more willing to use it to influence politics. Charles and David Koch, the pioneers of the conservative capture of American politics, believed—as did one of their major influences, Friedrich Hayek—that Americans were by and large too stupid to know what was good for them. Instead of explaining economic theory, they could better get their point across through public relations campaigns that relied on simple and relatable language. And so, beginning in the 1970s and ramping up especially in the 1980s, the Kochs and other billionaires funneled millions into university programs that preached maximum economic freedom and the benefits of a "marketplace of ideas."[12] Their work paid off. Soon, intellectuals had produced a catalogue of new scholarship about the liberal war on ideas.

In 1987, Allan Bloom, a philosophy professor at the University of Chicago, published a tome called *The Closing of the American Mind*. The main premise of the book was that, thanks to cultural changes brought about by phenomena like the hippies and rock music, as well as the popularization of postmodern philosophers like Michel Foucault, who challenged both the supremacy of American thought and power in the world and the very basis of the accumulation of knowledge in the university, most university students now saw all knowledge as relative, contextual, and ever-changing.[13]

Students were beginning to think, he continued, that "all the world was mad in the past; men always thought they were right, and that led to wars, persecutions, slavery, xenophobia, racism and chauvinism."[14] The problem was not that students had an alternate view of history, but that they only know how to *refute* history:

If I pose the routine questions designed to confute them and make them think, such as, "If you had been a British administrator in India, would you have let the natives under your governance burn the widow at the funeral of a man who had died?," they either remain silent or reply that the British should never have been there in the first place. It is not that they know very much about other nations, or about their own. The purpose of their education is not to make them scholars but to provide them with a moral virtue—openness.[15]

While couched in slightly different language from that used by the free speech worriers of today, Bloom's claims were essentially the same: If we allow modern students to have their way, all thought they disapprove of will be banished, and we'll end up with a very pessimistic view of American history and politics. Bloom diverged from our current era of free speech prognostication in that he saw *too much* speech as one of the reasons for the academy's predicament. We were allowing some—namely liberal and leftist college students—to speak and express themselves, not recognizing that sometimes speech should be reserved for the elites, who appreciate history. Because of that, we were losing a conservatism essential to American thought.[16] The only solution, Bloom believed, was to double down on a Great Books approach to education—teaching students the (white, male) western canon, and little else.

The book was a surprise bestseller, with more than 500,000 copies sold, and became somewhat of an odd cause célèbre for the conservative movement: Bloom was a semi-closeted gay man who espoused the value of cultural and educational elitism, and his book was published at a time when many conservatives were openly antigay and pushing a populist image of the Republican Party. Still, his book was taken up as a rallying cry by conservatives against encroaching liberalism on college campuses.

Bloom was part of the Koch and conservative billionaire intellectual funding wave: he was funded by the John M. Olin Center for Inquiry into the Theory and Practice of Democracy at the University of Chicago. The Olin Foundation, which backed the center, was started by its namesake, a multimillionaire and executive at his family's ammunition and chemical manufacturing company, the Olin Corporation. The foundation spent up to $55 million a year pushing foundations and institutions that believed in "private enterprise."[17]

With financial backing and the blessing of conservatives, the mainstream media latched on to the book. The New York Times gave it a rave review, calling it the "rarest of documents, a genuinely profound book, born of a long and patient meditation on questions that may be said to determine who we are, both as individuals and as a society."[18] (Wow.) Not revealed by the Times was the fact that the reviewer, Roger Kimball, was another recipient of Olin Foundation money.[19] Kimball would go on to publish the influential Tenured Radicals, another book about how colleges were places of leftist indoctrination, a few years later.

Then, in 1991, the up-and-coming conservative commentator Dinesh D'Souza released Illiberal Education. D'Souza's book focused mostly on affirmative action and how the liberal insistence on equality was actually making campuses less equal and less intelligent. The Atlantic ran 12,000 words of the book as a cover story one month before its publication.

As Moira Weigel has pointed out in her exhaustive history of the term "politically correct," none of the three books centered the term (D'Souza's was the only one to use it), or even the term "free speech," yet the media used the books as a jumping-off point to explore the concepts, and the general narrative that free thought was being suppressed in the country, especially on college campuses.[20]

In 1990, after returning from a reporting trip to Berkeley, California, Richard Bernstein wrote a column for the New York Times called "The Rising Hegemony of the Politically Correct."[21] The article, which included one of the first mainstream uses of the term, argued that there was a "cluster of opinions about race, ecology, feminism, culture and foreign policy [that] defines a kind of 'correct' attitude toward the problems of the world," and a "pressure to conform" to those opinions. Four years later, Bernstein followed up his report with a book called Dictatorship of Virtue, in which he argued that multiculturalism had run astray, and risked threatening free speech for all.

Later in 1990, *Newsweek* ran a cover story titled "Thought Police," also about the supposedly politically correct culture on college campuses, dispensing *six* reporters around the country to report on the apparent crisis. The next month, *New York* magazine ran a cover story referring to the trend as "the new fundamentalism" which also posited that universities were being taken over by leftists and progressives on a mission to silence conservatives. Weigel found that before 1990, the term "politically correct" was virtually nonexistent in the pages of America's newspapers and magazines. By contrast, in 1990 it was mentioned 700 times. In 1992, it appeared more than 2,800 times.[22] But nothing had really changed on college campuses in those two years. There were no nationally infamous incidents of speech being suppressed. *Newsweek*'s main two examples of thought-policing were the University of Connecticut's decision to discipline a student for putting up a sign on her dorm room door that included "homos" in a list of "people who are shot on sight," and protests over an anthropology professor named Vincent Sarich at UC Berkeley, who believed different races and people with different brain sizes held differing intellectual abilities. The magazine wrote that "Sarich was left in doubt whether he would be allowed to teach the introductory anthropology course he has taught off and on for 23 years." (He kept teaching at the university until he received emeritus status in 1994).[23]

But the trio of conservative books, and the mainstream media's insistence on following their warnings, had done their job in convincing the country that there was something nefarious going on, especially on college campuses.

The free speech crisis of the early 1990s culminated in President George H. W. Bush giving a commencement address at the University of Michigan in 1991 during which he railed against political correctness. "Ironically, on the 200th anniversary of our Bill of Rights, we find free speech under assault throughout the United States, including on some college campuses," he said. "The notion of political correctness has ignited controversy across the land. And although the movement arises from the laudable desire to sweep away the debris of racism and sexism and hatred, it replaces old prejudice with new ones. It declares certain topics off-limits, certain expression off-limits, even certain gestures off-limits."[24]

As Weigel points out in her history, conservatives' worry about free speech and political correctness was based at least partially on an accurate perception that college students were demanding more of a say in their education, and that educators were challenging the heterodoxies of the day. It's hard to say there was a crisis of free speech across the country, but conservatives were responding to something real—namely that people were less interested in listening to them.

But none of the books or articles seriously grappled with what college campuses in the early 1990s were actually challenging. The students were not simply shutting down speech, or policing it, but advocating for explicitly antiracist and profeminist educations. As the *Times*'s "Rising Hegemony" article mockingly put it, students believed "that everybody but white heterosexual males has suffered some form of repression and been denied a cultural voice or been prevented from celebrating what is commonly called 'otherness.'"

That, it seems clear, was the real worry of conservatives in the early 1990s, and it's the same worry we hear today; free speech is no more under threat than it ever was (and as American history shows, it never really *wasn't* under threat). Obfuscated by conservatives' proclamations of being silenced is an intense fear about losing the grip on the world they know, in which white men dictate the course and bounds of education and society writ large. It's as true then as it was back in the 1980s. We're relitigating the same debate after a new round of campus activism.

I'd mark the start of our new era of free speech worry in late 2015, with the publication of "The Coddling of the American Mind," an article in *The Atlantic* by social psychologist Jonathan Haidt and Greg Lukianoff, the head of a nonprofit called the Foundation for Individual Rights in Education (FIRE). The piece, shared millions of times online, claimed that the new free speech crisis was even more extreme than it had been in the 1980s and 1990s because students were no longer just challenging historical canon.

"The current movement is largely about emotional well-being," the authors wrote. "More than the last, it presumes an extraordinary fragility of the collegiate psyche, and therefore elevates the goal of protecting students from psychological harm. The ultimate aim, it seems, is to turn campuses into 'safe spaces' where young adults are shielded from words and ideas that make some uncomfortable."[25] The article was later turned into a book.

Since then, we've been in a semipermanent free speech panic, seeing examples of violations everywhere. It gives one the impression that there was some golden era of speech, during which Americans could agree that everyone had the right to speak, from which we are now receding. But the idea that free speech is constantly being trampled on is very recent. It's a product of the 1980s, and it has less to do with an increase in violations of the First Amendment, or a decrease in Americans who care about it, than with a well-funded conservative campaign to rework how we think of speech. There were no precedent-setting court cases that severely limited speech on college campuses (or anywhere else) in the past few decades. The complaints today are the same as they were in the 1980s and 1990s, with little to no proof to back up the idea that campus politics have meaningfully gotten more restrictive.

In the middle of the latest wave of free speech media controversy, amid thousands of articles being published fretting over PC culture, no-platforming, and campus protest, two articles on the subject were published by the New York Times, both by older, white male columnists: David Brooks and Frank Bruni. They were, in my opinion, the most honest of the thousands of free-speech-worrying articles we've seen so far. Stripped away were the usual broad claims about political correctness and campus activism. Instead, they were much more personal: Both men earnestly asked if anyone was still interested in listening to them, given that they were old white men.[26] Bruni's piece was published the morning of August 12, 2017—Charlottesville.

## chapter three

# CAMPUS WARS—MIDDLEBURY

T HERE ARE SEVERAL REASONS COLLEGE CAMPUSES HAVE BECOME THE central focus of the free speech debate in the United States. For one thing, colleges are harbingers of politics and discourse in the country. Before political correctness hit the mainstream in the 1990s, it was discussed earnestly on liberal-leaning college campuses. Before trans-inclusive language was widely accepted by the mainstream media, activists and trans students on college campuses pushed for the use of their correct pronouns in classrooms. The Vietnam War protests, along with protests against capitalism, racism, and all the rest, often centered on college campuses in the 1950s, '60s, and '70s.

Colleges are also quietly yet intensely influential: though students get made fun of as party-obsessed goofs (or as anti-fun, anti-free-speech nerds), and professors as out-of-touch elitists, what happens at colleges and universities vastly influences our world. The entire philosophy of neoliberalism, perhaps the most (in my opinion, destructively) influential idea of the last century, was essentially birthed out of the economics department of one school: the University of Chicago.[1] Stanford and MIT were central to the creation of the internet. Colleges contract with our military; their professors serve in presidential cabinets and as advisors to politicians. They produce the studies upon which policy is based. In those ways, colleges are a kind of collective rehearsal space for America: they are projections of whom we may become and whom we fear we are.

Colleges are also easy targets. Because college students are by their nature part of temporary communities, they don't have a lot of opportunities to push back: a controversy boils up, is dealt with on campus, and pontificated about in the media, and then the next class of students comes in. And despite the fact that two-thirds of Americans now attend college, the institutions have retained an image of elitism in the American imagination, all of which allows free speech opinionators to frame college students as brats who don't understand the real world.

And yet those same opinionators tell us that what is happening on college campuses is of extreme importance. They tell us, for example, that a medium-sized protest over a planned speech by right-wing author Charles Murray at Middlebury College is, in the words of conservative commentator Bill Kristol, a grave threat to "not just campus free speech, but free speech—indeed freedom in America—generally."[2]

And yet for incidents like the one Kristol was describing, which supposedly strike at the very core of freedom for the entire country, remarkably little reporting has been done to suss out what actually happened on these college campuses. How did college students protesting speeches become mainstream news? Why were they even protesting in the first place? I wanted to figure out exactly how a protest at a tiny liberal arts school surrounded by a bunch of farms became a national referendum on freedom for us all. And once I started poking at that free speech bubble on college campuses, I found that what happened at Middlebury, and at dozens of other schools with similar stories, was really about much more than free speech, but about everything that free speech can mask: namely, our unsettled history of racism.

◇◇◇

The temporary nature of college communities means that every four years campuses are washed of the previous classes' controversies, and debate and protest begin anew. There have been countless controversies on American college campuses over the decades about race, cultural appropriation, and the bounds of acceptability. Most just don't make national news. For the class of Middlebury students on campus in the mid-2010s, who would end up pushed up against each other in a riled crowd, corralled by police officers, blamed for violence that left one professor with a neck injury, and eventually placed at the center of perhaps the most infamous free speech fight in recent memory, the controversy started two years prior to Murray's planned talk, with a white girl wearing a sombrero.

In the fall of 2015, a white student wore a sombrero to Proctor, the dining hall on Middlebury's campus, where she was confronted by a Latino student who asked her why she thought it was okay to wear the headpiece. "I like to get turnt," the girl reportedly said.[3]

Rapidly, the campus splintered into supporters of "Sombrero Girl" and those who thought her cultural appropriation was offensive. On the anonymous chatting app Yik Yak, students began posting their opinions, with some Sombrero Girl supporters using racist slurs. In an attempt to get ahead of the fights, the college held a town hall to address racism on campus. It was, by most accounts, a mess. White people at the meeting began referring to themselves as "people without color"; several students expressed confusion about what cultural appropriation even was; Sombrero Girl cried; and no solutions were offered by campus administrators. "Town hall meeting designed to help Middlebury confront racism perpetuates racism by leaving students of color more exhausted than when they entered," one student wrote in a sum-up of the event.[4] "Crowd more moved by story of brave white victim than angry Latino man who called her out and lives this everyday: white feelings worth ten times black and brown feelings."

The focus on Sombrero Girl might seem silly, but it was the last straw for a lot of Middlebury students. Middlebury is exceedingly white. Only about 4 percent of its students are African American, and the college is surrounded by the blindingly white wilderness known as Vermont. Yes, it's a liberal school, but according to students of color there, white students weren't really getting what it was like to be nonwhite in 2015.

A year before the Sombrero Girl incident, Michael Brown had been killed by a police officer in Ferguson, Missouri, sparking an uprising around St. Louis and protests nationally. The dialogue kicked off by Black Lives Matter had begun trickling into college campuses. And while the majority of Middlebury's white students would likely identify as progressives, it seemed to the students of color that many did not understand just how pressing racial matters felt to them. While a debate raged on around the country about the value of the lives of people of color, white Middlebury students cried victim when they were told they were being racially insensitive: they didn't understand why students of color didn't want them to appropriate their culture's clothing.

"They would, like, dress up as Lil Wayne for Halloween, but then when it comes to talking about police brutality, where are they?" Joshua Claxon, a political science student, told me on a wintry day in the college's modern, spacious library. "And then, even if they were willing to talk about Iggy Azalea and Macklemore, who appropriate black culture in the rap space, they were nowhere to be found with the conversations around Trayvon Martin and so on."

Students of color felt unsafe at Middlebury for the same reasons they felt unsafe on college campuses across the country. Incidents of hate have been on the rise on college campuses in recent years, with a steady increase in antiblack acts of violence since 2014. According to one survey, the 2017–2018 academic year saw 77 percent more instances of white supremacist propaganda distributed at colleges and universities than the year before. In 2017, the FBI documented 280 hate crimes on college campuses, up from 194 in 2015.[5]

But students of color also simply felt alone and isolated. It's a feeling I can somewhat relate to. As a queer person in college, even at one of the most progressive colleges in the country, I remember feeling isolated. Colleges can be so insular, their worlds so constricting. I did not feel like I had a real community, and having recently come out to my parents, I felt I had few places to turn in rural Massachusetts to explore my identity. Any change I made in my appearance would be quickly noticed by the tiny student body of Hampshire College. It felt claustrophobic. I can imagine it feeling even more so for students of color at Middlebury.

"These incidents made me afraid," the student who confronted Sombrero Girl said at one of the three town halls Middlebury ended up holding over the incident.[6] "However small you see them, I spent the next few weeks scared because someone on this campus considered this behavior okay. . . . So when you say, 'You're too sensitive' or, 'Have a thicker skin,' I need you to understand, I have had my thicker skin. I am exhausted. I have had enough. These incidents have been eating away at me all semester, made me afraid to go to class, made me angry with myself and the strangers around me because I do not know whether you are the ones doing these transgressions. It's incidents like these that forced me to move off campus because I do not feel safe in this community anymore. I don't want to be here anymore."

Discussions about the Sombrero Girl incident continued on Facebook and other social networks, and they rapidly turned into a debate about what freedom of speech means, and whether it should include the right of a white girl to wear a sombrero.

Long before the Charles Murray incident, the terms of the free speech debate were being set by Middlebury's warring students: there were the defenders of Sombrero Girl, who thought free speech trumped all else, that to silence what many considered an offensive act would be to impinge on the freedoms of all, and those who thought that free speech either did not apply to a private institution with a pre-existing conduct code that forbade many activities and forms of speech, or should at least be used with greater caution to protect the safety, feelings, and comfort of the college's most marginalized students. For maybe the first time at Middlebury, these conversations weren't happening just among activists, but among everyone on campus.

In one campus newspaper op-ed that went as viral as something can go on a campus that houses around 2,500 people, a white student wrote she was "sick and tired of all this politically correct talk of racial equality and white privilege and 'microaggressions.'"[7]

"That's where the schism began," Josh Claxon told me. "Half the campus was pro-free-speech. And half the campus wasn't. You had this cycle of bad things happening—cops shooting black boys, this cultural appropriation, then Donald Trump's candidacy and election, and each time these divisions were created."

The tension built. But the administration's response was essentially to tell students of color to ignore the racism and not to attend parties they did not find politically appropriate. Then Donald Trump was elected, and the following morning two Muslim students found "Fuck Muslims #Trump2016" scrawled on their dorm room door's whiteboard.[8]

"All this stuff was getting pent up," one Middlebury professor told me. Then, in the spring of 2017, less than a week before he was scheduled to speak, everyone found out Charles Murray was coming to campus. "And then here's this space for students to reassert their power and say, 'Actually, enough is enough.'"

For years, students of color and their allies had been banging their heads against the wall, trying to get the majority-white campus to deal with what they saw as pressing issues of racism on campus, and no one was listening.

"It's classic social movement theory," the professor said. "People who have no other power have the power to disrupt."

Middlebury had hosted conservative speakers before Murray came in 2017, and with much less of a ruckus. The campus had even hosted Murray once: in 2007 he spoke to a crowd of about one hundred, most of whom were there to protest his appearance. But they didn't shout him down. Instead the students and professors sat silently in the middle of the auditorium, with students and faculty of color front and center, staring at him as he explained the premise of *The Bell Curve*. Some remember Murray telling a black student during that 2007 talk that they would have been a better fit at a state university (Murray denies this).[9] There was almost no press coverage of the event, no protest beyond the sitting students and faculty, and no subsequent think pieces about the value of free speech.

Things had changed in the ten years since. Donald Trump had been elected president, and that was a big part of it, but it seems students at

Middlebury and at other colleges and universities had also come to expect something different from the institutions they attend. Like the students chastised by *New York Times* critic Richard Bernstein in the 1980s for demanding their curricula better reflect their understandings of race, sex, and class, they wanted to have more of a say in their academics.

"I look at it more as a tenants' rights perspective," one Middlebury alum told me. "This is your home, you should feel comfortable. It's not about threatening our ideological standpoint, it's someone coming into your home and taking a shit on your rug and a shit on your identity."

The question for Middlebury students before Murray's second visit was where the line stood between a productive challenge to ideological orthodoxy and a deliberate provocation of students, particularly students of color. This time around, Murray was not only coming to campus, but was to be introduced by the president of the college, Laurie Patton, and interviewed by one of its most prominent faculty members, politics professor Allison Stanger. Some read that as an endorsement of the respectability of his ideas. After several years of racist incidents at Middlebury, with a Black Lives Matter movement burgeoning off campus and a president in the White House with ties to white nationalism, students felt they needed to make their line clear: having Murray at Middlebury would signal that students of color, who already felt isolated and underserved by the institution, and sometimes even unsafe, were less of a priority than presenting racist ideas as worthy of debate.

What students most took issue with was not Murray's conservatism, but the way it was framed—as science. Murray's most famous book, *The Bell Curve*, coauthored by Richard J. Herrnstein and published in 1994, has a relatively simple thesis: intelligence is largely genetic and can be measured through testing, especially IQ testing. The book argues that IQ is a better predictor of a person's socioeconomic status than anything else (employment opportunities, the wealth of your parents, geography, etc.). The authors explicitly state that black and Latino people have lower intelligence scores than white people (and that Asians are more intelligent on average than white people), and that if you control for the IQ of each group it "explains away much of the disparity in welfare recipiency among blacks, whites, and Latinos."[10] In other words, Murray and Herrnstein believed that if black and Latino people were on average as intelligent as whites, they would require less welfare and other government assistance. The authors also argued that the United States as a whole is getting less intelligent because those with greater intelligence have fewer babies, and those with less have more, and they recommended eliminating social safety nets that make it easier for low-income people to have children.

In case you think this is an oversimplification of the argument from a biased author like me, here is a direct quote from the book: "The technically precise description of America's fertility policy is that it subsidizes births among poor women, who are also disproportionately at the low end of the intelligence distribution. We urge generally that these policies, represented by the extensive network of cash and services for low-income women who have babies, be ended."[11]

Murray's work was covered widely in the media when it first came out. *The New Republic* devoted an entire issue to exploring and critiquing it. It was praised by conservatives and many liberals, but scientists took issue with its lack of original research. Stephen Jay Gould, the renowned biologist, wrote in *The New Yorker* that the book "contains no new arguments and presents no compelling data to support its anachronistic social Darwinism. . . . I can only conclude that its success in winning attention must reflect the depressing temper of our time—a historical moment of unprecedented ungenerosity, when a mood for slashing social programs can be powerfully abetted by an argument that beneficiaries cannot be helped, owing to inborn cognitive limits expressed as low IQ scores."

That might well have been Murray's aim: not to publish peer-reviewed science, but to use data and statistics to make a controversial, racist, political argument seem more valid. Murray is not a hard scientist, or even a professor, though he holds a PhD in political science from MIT. His main appointment has not been at a university, but as a fellow at the conservative American Enterprise Institute. His work was funded by millions of dollars from right-wing foundations, including $100,000 per year during the time he was writing *The Bell Curve* from the Lynde and

Harry Bradley Foundation, a Wisconsin-based charity that, among other things, pushed Governor Scott Walker's candidacy and welfare-slashing agenda. During the 1980s and 1990s, the foundation also funded the professorships and publications of hundreds of scholars focused on anti-affirmative-action research and other research that pushed a far-right agenda, along with various other right-wing causes and propaganda outlets. And much of the research cited in *The Bell Curve* was funded by the Pioneer Fund, which supports eugenics research, and whose main founder advocated for the sterilization of people with mental disabilities. One of the main assertions of the book, that black people's IQs are lower than that of whites, comes from researchers who received $400,000 from the Pioneer Fund. [12]

The ultra-right-wing nature of Murray's work did not stop it from becoming influential among the country's elite. Bill Clinton called Murray's analysis of welfare programs, specifically that they encourage single mothers to have more kids and not work, "essentially right." Murray's work is thought to have been an inspiration for President Clinton's Personal Responsibility and Work Opportunity Reconciliation Act, which set work requirements for welfare recipients (Clinton once said that there was "no question" that Murray's policy recommendations to end welfare for single mothers would alleviate poverty).[13] And Murray is still a popular author. His work is regularly reviewed by publications like the *New York Times* (often favorably).[14]

All of that factored into many students' decision to protest Murray. To them, the talk was not about a scientist presenting controversial findings, but about a racist who had deeply and materially influenced American policy, and who was at no risk of being silenced if he were not to speak at Middlebury—he was one of the most popular conservative authors of the day.

Still, the protest against Murray was not taken lightly by even the students most adamant about doing it. The media largely presented Middlebury's students as rabble-rousers, unthinking kids unable or unwilling to engage with Murray's ideas. But a look at the school's paper, dozens of blogs written by students, and students' Facebook posts shows that they were in fact thinking deeply about the implications of their protest. They especially struggled over the tactic of "no-platforming"—denying a speaker a platform by shouting them down or otherwise blocking a stage. Many students thought that shouting down Murray could lead to a slippery slope of no-platforming any speakers the students did not like. But the leaders of the protest thought that Murray was far enough over the line between simple dislike and presenting ideas that posed an actual danger to people of color, as his ideas had been used in the past to create national policy, that it was safe to shut him down.

"We were asking, So where is the line?" Alex Brockelman, a political science student who wrote extensively about the incident and supported the protests, told me. "The first line is whether or not you're advocating for specific policy—being an academic doesn't shield you from protest, but I do think it's particularly nefarious that Murray acts as if he's reluctantly discovering these things, not pushing for them."

The second line for the students was the quality of his research. Several students pointed out that Middlebury would not invite a climate change denier to the campus, especially since the college's most famous professor is Bill McKibben, a well-known climate researcher and activist.

"Global warming is settled science," one student said. "It's also settled science that people of color aren't genetically inferior to white people. You're not just bringing in any random ideas here. This is a curated environment. So it says something that they would bring this kind of racist thought."

What this all suggested, to Brockelman and other students, was that while things like climate science were a settled matter for Middlebury's administration, the question of black people's intelligence was not.

Emma Ronai-Durning, a senior at the time of Murray's visit, wasn't much of a protester until she got to Middlebury. And it wasn't really Middlebury that got her into organizing. Though the campus has a liberal reputation, the school feels closer in ethos to Brown or Dartmouth than to UC Berkeley. Its century-old stone buildings sit on a sloping, often frost-covered campus, and many of its students wear khakis and button-downs as they trudge through the Vermont winter on their way to classes. They are mostly serious and studious, not rowdy.

But Emma had fallen in with some activists in relatively nearby Burlington (it's the closest big city, an hour's drive away) who were protesting the construction of a proposed gas pipeline through the state. Emma had also been active in Wonderbread, a campus group of white students who wanted to work on issues of racism. But she didn't consider herself the kind of person to disrupt much of anything.

But in late February 2017, while she was studying at the library, a professor walked by, slammed down the campus newspaper on Emma's table, and pointed to an advertisement announcing Murray would be speaking the following week. The ad was the first time anyone outside of the campus branch of the American Enterprise Institute or the school administration had heard about the event. Emma had heard about Murray's ideas as a high school student in Oregon, and remembered feeling viscerally disgusted by them. She grew up in predominantly white areas, and the idea that anyone around her could think what Murray thinks—could accept that other races were inferior—was repulsive to her. She wasn't aware that people still paid attention to Murray until the professor showed her the paper.

Emma immediately messaged her friends Shaun and Madeleine about it, and they decided to attend a meeting that weekend in a small building near the campus library. Dozens of students showed up.

"There were so many people like me who had never participated in anything before like this, but we were like, 'This is something I have to act on,'" Shaun told me the next winter. We were sitting in an empty room above the campus dining hall and eating stale salad and mushy pasta—typical campus fare. "And we didn't know what that meant. But we were ready, and we were showing up."

There were several meetings after that, all tense, some with members of the Middlebury administration, others with faculty, and a few with just students. The administration pleaded with students not to shout Murray down. Allison Stanger, the selected moderator for the Murray event, had written on Facebook, "Please ponder how Charles Murray can be a white supremacist when he married an Asian woman and had two children with her. How does that work?" She asked students a similar question at one of the meetings. It rubbed many as tone-deaf, and reaffirmed their commitment to disrupt the event, to call out the liberal ideology espoused by that post: that one cannot be racist if one knows or cares for people of different races—after all, that's exactly what the campus had done.

Emma called her activist friends in Burlington, many of whom had been arrested at pipeline protests before. They said they'd come to the Middlebury protest but not lead it, and told Emma there could be consequences—expulsion, arrest—for her actions. The activists suggested it might be an opportunity to highlight Vermont's history of eugenics. Like many states, Vermont had adopted a sterilization program for criminals and others deemed mentally unfit in the early 1900s. But they also wanted students, not outsiders, to take the lead.

Emma calculated the risk to herself and decided it was worth it: She would participate, and she would invite her activist friends. If anything happened to her, she had a girlfriend she'd recently called it quits with back in Oregon to whom she would gladly return. Staying at Middlebury didn't seem worth remaining silent over Murray.

The afternoon of Murray's talk, Emma ditched her usual athletic look and dressed up in a button-down shirt. She wanted to look respectable for her first big action. And then she headed to the auditorium. The plan was for her and other activists to fill up the auditorium with dissenters before too many Murray supporters got there. So they sat for hours as more protesters gathered outside. Finally, Murray walked on stage.

The student activists stood up and turned their backs, and joined, one line at a time, in reading from a statement, so that their collective voices built into a booming chant. "This is not respectful discourse, or a debate about free speech," the statement read. "These are not ideas that can be fairly debated. . . . Science has always been used to legitimize racism, sexism, classism, transphobia, ableism, and homophobia, all veiled as rational and fact, and supported by the government and state. . . . Middlebury College was one of forty-four colleges with a eugenics-zoology program. . . . There are countless groups of people affected because of what claims to be academia, which then makes its way into the public, which then makes its way into the White House."[15]

After it became clear that Murray would not be able to speak to the audience, Middlebury President Laurie Patton and Murray left the stage. They moved to a backstage room to continue their conversation, which was streamed online for anyone who still wanted to hear Murray speak (so he was not exactly no-platformed, but different-platformed). Protesters spilled outside the auditorium, where the chanting and protesting continued. After the livestream ended, Murray and Stanger, along with Bill Burger, the college's vice president for communications, left the building and were confronted by protesters, including those who had come down from Burlington, some of whom were masked. Murray and the college administrators tried to make their way through the crowd to Burger's Subaru. What happened next is unclear—either some protesters deliberately pushed Stanger, or campus public safety officers pushed the protesters into her. In the jostling, Stanger's neck was hurt.

When the trio made it to the car, they were directed by public safety officials to drive through the crowd slowly to make their escape. One protester ended up on top of Burger's car as he drove away and was either safely let off (according to Burger) or flung off the hood at twenty-five miles per hour (according to students), before Burger, Murray, and Stanger drove off campus.

Middlebury spent months combing through security camera footage to identify students at the protest. The college would end up disciplining dozens of students, including Emma, who was placed on academic probation, meaning if she was caught doing something the college did not like again, she could be expelled or suspended. Campus security caused controversy again when the public safety department, in tandem with the private security company it had hired to investigate the protest, claimed that a black student named Addis Fouche-Channer was at the protest, with no evidence to back up the assertion. She insists she was never there, and this led to a new round of claims of racism on the campus, which continued until the end of the semester.

◇◇◇

What happened at Middlebury was not a random occurrence—it took place in the context of political movements that have been bubbling up on college campuses across the country for years, most of which have received far less media attention than the Murray incident. Most mainstream media accounts presented the Middlebury fights as if they were something new, as if college students were suddenly allergic to the concepts of free speech and tolerance.

Perhaps what pundits were responding to is that the language around activism has changed. No-platforming, trigger warnings, safe spaces, accountability—these buzzwords can make it appear as if something new is happening on college campuses, when really what we're seeing mirrors fights that date back to the civil rights movement. The intensity of that activism has ebbed and flowed over the decades. The tactics the students are using are in some cases more militant than they have been in decades (but still much less militant than the armed struggles of the 1960s and 1970s), but the issues they're protesting are the same as they were fifty years ago: namely, students are asking for an end to racism on college campuses and for more control over the administrative functions of schools.

Ironically, the idea of college campuses as open places for political debate came from the left. Before the civil rights movement, protests were relatively common at colleges and universities, but it wasn't until the 1960s that students began advocating for the concept of a universal ability to express oneself on campus, most notably during the Free Speech Movement at UC Berkeley.

The intersection of Bancroft Way and Telegraph Avenue in Berkeley, California, right at the south entrance to UC Berkeley, was a popular spot for student groups to gather, hand out flyers, and recruit newcomers to political causes. But as student activism increased in intensity in the early 1960s, administrators worried that it would spread if they did not tamp it down. In 1964, Dean of Students Katherine Towle sent a letter to the entire campus saying that setting up tables would be banned from the intersection, as would collecting money and recruiting anyone for political activity that took place off campus. Two prominent civil rights student groups—CORE and SNCC—refused the orders, and when the school held a disciplinary hearing to discipline the students involved, more than 500 supporters participated in a sit-in at the college's Sproul Hall.

"We ask only the right to say what we feel when we feel like it," student leader Art Goldberg said. "We'll continue to fight for this freedom, and we won't quit until we've won."[16]

A few days later, another CORE activist refused to remove his table from the college's south gate and was arrested. This time, more than 7,000 students came to protest and used the top of a police car they'd surrounded as a podium for their speeches. Joan Baez sang some songs. Berkeley administrators blamed the events on "communistic, nonstudent agitators."[17]

Over the next few days, students, led by local civil rights activist Mario Savio, decided on the name for their group: the Free Speech Movement. Protests continued, culminating in a student-led strike in December that shut down campus. As the protests grew, the media began paying attention; eventually, the school relented and allowed most forms of political organizing to take place on campus. Several administrators, professors, and even the college's chancellor resigned as public support turned against them.[18] Some of the students continued their protests, arguing for even more rights on campus, but the Free Speech Movement at Berkeley fizzled out.

From its outset, the movement wasn't only about speech. It was largely about the ability of students to take control of their education. The metaphor of colleges as factories, pumping out students primed for the corporate and military worlds, was a popular one among organizers. Students were protesting because of "distress, disaffection, disillusion . . . the fact that the imperialist social order is in general and acute crisis," as Bettina Aptheker, one of the leaders of the Free Speech Movement, put it. "Society is moribund. . . . A university in the midst of such madness must shed any illusion of social neutrality; it must become an instrument for progressive social change."[19]

It's a remarkably similar argument to the one being made by college students at places like Middlebury today—that colleges are not neutral actors that impart knowledge on their students but agents of politics that can be swayed in one direction or another, that must be influenced in order to influence the outside world, and that students have a central role to play in the struggle.

The big difference is that sixty years ago, that leftist argument was couched in the language of free speech, codified as the Free Speech Movement, whereas today it is couched in essentially the opposite, in what might be called a Fuck Free Speech Movement. This radical departure in rhetoric signals two things: how successfully the right has co-opted the language of the left over the past half-century *and* how empty a signifier that rhetoric was in the first place. Leftist Berkeley students didn't want just any speech on their campus; they wanted *their* speech, their politics, their views. The same can be said of conservatives today who expound the virtues of free speech whenever a conservative is shut down on a college campus, but who remain silent when leftist professors are fired or disciplined (more on that in the next section of this book). Free speech is a great guise for actual politics.

As literary theorist Stanley Fish wrote in 1994, "Free speech, in short, is not an independent value, but a political prize, and if that prize has been captured by a politics opposed to yours, it can no longer be invoked in ways that further your purposes, for it is now an obstacle to those purposes." In other words, political actors—college students, politicians, lobby groups, whoever—use free speech to universalize their goals, to make them seem beneficial to everyone. The "liberal left" has often fallen into the right's trap in this regard. But at some point, at least in the 1960s, the left *did* seem to understand this principle: free speech was not in and of itself a value to fight for, but a crowbar to open the door to debate larger, material issues about race, sexism, the purpose of education, and capitalism.

Those issues became front and center when, in February 1968, after weeks of student protests at South Carolina State College against segregated spaces in the college town of Orangeburg, police shot a group of black student protesters outside a segregated bowling alley. Three were killed and dozens more were injured.[20] The violence against the students sparked further uprisings on college campuses, particularly at historically black institutions like Howard, where the next month thousands of students staged an occupation of university buildings, demanding that administration officials, whom students felt were out of touch with the needs of most African Americans, resign; that African American history be made more central to the school's curriculum; and that the school make more of an effort to reach out to the community surrounding the campus.[21]

A few months later, thousands of Columbia University students in Manhattan occupied administrative buildings to protest the university's proposal to build a gym on public land in Harlem, which the students viewed as imperialist (the word "gentrification" was not in popular use yet). The students took Dean Henry Coleman hostage in one of the buildings. Supportive residents from the surrounding neighborhoods used homemade catapults to fling food through university windows to the occupying students for sustenance. Eight days after the occupation began, between 1,000 and 1,500 New York City police officers flooded the campus and ended the occupation.[22] But Columbia agreed not to build the gym on public land.

Despite sporadic success, the student movement splintered throughout the 1960s and '70s, reflecting the fractures in the political culture at large. Universities' and the government's escalating responses to student demonstrations—which culminated in the killing of four students at Kent State in 1970 during an antiwar protest—made it clear that the cost of activism on college campuses was higher than it once was. Some students became more radical, aligning with groups like the Black Panthers and the Weather Underground, and some became more reformist, arguing for more inclusion at universities.

But university administrations also found a new tactic to quell protest: instead of battling against students and using the cops to break them up, arrest them, and in the worst cases kill them, they absorbed student demands into their academic machines. According to Mark Edelman Boren, a professor of English at the University of North Carolina, Wilmington, and the author of *Student Resistance*, a history of student uprisings, gender, race, and sexuality studies programs were started at universities and colleges across the country not only in response to student demands, but as a way to take some steam out of protest movements.

"Under the official stamp and control of academia, specialized programs forced student radicals to join them or further isolate themselves, especially since the more politically moderate would be placated by the university's 'progressive' innovations," Boren wrote.[23] Students were left with a choice: keep protesting for radical change and face persecution from administrations and police, or accept the colleges' compromise—there would be no systemic change, but at least there would be the study of it. It was a "good cop, bad cop" approach, and it worked.

It's likely that this reformist approach helped lead us to the situation we're in today: thanks to the protests of the 1960s and '70s, colleges have become more diverse, their curricula have become less focused on white and Eurocentric histories, and their administrations have become more concerned with student input than ever before. But in the mid-2010s, influenced by the battles and movements taking shape outside of colleges, particularly Black Lives Matter, it was as if college students looked around and thought, "Wait a minute, we're not done yet." You can now study gender at Middlebury, but gender discrimination and sexual assault are still problems there. You can study race, but as the series of incidents culminating in the Charles Murray talk showed, racism is not dead at Middlebury.

I asked several students at Middlebury why they were so appalled by Murray in particular, and they all gave similar answers: because racism today is less obvious than it once was, but it still exists. The protests of the 1960s and '70s had brought progress, but now it seemed like most white students, faculty, and administrators had patted themselves on the back for addressing race and gender while ignoring pervasive inequalities. Many of the students who participated in the protest were convinced that the majority of their fellow students, and the administration, would privately agree with Murray's ideas about race. What's more, they believed no amount of debating Murray was going to change that.

◇◇◇

The Murray incident spawned hundreds of news articles and opinion pieces, most of which blamed the students for what happened. There were no fewer than eight opinion pieces in the *New York Times* following the event, and all but one came out against the student protesters. In one piece, the paper's editorial board wrote that "true ideas need testing by false ones, lest they become mere prejudices and thoughtless slogans. Free speech is a sacred right, and it needs protecting, now more than ever." Another, by Frank Bruni, posited that the students at Middlebury, whom he called "our future leaders," may have gotten "the idea that they should be able to purge their world of perspectives offensive to them."[24] A *Washington Post* writer even compared Murray's plight to that of the Little Rock Nine—the nine black high school students who faced a barrage of hate as they attempted to walk into a newly integrated school.[25]

Allison Stanger, the professor who was injured during the scuffle outside the Murray talk, wrote *two* op-eds in the *Times* about what happened at her college. In one, she argued that while it was okay to protest white nationalism, Murray wasn't truly a white nationalist. She also said that it was important to engage with ideas you find distasteful. "Our constitutional democracy will depend on whether Americans can relearn how to engage civilly with one another," Stanger wrote, linking the incivility of Middlebury's students to that of President Trump and his supporters.[26] Stanger would go on to make several public appearances—at Yale University, Elmhurst College, and Arizona State University; on C-SPAN; and in front of a Senate Committee called Exploring Free Speech on College Campuses.[27] Charles Murray still commands $30,000–$50,000 a speech.[28]

The vast majority of the thousands of opinion pieces published in the wake of the Murray protests had two things in common. First, they invoked the First Amendment and the need to protect it, lest we ruin our democracy—even though the protests at Middlebury had nothing to do with the First Amendment. Middlebury is a private school, and therefore the protest took place on private property. The government was not involved. Speech at Middlebury is already severely limited. The school, for example, makes hiring and admissions decisions all the time, effectively limiting who is and is not allowed to speak on campus—but these are not presented as affronts to the Bill of Rights.

The second commonality was the broad brush with which the op-eds painted the college students. Most did not grapple with the actual opinions of the students involved, but instead declared that the students (who represent a fraction of Middlebury's student body, which in turn represents about .000125th of the total college population of the United States) were indicative of students, or even millennials, writ large. Shortly before the Middlebury protests, the *Daily Beast*'s Robby Soave summed up the general anti-college sentiment in the media, writing "the modern college student thinks he or she (or xe) is uniquely oppressed, mistreated and unsafe. . . . They think a university education is too hostile, triggering, difficult."[29]

It was an unfortunate flattening of opinion and information, because in truth the Middlebury students and the professors who supported them had thought long and hard about what they were doing and about the potential consequences for themselves, Murray, and free speech. They felt the least the world could do was offer them a chance to explain themselves.

Less than two weeks after the protest, a group of about 150 Middlebury students signed on to a 3,100-word treatise called "Broken Inquiry on Campus."[30] It was a response to a letter called "Free Inquiry on Campus," which was signed by more than one hundred professors from a wide array of disciplines at Middlebury and published in modified form in the *Wall Street Journal*. The "Free Inquiry" letter argued many of the same points that the hundreds of other op-eds had argued: that listening to opinions you disagree with is necessary to learn.

In "Broken Inquiry" the students argued that the protesters were actually in favor of civil debate, but that there was no way to civilly debate the racism of Charles Murray. "We hope that Middlebury College would not allow a classroom debate in which a white student argued that the black students in the class, due to inferior intellectual inheritance, did not belong," they wrote. By framing all ideas as worthy of debate, the college risked conflating baseless opinion with well-studied fact (the global warming analogy is again useful here). "We risk elevating biased opinions with no solid, factual foundation into the realm of 'knowledge' and affirming the unconscious biases many hold," the students wrote. The open letter also argued that in a racist, sexist society, there is a difference between debating controversial ideas and legitimizing those that fundamentally challenge the humanity of certain people. *That* was their line in the sand: there was no risk of college students closing their eyes and ears to anything and everything they disagreed with. They simply did not feel it was appropriate to give a platform to Charles Murray, especially in 2017.

In the coming months that philosophy would be tested twice. In the dead of winter of 2017, half a year after Murray's talk had brought protest and a media frenzy to campus, students at Middlebury received an email informing them that James O'Keefe, the conservative provocateur known for his undercover videos that attempt to expose liberal and progressive organizations as frauds, would be speaking at a nearby hotel. It appeared that a group called the Leadership Institute, which is partly funded by well-known conservative billionaires like the Koch brothers and runs a conservative college news website called Campus Reform, had attempted to get a college club to sponsor O'Keefe's talk on campus, but none would bite. The College Republicans turned down the offer, as did the Middlebury chapter of the American Enterprise Institute. No faculty member would sponsor the creation of a new club, and the administration did not want him on campus either. O'Keefe was essentially blacklisted from Middlebury, banned from campus not only by leftists but by conservatives too, so he gave his talk to just a couple dozen listeners in a dingy hotel conference room. But there were no op-eds in the mainstream press about Middlebury's intolerance following the event.[31] "There are plenty of people who the college would not invite to Middlebury," student Alex Brockelman told me. "The administration believes there's a line too, they just didn't think that Murray was the line."

In the spring of 2018, a little more than a year after the Murray debacle, Middlebury College Republicans invited Richard Sander, a UCLA law professor who argues against affirmative action because he believes that many students of color do better when they attend less elite institutions. The invitation felt like a direct provocation to the protesters who had shouted down Murray: here was another conservative scholar who held controversial opinions on race and equality—his book *Mismatch*, for example, argued that affirmative action puts students of color in academic environments that are too challenging for them, and should therefore be ended. The book was criticized for many of the same reasons Murray's was: data being misused to form thinly veiled racist conclusions.[32] But unlike the Murray event, the Sander talk was scheduled to take place in a small building near the college's golf course, as far off campus as you can get without going off campus. It would not be introduced by the president of the college. The college was hosting Sander, but not giving him the main stage. Some student organizers debated whether to protest the event, but it seemed not to be worth it.

"If there's a platform that we can affect, maybe it makes sense to protest," Josh Claxon told me. "And Sander's not being given a large enough platform for us to really care."

Another reason the students didn't protest was that they had in some ways stopped caring. What had started as a protest over one speaker had turned into an international referendum on the meaning of free speech. It had turned the campus into a media circus. It had ended with the disciplining of dozens of students, and increased tensions on campus. Students felt exhausted, and in some ways they felt like they had lost. They had wanted to bring attention to the everyday racism that students of color experience, which often comes under the guise of academic and scientific inquiry. They had wanted to bring attention to how a well-meaning liberal institution like Middlebury could still be complicit in racism. Instead, they'd been painted as unthinking brats, ready to disrupt whomever disagrees with them, and unworthy of education. The website where the "Broken Inquiry" letter was posted had been visited by only 7,000 readers. The opinions of those who disagreed with the students, which were published in the pages of virtually every mainstream paper in the country, were undoubtedly viewed many thousands of times more than that. Their message had been drowned out by those claiming that free speech had been violated.

## chapter four

# CAMPUS WARS—EVERGREEN

COLLEGES ARE MICROCOSMS OF THE WORLD. THEY REFLECT, AND IN some ways magnify, the problems of their surroundings. When US popular opinion began to turn against the Vietnam War in the 1960s, colleges became the epicenters of protests against the war. The same is true today: as Black Lives Matter, for example, pushed for an end to police brutality in black communities, many Americans were free to ignore the struggle, encountering it only in news articles and on television. That's not true on many college campuses, where social movements are debated and supported, and students frequently push the bounds of their education and push their administrations to respond in ways more progressive than the culture at large. This is in large part why they've become laboratories for a new kind of free speech politics. Students are able to test out their theories of political change—no-platforming, demonstrations, demand letters—in a more controlled environment than in the outside world. And because politics and tactics popularized on college campuses often seep into the mainstream, campuses have become laboratories too for a kind of politics of pushback: those opposed to the students' demands and strategies must figure out how to stop them before they get off campus. And so those most deeply opposed to the burgeoning demands of equality on college campuses have developed strategies of their own, attempting to shut down movements before they spread and leaving paths of personal pain in their wake.

In November 2016, dozens of Evergreen State College faculty, administrators, and students gathered in a lecture hall on the college's brutalist-inspired campus in the middle of nowhere (otherwise known as Olympia, Washington) to hear a presentation from the school's president, George Bridges, and his "Equity Council." As the sound of the ocean's lapping waves played over the speakers and a drummer from a local Native American tribe beat a drum, the president and dozens of others spoke about how to encourage diversity at the school and better serve its LGBTQ students and its students of color. Then, Bridges asked everyone gathered who so desired to get into a metaphorical canoe on the stage, as a symbol of their shared commitment to be in the fight for diversity.

The whole event was very Evergreen, very Pacific Northwest (or at least what people outside the area associate with it): hippieish, overly sincere, with serious nods to equality, but also easily mocked. Nice white people doing nice white people things. What the Equity Council had proposed, after months of deliberation, was pretty straightforward, and probably less mockable: the school wanted to hire someone to oversee equity initiatives; institute hiring practices that would help bring about more diversity, including by considering whether each new faculty candidate would not only be a good fit academically but also help the college achieve its equity goals; and ask all faculty to write a year-end note reflecting on progress and setbacks toward achieving equity on campus.

Naima Lowe, a professor of media studies who had been chosen to be part of the Equity Council, sat in the room. She even got in the canoe.

"I'll be honest: I wasn't personally, like, into the canoe thing," she told me later. "But I got it. I understood why it was meaningful."

At least the college was trying. It had been a tense few years for Evergreen. In May 2015, police had shot two black men at a Safeway supermarket a few miles from campus. One was partially paralyzed. Amid the nationwide protests over police violence, the shooting so close to campus had heightened antiracist activism among students, and the sense that race needed to be addressed more directly by the administration—the college is more diverse than some other similar liberal arts schools, but black students still make up only about 4 or 5 percent of its enrollment on any given year.[1]

Later that year and again in the following one, flyers were found across campus with white power slogans like "White Lives Matter" and "Protect Your Heritage." Students figured out that many had come from a local chapter of Identity Evropa, a notorious white supremacist group. Despite its progressive reputation, the Pacific Northwest is actually a hotbed of white supremacy—in 2016, a white supremacist stabbed a black man in a random act of hate in Olympia, claiming he was seeking retribution against Black Lives Matter.[2]

But beyond the direct violence, students and some faculty members, like Naima Lowe, were mostly concerned with a kind of mundane, but still pervasive, racism they saw displayed at the college: there were few black students, fewer black faculty, and the education did not center race. Retention rates were falling for all students, but some members of the campus community, including Lowe, were particularly concerned that students of color did not feel welcome in this extremely white part of Washington (the county that surrounds Evergreen is 2.7 percent black).[3]

"When you come here you pretty quickly realize that in pretty much every class, you're going to have to deal with people who are racist but don't realize they are," one student told me. "There are a lot of people who are really well-meaning here but who have been totally insulated from people of color."

More than the white people with dreads, or the vegan students comparing animal abuse to slavery, it was the everyday drudgery of feeling burdened by the ignorance of the campus. Georgie Hicks, a black student who worked at the school newspaper (she uses a pseudonym to write her articles and when talking to the press so that she doesn't get doxxed by right-wingers), told me it felt isolating to be one of two or three students of color in every class, always burdened with explaining to white people why what they said was offensive. She had tried to engage with the administration several times to address her concerns, to no avail.

"I was basically writing articles calling out the administration, saying, 'Hey, this is what we want from you,'" Hicks said. "But they're not listening. They're not reaching out to try to really change anything. It gets to a point where you're like, they're not going to listen to us. So what else do you do?"

In an article in the student newspaper, one black trans student explained that the problem wasn't just at Evergreen, but in the world in general these days: It seemed like the fight for social justice had plateaued, because white progressivism had slowed the pace of change. After the tumult of the 1960s and '70s, it was as if a kind of grand bargain had been reached: Diversity would be fought for, but it would be assimilationist and would require that the radicalism practiced by leftists be toned down. The term "color-blind" spread through America in the 1990s. Barack Obama's election was supposed to signify that we were living in a "post-racial" America.[4] Colleges and workplaces got more diverse, but the grand bargain got no closer to solving the deep imbalances in the country. The racial wealth gap, for example, has only worsened since the 1980s.[5] Students were fed up with politics-as-usual on college campuses, which seemed increasingly to favor superficial diversity and civility over actual efforts to increase racial and economic equality. "I've gotten to this point where I feel that liberation is going to be messy and hella violent," the student said. "Yes, non-violence has gotten us to a certain point, but also, we are still here living in a neo-colonialist, white supremacist society."

At the school's convocation in September 2016, as President Bridges sat down for a Q&A with Naomi Oreskes—a prominent historian of science and commentator on global warming—two students walked onto the stage holding signs reading, "Evergreen cashes diversity checks but doesn't care about blacks." Bridges was flustered, but the talk went on. The students were given an opportunity to address the assembled crowd at the end of the event. Orientation week continued with little fanfare, yet the disruption made it clear that students were running out of patience. Still, in November, as Naima Lowe got into the invisible canoe with her colleagues, she thought things might be heading in the right direction at Evergreen, even if they were moving about as fast as a canoe.

And then the emails started.

A few days after the Equity Council event, Bret Weinstein, a professor of evolutionary theory and biology, sent an email to the faculty listserv, which reaches about 1,200 faculty and 400 student workers, and which is all public record because Evergreen is a publicly funded school. You may have heard of Weinstein by now, because what happened next took him from a little-known professor at Evergreen to an internationally recognized figure praised by many in the mainstream media as a fighter for free speech.

In the email, Weinstein listed a few concerns. Mainly, he felt that the diversity canoe was more of an "unstoppable train" than a canoe, and that professors who disagreed with the equity plan would be silenced.

"We have now imposed on ourselves a de facto hierarchy based on skin color, and hooked it directly to mechanisms of hiring, promotion and dismissal—empowering some, and disempowering others," he wrote. "One could argue that, because the direction of this empowerment runs counter to the historical pattern, this new asymmetry was needed to close an equity gap. I find that idea disturbing, but not nearly as disturbing as the fact that the asymmetry was never discussed."

In another email Weinstein claimed he was part of a "silent majority" of professors too scared to step up to the politically correct Evergreen administration. He posited that a negative review of him left on Ratemyprofessors.com a few days after the equity event, which claimed Weinstein "refused to responsibly address matters of race and gender" in his classes, was a coordinated character assassination.

Weinstein's email launched an exchange that went on for months. The professors divided into two distinct camps: one that believed that Evergreen's new plan for racial and gender equality was an attempt to silence the academic freedom of its professors, and one that saw it as a necessary step forward for diversity on campus.

"Being called racist won't cost you your life, health, livelihood, sanity, freedom," Naima Lowe wrote in one email to the listserv, imploring her white colleagues to do some self-reflection. "Being faced with un-checked racism can and does all of those things."

Lowe felt frustrated. Students had been asking for the same things back when she was in college, and yet little had changed. "When I was young and heard fucked-up and horrible racism in class all the time, I just had to deal with it," she told me. "But should I have? In a way it made me who I am, but I'm like, maybe it would have been great if there had been other tools to deal with it."

That, to Lowe, was all the students were asking for: more tools to deal with the same problems college students had been facing for the past several decades. She was surprised such a simple request would prompt so much pushback.

In the winter of 2017, word began circling on campus that an annual event held every spring would be tweaked that year. Since the 1970s, Evergreen students have participated in something called "Day of Absence." Every spring, students of color had been invited off campus for a day of socializing, workshops, and discussions about race. Since 1992, white students had been encouraged to stay on campus and create their own programming. The workshops were always optional. The events never solicited much controversy. Those who did not want to participate stayed home. Those who wanted to participate simply were excused from class to do their own learning for the day.

This year, students proposed reversing the locations of the workshops: students of color would stay *on* campus, and white students who wanted to participate would meet in a nearby Unitarian Universalist church. As always, the programming was voluntary—even if the entire white population of the campus wanted to participate, the church couldn't accommodate more than a tenth of them.

But Weinstein saw this reversal of locations as an attack. "There is a huge difference between a group or coalition deciding to voluntarily absent themselves from a shared space in order to highlight their vital and under-appreciated roles and a group or coalition encouraging another group to go away," he wrote. "The first is a forceful call to consciousness which is, of course, crippling to the logic of oppression. The second is a show of force, and an act of oppression in and of itself."

The email exchanges continued, but the Day of Absence / Day of Presence went by with little fanfare. Then, in May, two black students who had gotten into a Facebook argument with another student over race at Evergreen were detained and questioned by campus police for several hours in the middle of the night for supposed threats they'd made against the student. A few days later, a small group of student protesters disrupted the campus's public discussion with one of the candidates for the newly created position of diversity and inclusion chair. The email exchanges among faculty continued, as the fervor among students built up—everyone on campus had read the emails by now. For some, it seemed Weinstein represented everything wrong with Evergreen's brand of liberalism—someone theoretically progressive who nonetheless was totally unwilling to listen to the concerns of students of color.

On May 23, students decided to disrupt one of Weinstein's classes, and called on him to be fired. The police were called. The next day, hundreds of students occupied the campus's library and administrative building. They asked professors to show their support and join them. Naima Lowe was one of the few who did.

"Not a single member of the faculty has a job without the students. Period. No configuration of our curriculum is viable without clear input on the very issues that the students are protesting. Period," Lowe wrote to her fellow faculty the day of the occupation. "If our students are suffering in this way, then our job is to respond, listen and understand what they are trying to tell us."

Lowe had had it—she had spent months trying to convince her white colleagues that students of color had legitimate demands, that being black on campus really was as hard as they were saying it was. And in return she had been accused of reverse racism by Weinstein, and largely ignored or told to remain calm by others. Outside the library, Lowe told her colleagues, "We are literally asking for the same shit that students have been asking for since the '70s. None of this is new. None of it!" A crowd of students gathered around her and applauded. People were filming. Naima continued, obviously exasperated: "I don't have time for anything else. I'm too tired. This shit is literally going to kill me." After a few minutes the students surrounding her outside the library began to chant at the white professors, "Go inside or go home," trying to implore them to engage with the students in the library and administrative offices. Lowe briefly collapsed on the floor from the stress of the moment, and was immediately surrounded by a wall of student protesters who helped her to her feet, prevented onlookers from disturbing her, and brought her water and a medic.

Inside, students surrounded the office of President Bridges and barricaded the doors to the library building so no police could get in. The confrontation was intense. There was yelling. The students corralled other administrators into the office. The idea was to negate the excuse they'd heard from administrators before: "Well, I'll have to talk to someone else about that before we can move forward with the initiative." With everyone in the same room, they'd have no excuses.

Bridges mostly listened. The group, largely students of color, drafted a list of demands on scrap paper and laptops. They included the firing of the police officer involved in detaining two black students earlier that month, the suspension of Bret Weinstein, mandatory cultural competency training for staff and faculty, and the creation of a center for equity that could focus on making the campus more diverse and hospitable to queer students and students of color.[6] After about four hours, the protest dispersed with no arrests.

Two days later, Bridges addressed the school. The administration would not fire Weinstein or the campus cops, he said, but Evergreen would create a full-time equity center and begin to institute mandatory training for cultural sensitivity. Bridges had acquiesced to some of the students' demands.

Students planned no more protests. They had at least partially won. They were also exhausted. The semester was almost over. It's impossible to know how things would have shaken out if Bret Weinstein hadn't decided to go on Fox News. The night after the library occupation,

Weinstein appeared on *Tucker Carlson Tonight* in a segment called "Campus Craziness." Carlson said that students of color at Evergreen had told white students to "leave campus or else," and presented the protest as a kind of hostage situation, comparing it to the Khmer Rouge. "They imagine that I'm a racist. That I'm teaching racism in my classroom, and that I therefore have no right to speak," Weinstein said in the segment. He returned as a guest two weeks later.

Right-wing news sites and blogs ran wild with the story. Eric Weinstein, Bret's brother, the managing director of Silicon Valley investment firm Thiel Capital (owned by Peter Thiel, a right-wing billionaire who has helped fund lawsuits to shut down the left-leaning media site Gawker), began tweeting about the incident, calling the students Maoists and fascists, and garnering tens of thousands of retweets. Hundreds of YouTubers made videos about the incidents. Many manipulated images of Naima Lowe and other prominent protesters, drawing attention to her race and size. Some professors at Evergreen wondered if Eric Weinstein and perhaps even Peter Thiel were coordinating media for Bret. Many of the headlines used the same words to describe the students. Zoltán Grossman, a geography professor at the school, found a blog post in which Eric Weinstein espoused the benefits of twisting media language to influence people to favor certain policies. "He was almost laying out a game plan for how to do propaganda," Grossman said.[7]

After Fox and the right-wing media latched on to the story, Lowe and others began receiving hundreds of emails and messages on social media from people who had seen her on Fox News and conservative websites. Many were angry, some explicitly violent. People called her ugly, fat, the N-word. She would forward a digest of the emails to the college administration each week. She took leave for her mental health.

A few weeks later, Patriot Prayer, a white supremacist group, planned a rally on campus that organizers originally called "March Against Evergreen State College" but which they quickly redubbed "Free Speech Evergreen State College."[8] White supremacists had killed several people in the Pacific Northwest that year, including two men who were stabbed to death on a train in nearby Portland after defending two Muslim commuters from a man's racist attacks. Months earlier, Naima Lowe said she had seen a custodian at Evergreen walking around with a jacket adorned with patches associated with white supremacist groups.

At the Patriot Prayer protest, cops in riot gear separated the participants from students and outside groups of black-clad leftist demonstrators, who sprayed silly string at the white supremacists. The confrontation was tense, but it did not lead to violence.

Then, one day in June, a man called Evergreen and told an administrator he planned on coming to campus with a .44 Magnum to "execute as many people on that campus as I can get ahold of."[9] The campus shut down and classes were canceled, but students were left in their dorms with no additional security. Some students went to local big-box stores and purchased baseball bats for self-protection against what they perceived to be a credible threat. When a photo of a few students striking poses with the bats while smiling leaked, it was picked up by right-wing websites, which used it as evidence of the students' willingness to resort to violence. Bret Weinstein tweeted the photo out and claimed that some had already been hit by the students.[10]

Nearly two years later at Evergreen, things were largely the same as they were at the start of the protests. Weinstein and his wife, who was also a professor at the school, had left and received a $500,000 settlement from the school. Lowe ultimately decided to leave too and settled with Evergreen for $240,000. The school's enrollment numbers had dropped, though it's not clear by how much. Evergreen was already struggling to enroll students before the 2017 protests.[11] It's likely the school's admissions and financial situation will get worse. Several students central to the protests have left Evergreen as well. Nearly all who stayed refuse to talk to the media, some because they're afraid they'll be doxxed by right-wingers, some because they feel traumatized by what happened and don't want to relive it, and some because they're just sick of seeing their story told over and over again. Most have done a remarkably good job of keeping their names hidden from public view—Naima Lowe became a public figure and was smeared by alt-righters, but many students managed to avoid the same fate. In general, the feeling of defeat was pervasive on the gloomy, often-gray-skied campus.

✕✕✕

It's important to acknowledge something: conservatives are in some ways right about the college issue. When they fret about no-platforming, when they complain that students no longer want to do things their way, when they express fear that if the culture on campuses continues to move in the same direction it's unclear who *will* be able to speak, they're tapping into something real: college students *do* want change. They want more of a say in their academics, and they want fewer conservative white men taught in classrooms and taking the stages of the lecture halls. That's explicitly what students were arguing for at Evergreen.

What conservatives (and many liberals) are wrong about is the idea that these changes have anything to do with a universalist definition of free speech. Colleges—indeed, all institutions—have *always* limited what can and cannot be said on their campuses.

In September 2017, Carolyn Rouse, an anthropology professor at Princeton, presented a lecture she called "F*** Free Speech." Rouse censored the "fuck" because she knew she couldn't write the full word out on posters, but also to prove her point: you only understand what the title really means because of context. Rouse argued that's true of all speech. She began the talk with a few examples. If you're a doctor, giving medical advice that could lead to someone's death is generally accepted in a hospital. But if you give the same advice to someone at a party, you could be sued. If you are a bereaved parent attending a support group for bereaved parents, you might say, "I'm so sad I want to die." It would be an appropriate thing to say. But if you say that to your therapist, they may ask for you to be institutionalized. And if you say it in a college classroom, the cops or medics might be called. All speech is contextual. You might be free to say anything you want in any context legally, but it never happens that way. That's *especially* true in academic settings: there are countless rules internalized by professors and students that are so uncontroversial they are most often left unstated. If you began a paper with "Hi. How are you?" you'd likely get an F.

Even what we call polite speech, Rouse said, is a form of self-censorship. You don't walk up to someone and say, "Fuck you." There are rules about what speech is allowed where—in courtrooms, at dinners, at your office, and at school. We usually make judgments about which speech is allowed where internally, and self-censor, so that society can function, with little complaint. Being polite, beginning school papers in an academic, formal manner, not talking about porn you watched while in church—these forms of censorship do not worry the free speech defenders.

"Speech is suppressed, censored, and self-censored all the time, in ways big and small," Rouse told her audience. "So the question we need to ask is why do some incidents get the attention they do, and some do not?"

To pretend that colleges are places of free speech would be to ignore that they are places where expertise and knowledge is built. Professors are credentialed. Students are admitted and denied admission. (Is each rejection letter a rejection of free speech? Well, in some ways, yes, but according to Rouse, that's okay, or at least inevitable.)

It's somewhat ironic that colleges are the main locus of today's battles for free speech because they are, and always have been, some of the most restricted speech environments in the country.

"You don't just write papers as if you're the first person to invent something," Rouse told me later. "We have a very specific form of knowledge production." That form of knowledge production has, historically, respected hierarchy and self-referentiality: Studies conducted at universities are built on previous studies conducted by universities; there are respected and followed Socratic methods; professors are, generally, thought to know more than students. To an extent, the far-right defenders of free speech are responding to something real when they point to Evergreen, Middlebury, and other colleges and universities as harbingers of a new (and, to them, scary) paradigm: students *are* challenging the once-respected methods of institutional knowledge transfer, expecting their institutions to listen to them more and to place a greater emphasis on race and gender and class. But this is nothing new, and to couch it as a free speech issue ignores the fact that colleges are already anti-free-speech zones. We are not arguing over speech versus restriction, but over two forms of restriction: one that respects traditional teaching methods developed largely by white men and a newer one, with different values.

Rouse did not allow her speech to be posted online. She doesn't use social media. But after she was asked on Fox News in part to defend her speech (and in part to talk about the Charles Murray incident at Middlebury), she began receiving racist and misogynistic hate mail. Her colleague Keeanga-Yamahtta Taylor, another black woman who is a professor at Princeton, had received death threats after giving a speech critical of President Trump a few months earlier at Hampshire College (my alma mater). Rouse knew she was lucky that she didn't receive more threats. But the controversy signaled something to her: people weren't really mad about free speech on college campuses because, in her mind, free speech did not exist on college campuses—or anywhere else. It never had. They were mad about the *specifics* of what was and wasn't allowed to be said on college campuses. It was the same at Evergreen: what Bret Weinstein had couched as a debate about free speech was actually a debate about the college listening to students of color.

In September 2016, three black men—Terence Crutcher in Tulsa, Oklahoma; Keith Lamont Scott in Charlotte, North Carolina; and Alfred Olango in a suburb of San Diego, California—were killed by police. On September 20, the actor Isaiah Washington posted a status to his Facebook page in which he wondered what would happen if everyone stayed home on September 26 to protest the death of black people at the hands of police. "I'm very sure that within 72 hours . . . Black Lives Would Matter," he wrote. On September 26, virtually everyone in the United States ignored that call—except a group of students at Reed College, a tiny liberal arts school on the outskirts of Portland, Oregon, who decided to test Washington's theory by boycotting class for the day.

September 26 did not change much nationally, or at Reed, but some students, members of a group called Reedies Against Racism, took the message to heart: they would disrupt normal life until black lives mattered. Their daylong boycott turned into a weeklong occupation of a classroom, which turned into a yearlong protest.

Reedies Against Racism had twenty-five demands. Among them: Reed should disinvest from its operating bank, Wells Fargo, because of its unethical investments, create a more formalized system to recruit and retain students of color at the school, make the student meal plan more affordable for students in need, and hire more tenure-track black faculty.[12] The demand that became the protesters' cause célèbre, demand number thirteen, focused on a course central to Reed's philosophy of education. Humanities 110 (also called Hum 110), a required first-year course, is made up of lectures and small group sessions in which students debate and discuss assigned readings. The problem, according to RAR, was that nearly every reading assigned in the class was written by a white man hundreds or thousands of years ago, with a special focus on classic Greek art and literature.

To RAR members, it was time for a change. Students had tried for years to add literature from other cultures to the course, to no avail. And so starting in 2016 RAR occupied the Hum 110 classroom every class for the entire school year and into the next one. The occupation not only challenged a fundamental course at Reed; it challenged one of the school's fundamental philosophies—that debate, discussion, and analysis were a way toward better understanding and social justice. That was the very point of Hum 101. RAR students were saying that wasn't enough, that Reed had already set the terms of the debate in the form of the western canon, and that there was no point in playing ball on a racially biased playing field.

RAR had an uphill battle to fight. The course was popular among students—overall 70 percent said they enjoyed it (a deeper dig into the numbers showed that 47 percent of students of color and 75 percent of transgender students voiced concerns about the course in 2016).[13] Many professors relished the opportunity to teach the course. It was truly central to the school's identity.

At the beginning, the disruption often prevented the class from taking place. Professors would walk out or teach their class elsewhere. But for the rest of the year, most of the protests involved RAR members sitting silently on the floor at the front of the class, holding up signs, including ones with quotes from black authors. As the protests dragged on and the administration refused to budge (it banned many of RAR's leaders from entering the Hum 101 lecture hall in perpetuity), Reed students began to experience much of what happened at Evergreen—doxxing from right-wingers; a few actual threats on campus, including racist and homophobic graffiti and swastikas painted in the school's library; and a flurry of unsympathetic news coverage. The mainstream press, like it did at Evergreen and Middlebury, painted the protesters as anti-free-speech, anti-intellectual, and just plain irrational.[14] RAR supporters thought everyone was missing the point.

"One of the big pillars of intellectualism is this ability to question everything you already know," Maddox, a nineteen-year-old member of RAR, told me. We were secretly meeting in a musty-smelling dorm common space at night because the college had banned all media from campus after RAR's actions caused an international news event. "We, as a society, accept this foundational idea that the western canon, and most western texts, and all the textbooks I received when I was younger—all of them telling me that, 'Oh, this place's economy was trash and they didn't have running water until the white people got there.' Are you saying it's not intellectual to question those truths? Why is it anti-intellectual to question our obsession with the western canon?"

In the context of the United States in the mid-2010s, many, especially students, seem to be realizing that no matter how many times they ask for their voices to be heard, the playing field, platform, classroom, country, whatever—it was still designed to disadvantage their viewpoint, and it's a losing game to play by its rules. Instead, they prefer to shut it down, or at least call attention to how little power they have and why they feel the game has been, all along, rigged.

In the early 1990s, the literary theorist Stanley Fish and the conservative provocateur Dinesh D'Souza participated in a series of debates about political correctness, affirmative action, and the role of politics on college campuses. D'Souza's line of argument was that colleges were becoming too image-conscious, reducing the standards of their academics in order to prove themselves as nonracist and nonsexist.[15] Fish's argument was essentially the opposite: that colleges were indeed still predominantly white, male, and rich, and that all students and professors were asking for was to level the playing field.

Fish later wrote a book called *There's No Such Thing as Free Speech . . . And It's a Good Thing, Too*, in which he expanded on his thoughts. What Fish saw on college campuses was a battle between two modes of thinking: a conservative one mostly espoused by white men and one that demanded that different cultures, races, and genders be taken into consideration. But what the former had succeeded in doing was claiming *their* mode of thinking as the unbiased one, the natural order. "One can reduce the strategy to a formula," Fish wrote. "First detach your agenda from its partisan origins, from its history, and then present it as a universal imperative, as a call to moral arms so perspicuous that only the irrational or the godless (two categories often conflated) could refuse it. . . . This is precisely what has been done, and done brilliantly by the neoconservative participants in the recent culture wars. Perhaps their most stunning success has been the production (in fact a reproduction), packaging, and distribution of the term 'political correctness.'"[16]

It's remarkable how similar the discourse Fish was addressing twenty-five years ago is to today's debates, in which conservatives and some liberals like Weinstein claim that a threat to their privileged place within academics is in fact a universal threat to the modus operandi of our entire language and institutions.

Fish warned liberals not to fall into the trap set by conservatives; if they claimed that they prized the same things—free speech, universal truth—they'd be playing the game on conservatives' terms. Fish posited it would be better for everyone to acknowledge that debates over curricula and speakers on college campuses are not debates "between political correctness and something else, but between competing versions of political correctness." In Fish's view, and in mine, most conservatives do not care more about free speech than liberals do. They simply define acceptable, correct speech differently.

These different versions are easy to see on college campuses. Conservative Christian universities, for example, do not regularly invite atheist, leftist speakers. Their curricula do not give equal weight to the opinions of leftists in the interest of maintaining open debate. You don't usually learn Marx at Wheaton College, just like you don't usually learn the teachings of Jesus at Hampshire College (though you can create a self-directed course of study that focuses on him, if you wish). Colleges are curated environments. Most liberal arts institutions, like Middlebury and Evergreen, just happen to be curated in ways conservatives don't like.

Although colleges may be increasingly curated to match the desires and interests of more diverse and more progressive student bodies, they're still overwhelmingly white and classicist, much like they were in the early 1990s: When Fish and D'Souza debated, more than 80 percent of the country's professors were white men, and 97 percent of colleges were found to put no "undue pressure" on conservatives.[17] Conservative commentator Christopher Clausen once said that colleges were teaching Alice Walker's *The Color Purple* more often than Shakespeare. It became such a common refrain that D'Souza, Lynne Cheney, and countless other conservatives repeated it. But, according to Fish's calculation, Shakespeare was still taught forty times more than *The Color Purple* at the time.[18]

Conservatives might have more to worry about this time around: only 41 percent of professors were white men in 2016 (though most of the diversity gains came from white women; black and Latino professors still make up a tiny fraction of America's academic field).[19] The content of what's being taught is changing too. That's harder to quantify, but you can get a clue from an annual survey done by the National Association of Scholars, which asks about the books that hundreds of colleges assign to their incoming freshmen—the books meant to set the tone for their college experience. In 2017, NAS found that, nearly uniformly, the books were recently published, and about race and social justice (Ta-Nehisi Coates's *Between the World and Me* was particularly popular).[20]

Of course, one book doesn't necessarily mean that racial and social justice are at the forefront of college curricula. It's impossible to know the general thrust of what is being taught in most classrooms, but from my reporting (and from my experience as a college student), I think it would be safe to say that the classics—Shakespeare, John Locke, and all the rest—still have a prominent place on campus, and that racial and social justice, while discussed more frequently, are by no means the center of most discussions in most classrooms. Even at Evergreen, one of the most liberal of all colleges, students complained that the topics were not discussed at all in their science classrooms. Still, conservatives are rightly sensing shifting sands. As Fish puts it, the story the academy teaches us about America, the world, and our place in it, is changing. And by privileging one story over another, we will inevitably piss off those who preferred the previous story, even if it was a racist one.

> Those we now criticize as racists . . . did not think of themselves as evil persons pursuing evil policies; they thought of themselves as *right*, and from the vantage point of the story they were living and telling . . . they were. In the years since 1960, that story has become less and less compelling to more and more people, which means not that its limitations have been transcended but that another story, with its own limitations, has become more compelling. The effect of telling that newer story has not been to eliminate impartiality, but to alter its shape. . . . The conclusion is perhaps distressing—especially if you are holding out for a vision rooted in no story but in the Whole Truth as seen by the eyes of God—but it is inevitable: alternative stories are alternative vehicles of discrimination, alternative narratives in which some interests are slighted at the expense of others.

There is not more or less speech on college campuses these days. And there is not a different view about free speech in America than there ever was. There is different speech, and those invested in the old story are freaking out about it.

## chapter five

# PUSHING THE LINE

THE EVENTS IN CHARLOTTESVILLE—NAZIS AND THE ACLU ALIGNED
over a permit to march; counterprotesters intent on shutting the Nazis down, free speech be damned; the media frenzy—all seemed so fright-
eningly new, unexpected, maybe even (to some people less pessimistic
than I about this country) un-American. But the march and its fallout
were foreshadowed by a series of events forty years ago. Charlottesville
was not new; it was just another in a long line of examples of Americans
battling over the lines between speech, action, and violence. After Charlottesville, when people asked, "How could this happen here?" or "Why
would the Nazis march here?" or "Why would the ACLU defend them?"
or "What can we do about Nazis without impinging on free speech?" the
answer was: look to Skokie.

In 1976, Skokie was like most postwar Chicago suburbs: blocks
upon blocks of brick, low-slung, single-family homes on small plots of
well-manicured grass, plus a few strip malls and bigger buildings toward
the town center. Its only defining feature was its residents: 40,000 out of

70,000 were Jewish, many of them Holocaust survivors who had moved to the suburb shortly after World War II ended. Almost nowhere else in America, save for parts of New York City, was the trauma of the Holocaust so concentrated.

That made Skokie a tinderbox, and that's what made it such an appealing place for Frank Collin, the leader of the neo-Nazi National Socialist Party of America, to hold a march.

The NSP was a breakaway group of members of George Lincoln Rockwell's National Socialist White People's Party (also at various times known as the American Nazi Party). The group had fractured in part because of the revelation that Collin's father was actually a Jewish Holocaust survivor who had changed his name upon coming to the United States. Despite the controversy, Collin was able to attract a few dozen followers and open an office for his tiny party on Chicago's South Side. The group held rallies in Jewish and black neighborhoods throughout the 1970s. In 1976, Collin began encouraging rallies in Marquette Park, which was surrounded by a neighborhood that until recently had been majority-white but which had seen an influx of black families. After several of Collin's rallies ended in scuffles between Nazis and counterdemonstrators, the City of Chicago first banned all rallies from Marquette Park and then, likely realizing the legally dubious nature of its decision, instead required any activist group that wanted to hold a rally to post a $250,000 bond.[1] Collin appealed to the ACLU for help, and the organization agreed to represent him and his party. The decision made almost no waves within the ACLU or outside it—to the organization, it was a cut-and-dry free speech case: the government was infringing on a group's right to peaceably assemble. But that also meant that the case got Collin little attention from the media and the public, which he needed to recruit.

So while the case worked its way through the courts, Collin decided to rouse residents of the Chicago area further by sending over a dozen letters to nearby municipalities declaring his intention to march. The suburb of Skokie was one of the only towns to respond, informing Collin he would be required to post $350,000 in insurance bonds for any march he wanted to hold. It's impossible to know what would have happened if

Skokie, like many of the other municipalities that had received requests, simply ignored Collin. But the Jewish residents of Skokie felt that they could not ignore the provocation.

Fred Huss, now a podiatrist who lives a few miles from Skokie, was a teenager when Collin requested a permit to march in the town. Huss had been a toddler when his parents moved to Illinois. His parents had spent years running and hiding throughout Germany, including in a cave, avoiding the Nazis until the war was over. Skokie felt like a safe space for them, but the trauma of the Holocaust infiltrated daily life. What could have been a relatively normal suburban childhood for Fred was instead filled with tumult.

"There's nothing normal about living under the anguish that goes on in two-survivor families," he told me one spring day in Chicago, shortly after his mother had passed. "There were fights. Some were physical, some emotional. My dad, he wore his pain clearly on his sleeve."

It was normal to feel so abnormal in Skokie, according to Huss. Parents waking up screaming in the middle of the night. Parents scared of large crowds, or just shut down and depressed, processing their trauma. Huss's father, a barber, would regale his clientele with Holocaust stories. His mother, a teacher, would tell kids about her history. They had outlets, but it was never enough to truly heal, and the Collin march was salt in the wound.

For that reason, to Fred Huss and many other residents of Skokie, it was obvious they couldn't let the march happen. Fred still has a picture of his mom holding a megaphone outside Skokie's Village Hall—one of hundreds of protesters asking the city not to let the Nazis in. The Huss family wasn't anti-free-speech, but Fred thought that the march could easily lead to violence, and that Skokie's residents might even ensure that it would, and so it needed to be shut down.

"They were coming into an area to cause anguish and agony for these people, and people were so hurt to have to relive it again," Huss said. "From what my father and my brother told me, there were quite a few things in the back of people's trunks to take care of business. . . . There would have been serious injury to a lot of people."

Responding to public pressure, the Village of Skokie asked a judge for an injunction on Collin's May 1 rally. Collin changed the date. And so the Village cobbled together a plan: it passed three new ordinances that effectively shut Collin out of town by requiring $350,000 in insurance for demonstrations, preventing the dissemination of any material that "incites hatred" against people for their religion or race, and prohibiting marches that include military-style uniforms (as Nazis were fond of wearing).[2] The ordinances mirrored an Illinois law passed in 1917 that had been upheld by the Supreme Court in 1952. But views on free speech had changed since then: Illinois had repealed that law in 1964, and the ACLU saw Skokie's attempt to locally reinstitute it as an affront to the First Amendment. The group sued.

The debate over what to do about Nazis wanting to traumatize people by marching has changed little since Skokie. Newspaper clippings from the time could be read as if they were from today, just by replacing "Skokie" with "Charlottesville" or "UC Berkeley."

"If I wanted to stand outside Wally's Polish Pump Room this Saturday and shout that everybody who eats Polish sausage is a pig, I suppose that would be my constitutional right. At least the ACLU would probably think so," one op-ed columnist wrote in the *Chicago Sun-Times*.[3] "However, I don't think I should expect the city to give me a police escort when I go there." The columnist's solution was the same: Let the Nazis march, but don't provide them with police protection.

Some advocated for ignoring the Nazis, starving them of publicity. "The people of Skokie should make it their business that nobody—and I mean nobody—be there to give them their audience," one Skokie resident said at a meeting in the Village Hall.

Others argued that the First Amendment didn't actually protect against hate speech. "Since when is the killing of 6 million people to be considered 'free speech?'" one demonstrator at an anti-Nazi protest asked. Village President Albert Smith said that the line was pretty clear: everyone, except those who advocated genocide, was entitled to free speech. "How do you decide who gets the First Amendment rights?" he asked a newspaper reporter. "I'll tell you how. The only people who can't are those who can be proven to be responsible for 10 to 20 million murders."[4]

For the ACLU of Illinois and its national counterpart, the decision to represent Collin's group against the Village of Skokie seemed like an obvious choice. They had already taken Collin's side in his fight for a permit at Marquette Park with little fanfare, and the ordinances in Skokie were even more restrictive. Who could determine what constituted a military uniform? What material was considered enough to incite hate? "We have no choice but to take the case," David Hamlin, head of the ACLU of Illinois, wrote at the time.[5] Just a few years earlier, the ACLU of Illinois had successfully argued to the Supreme Court that Dick Gregory, a comedian and civil rights activist, could not be arrested for leading a protest where some demonstrators participated in disorderly conduct.[6] Though the ACLU had until that point represented very few white supremacists, the Skokie case was an opportunity to affirm its place as the arbiter for *all* speech rights, not just the rights of leftists and unionists.

The organization knew it had a good case. Legal precedents in recent decades had made it clear that local governments could have a hard time placing "prior restraint" on speech or protest. In 1976, in deciding a case involving the State of Nebraska's efforts to prevent newspapers from revealing information about a murder trial, Chief Justice Warren Burger had called prior restraints on speech "the most serious and the least tolerable infringement on First Amendment rights."[7]

The ACLU first argued in front of the Illinois Appellate Court, which struck down Skokie's ban on distributing literature and wearing uniforms but upheld the town's right to ban the display of swastikas, which the court construed as "fighting words"—words that, according to a unanimous Supreme Court opinion from 1942, "by their very utterance inflict injury or tend to incite an immediate breach of the peace."[8] (The "fighting words" doctrine still exists today, but the Supreme Court rarely favors the suppression of speech because of it. In 2011, Justice Samuel Alito invoked it to defend banning members of the hate-spewing Westboro Baptist Church from military funerals, but was outnumbered eight to one by his fellow justices.[9]) The ACLU appealed to the Illinois Supreme

Court, arguing that allowing a swastika to be defined as "fighting words" would set a precedent that could allow municipalities to ban any groups with controversial ideas, like preventing black people from marching in white communities with a black power fist.[10] The court ruled in the ACLU's favor.

Since Skokie, this distinction—between speech and words meant to incite violence—has been the central battleground of free speech fights involving Nazis in this country. To the ACLU, almost nothing short of an actual call for murder is an incitement to violence, and therefore speech that must be protected. To many others, the residents of Skokie included, the choice to march through a town of Jews carrying a swastika was enough to be considered violence. What does a swastika represent if *not* a call to violence?

"The Nazis are a unique political tradition due to their advocacy of and history of mass genocide," the conservative sociologist Irving Louis Horowitz wrote in an extensive rebuttal to the ACLU's position on free speech, published two years after Skokie. "In the case of the United States, they advocate genocide against Jews and blacks. The general slogan of White Power can be asserted to fall within constitutional safeguards provided by the First Amendment, but the symbol of genocide, the swastika, is the direct link between Skokie and Auschwitz, between the invasion of a quiet Jewish town and the destruction of equally quiet European Jewish villages and neighborhoods by the hundreds in World War II."[11]

Horowitz was not only critical of the ACLU for helping Nazis incite genocide; he also blasted the organization for helping them become palatable. To represent them in court was one thing, but in order to win in court, the ACLU also coached the Nazis to stay away from inflammatory language, to mention white pride instead of genocide, free speech instead of the Third Reich.[12]

It's telling that a conservative like Horowitz could come down on the side of limiting the speech of Nazis at the time, when today's conservatives would more likely take the ACLU's position—favoring free speech for all over limiting the trauma it can cause. Just a decade later, conservatives like Dinesh D'Souza would use the terminology of free speech to push right-wing ideals and argue that any effort to limit free speech is antithetical to democracy. The abrupt switch from Skokie to the late 1980s, when hysteria over PC culture took over the country, shows how arbitrary free speech politics are: very rarely are people consistent in their approach. Instead, they tend to favor suppressing the speech they don't like and allowing the speech they do.

The Nazis seemed to internalize the ACLU's suggestion to tone things down: after the fervor from Skokie died down, Collin told a local paper, "Our only interest in agitating was to focus attention on the First Amendment rights we were being denied. We put pressure on the system and it worked." Today, the alt-right has internalized the lesson of Skokie: its leaders know to stay away from the language of genocide and violence, instead couching their message in universal values like free speech, and sometimes the ACLU is right there with them to help.[13]

If the courts had agreed with Horowitz, US free speech law today might look like those of many European countries. In Germany, hate speech is illegal in all contexts, even online (social media networks can be fined for not removing it). In France, publicly insulting someone because of their religion is grounds for arrest or fine—fashion designer John Galliano was put on trial after making drunken anti-Semitic remarks that sent ripples through the international media in 2011. Although the laws in those countries make a Nazi march like the one that almost took place in Skokie much harder, discrimination can still flourish: the far right is on the rise in France, Germany, and many other European countries. The laws are applied inconsistently at best (Muslims have pointed out that France's law has barely stopped anti-Muslim tirades in the press); at worst they are used to stifle legitimate political dissent: activists protesting Israel's treatment of Palestinians have been slapped with fines for "inciting racial hatred" in France. But the laws are at least an admission by governments that they do have an interest in curtailing some speech, and that those interests are inherently political. As the history outlined in this book shows, the United States does not curtail speech any less than other western countries—it's just that the bias of the US government is more hidden, cloaked behind the supposed neutrality of the First Amendment.[14]

Skokie did not set legal precedent—for the ACLU it was a rather run-of-the-mill case of fighting prior restraint—but the national uproar over the case turned the ACLU's fight into a referendum on the morality of free speech. People had to decide whether they thought that speech can be confined or whether they, like the ACLU, believed that to confine even the most despicable speech would mean giving the government the power to stop virtually anyone's speech. The country was divided. The *New York Times*, as it often does now, took the ACLU's side, with an editorial that concluded, "As long as the Nazis do nothing illegal, they are entitled to the protection of the law. The argument that they will provoke violence simply by appearing on the streets of Skokie only emphasizes the obligation of the police to keep the peace."[15] A roundup of opinions from the local *Skokie Life* newspaper found that some believed protests would give the Nazis more attention than they deserved, while others believed the Nazis should be "smashed" in the streets.[16]

The ACLU of Illinois lost almost 25 percent of its membership because of its decision to represent Collin. The national ACLU lost tens of thousands of members too (down from 270,000 in the early 1970s to 185,000 after Skokie, though it's unclear how much of the decline was directly related). It ended up half a million dollars in debt, but the organization persisted in defending its decision. At a panel discussion in a New York hotel about the limits of free speech just a few weeks before the scheduled rally, the head of the ACLU at the time, Aryeh Neier, and ACLU Illinois lawyer David Goldberger, who was part of the team representing Collin, were lambasted by representatives from other civil liberties organizations and professors who asked why the ACLU had decided to represent Nazis. One panelist pointed out that the ACLU could agree that the Skokie laws were bad, but still focus the organization's limited resources on more liberal causes instead. Asked whether the ACLU would feel compelled to represent Nazis holding signs that directly advocated violence, something like "Kill a Jew Today!" Goldberger replied, "The answer would have to be yes." [17]

The ACLU's decision to defend the Nazis in Skokie came after years of internal strife about whom the national organization should represent.

At its founding in 1920, the ACLU was more explicitly leftist. The organization defended union leaders and socialists against corporate and government persecution throughout the 1920s and '30s. Its leaders even advocated for free speech as a means to overthrow the capitalist oligarchy of the US government (more on that later). In the 1940s, the organization had lambasted the United States for the travesty of Japanese internment when few other organizations would, and in the 1950s, it represented dozens in important civil rights cases, including *Brown v. Board of Education*. But it had gradually taken on a more universalist approach to free speech—defending people regardless of political belief.

Its state affiliates had conflicting ideas about whom to give resources and legal counsel to. For example, in one Mississippi case shortly before Skokie, the ACLU had agreed to represent the Ku Klux Klan, but then reneged as the case went to federal court. In another case in California, the ACLU had battled itself in court: the branch in Los Angeles defended a group of black marines who had attempted to attack Klan members in the marines, and the San Diego chapter defended the Klan.[18]

Increasingly, the organization took a neutral approach to civil liberties: it would defend whomever it thought needed defending if the case had possible ramifications for civil liberties for everyone. And it saw its membership decrease less as a rebuke of this philosophy than as an inevitable dropoff after tens of thousands had signed on as a form of protesting Richard Nixon's election in 1968. As some leaders of the ACLU saw it, Skokie strengthened the organization—ridding itself of those who did not care about civil liberties that much in the first place, and proving that the organization would stand up for civil liberties no matter what. But it was clear that they had to defend their decision in order to retain the rest.

"The right to free speech is always tested at the extremes," Neier told those gathered at the free speech debate.[19] "It is almost always fringe groups of people who are provocative, who select that place where they are disliked the most because that is where they can get the most attention. Isn't that what Martin Luther King did at Selma? For that very reason it is the extremes that have the greatest interest in protecting the rights of their enemies. Once the freedom of one group is abridged, that infringement will be cited to deny the rights of others. The people who most need the ACLU to defend the rights of the Klan are the blacks. The people who most need the ACLU to defend the rights of Nazis are the Jews."

Shortly after Skokie, as the ACLU's membership rapidly declined, David Goldberger, the attorney who had represented Collin in court, sent a letter explaining the ACLU's reasons for taking the case to supporters. Think of what would happen if Skokie wasn't about Nazis but about antiwar demonstrators, he said. Think about the implications of a government's ability to limit free speech as it sees fit. The appeal worked: membership began rising by the thousands again. As Neier later put it: It's not that people forgot about Skokie, or supported the ACLU in spite of it; it's that the rest of America came around to supporting the ACLU's vision of free speech.[20]

The rally never happened in Skokie. Collin told supporters that he had made his point—free speech had been saved. Plus, he said, he was more interested in protesting again in Marquette Park anyway. He and his band of Nazis rallied there in July 1978, surrounded by thousands of counterprotesters. Afterward, his group trickled into nothing, and in 1980, Collin was convicted of molesting underage boys. Since then, he has converted from Nazism to a hybrid of New Age philosophies, and has abandoned his association with white nationalism.[21]

But the reason Collin never marched on Skokie is still up for debate. According to some, it wasn't because of the town's efforts to prevent the rally, but because Collin feared that if he had marched, he would have been killed. One group wanted to make sure of that. As the ACLU and much of the American media debated the merits of giving Nazis a platform, the Jewish Defense League, a militant right-wing band of Jews, vowed to severely beat or even kill Collin and his supporters if they ever marched on Skokie.

A disclaimer here: I deeply disagree with the Jewish Defense League on virtually everything the group stands for. It is not a Jewish version of antifa—antifa, as the name implies, is against fascism. The Jewish Defense League, in many ways, is a Jewish supremacist group. Its members do not believe in the right of Palestinians to have a homeland. Its members will openly discuss their belief that Jews are more intelligent than other ethnicities, including Anglo whites. But as I researched this book, I found myself drawn to the story of the JDL for three reasons. First, it proves that the idea of no-platforming is not just a left-wing concept—that when centrist establishment politics espoused by groups like the ACLU tend to favor free speech for everyone, including Nazis, some people, across the political spectrum, end up taking matters into their own hands. Second, JDL members' claims that they prevented Collin from speaking in Skokie need to be taken seriously, because if they're true, they may change the conclusions we draw about the best methods for defeating Nazism today. Although pundits argue about the merits of antifa-aligned activists blocking Nazis from speaking, we often forget that there is historical precedent, even if from organizations on the right like the JDL, suggesting that action taken outside a legal framework can work to prevent the spread of fascist speech.

And finally, as the grandchild of Holocaust survivors, and as someone who was nearly killed by a Nazi in Charlottesville, I'd be lying if I said I wasn't attracted to the JDL's militancy. I abhor the group's politics, yet part of me wishes I could stomp on a Nazi's face with some fellow Jews. I wanted to speak to some of the surviving members who still live in Skokie to find out what drew them to JDL in the first place, and whether they saw their tactics as applicable to today.

At the back of an unassuming office park in Skokie sits the Illinois Holocaust Museum, opened in 2009 after thirty years of work by Skokie residents in direct response to the planned Nazi march. As groups of schoolkids walked around the exhibits, I sat in a conference room with two former members of the JDL. Buzz Alpert is now eighty years old and looks like a militant—skinny with a gaunt face, dressed in a bomber jacket, and deadly serious about his mission. Bob Kandelman, sixty-three, is larger and more jovial—he'll laugh as he tells you about all the Nazis he beat up. Neither has any regrets about what he did.

Buzz Alpert came to the JDL in 1969. A former marine, he knew how to fight. He knew how to use guns. He'd majored in history in college, and it had deeply angered him when he learned how long it took for other countries, especially the United States, to stop the massacre of Jews in the Holocaust. Why hadn't anyone done anything?

"The JDL for me was the opportunity to . . . contribute to a battle that might avoid another Holocaust," Alpert told me. "I'm not trying to give us [outsized] importance. We weren't in another Holocaust. But all cancers start small, and there was a cancer: Frank Collin."

Alpert's first fight was in the Chicago suburb of Berwyn in 1972.[22] It was brutal. Twelve JDL members faced down twenty-two Nazis carrying signs with slogans like, "Free Speech for Whites." Alpert walked right up to one of Collin's deputies in front of City Hall and took him by the throat. He was kicked from behind and fell down on his hands and knees. A Nazi had him in a chokehold on the ground. His vision was going gray. Alpert managed to grab the attacker by the testicles until he let go, but then he was promptly kicked in the face by another of Collin's men.

Alpert and Kandelman fought Nazis on dozens of occasions. Alpert still has pain in his neck from his fights. But both feel like it was worth it. Kandelman said that without the JDL, there would be nothing stopping the Nazis from recruiting.

"We were sending a message to anybody who was like-minded, and this is what I think the bigger picture was," Kandelman said. "These groups by themselves are just a nuisance, we can deal with them. The problem is who they might stir up. When you send a message that, if you try to create some sort of movement against the Jews, you're going to have a hell of a price to pay, people are going to think long and hard before they pursue that course of action."

That's why the Nazis didn't come to Skokie, according to Alpert and Kandelman. "Collin knew he was coming into, so to speak, our territory," Kandelman said. "It wasn't the ACLU. The ACLU was in his corner. It wasn't the Anti-Defamation League that stopped him. It wasn't all the demonstrations or the letters or anything else. He knew that if he came in, he would be carried out."[23]

At the time, the JDL was denounced across the political spectrum, especially by those on the left, who saw the JDL as complicit in fascism. In part, it's because leftist groups felt that they should have been leading the fight against Collin and his supporters. The leftist paper *Workers Vanguard* wrote in 1978 that tens of thousands of members of labor unions would have been ready to counterdemonstrate against the Nazis in Skokie if the march had happened.[24] It's impossible to verify this claim, and given that few leftist groups were on hand in Skokie during the counterprotests leading up to the planned march, it seems safe to assume that it was an exaggeration. JDL members' belief that no one else would defend them was at least partially true in Skokie. The *Workers Vanguard* acknowledged this underwhelming response; without a militant response of its own, the labor movement and the left more broadly were ceding ground to the JDL and centrist groups like the ACLU.

Today, members of the JDL and residents of Skokie have changed their minds on free speech. Kandelman and Alpert told me they were against antifa shutting down Nazis. I expected them to be against antifa because of their right-wing politics, but it was more than that: they no longer believed people should be shut down for what they said. I heard the same thing across town at Fred Huss's house. Yes, we risk violence, Huss told me, but if we restrain speech at all, there's a greater threat. His millennial son, who sat beside him, agreed. Fred Huss's parents had been ready to use violence to stop the Nazis in Skokie, and Fred said that while he understood the desire, he has come around to believing in free speech for all. Fred's son similarly thought without a doubt that all speech, including that of Nazis, needs to be protected.

How had this family's views on free speech evolved so completely over three generations? It's not to belittle the legitimate differences in their opinions, but I wondered if the imminence of threat had something to do with it: Skokie happened when most survivors of the Holocaust were still alive, and still trying to adjust to American life. Today, white Jews still face threats, but we are also assimilated into whiteness, and therefore granted the protection of state powers more than other groups Nazis march against. Recent history has shown us that black and Latino people, for example, cannot rely on the police to protect them from hate as much as Jews can.[25]

So maybe that's where the Huss's differing opinions come from, and maybe that's what accounts for much of the differing opinion on free speech, from college campuses to living rooms in Chicago and beyond: those who see speech, even in its most hateful forms, as an abstract moral issue are willing to defend it. And those who regard that speech as a potentially deadly threat are willing to put their lives on the line to push back against it.

In post-civil-rights America, the conceptualization and politics of free speech have been dominated nearly completely by two groups: conservatives who insist they are being uniquely silenced by PC culture and liberal-leaning groups, especially the ACLU, that believe in an even-handed approach to free speech in which every individual has a right to say what they want, as long as they are not breaking any other laws.

The ACLU does not have a precise definition of free speech or exact criteria for what kinds of cases it chooses to represent, but the organization represents both leftists and Nazis, and everyone in between, and it helps win some cases that further corporate dominance of our politics and some that hinder it. In other words, while the ACLU is a semi-progressive organization, it is agnostic when it comes to speech. Its main process for deciding whether to take on a case these days is to ask, Does it further the protections offered by the First Amendment? That wasn't always the case. Before the ACLU became one of the largest nonprofits in the country, toeing a middle-of-the-road line on speech politics, it was a radical communist organization that saw the support of worker revolution as central to its mission.

On the morning of October 1, 1910, a bomb made of sixteen sticks of dynamite rigged to an alarm clock tore through the *Los Angeles Times*

building in downtown LA, killing twenty-one people. The *Times* was known as one of the most staunchly anti-union papers around, and soon police linked the bombing to a man named J. B. McNamara, who was a member of the International Association of Bridge and Structural Iron Workers. His union had been linked to over one hundred dynamite attacks in the preceding five years, though none until the *Times* bombing had been deadly.

To give you a sense of the radicalism behind the labor movement in the early 1900s: labor leaders did not distance themselves from McNamara. Instead, his case became a cause célèbre. Leftists accused the city's police department of framing McNamara. Job Harriman, a socialist who backed McNamara, nearly won the city's next mayoral election. And Clarence Darrow, who would go on to become one of the ACLU's most prominent lawyers, represented McNamara and his brother, who was implicated in another bombing, in court. When the brothers eventually entered a guilty plea, every newspaper in the country called on the labor movement and its representatives to denounce the bombing, but Darrow refused. The brothers were part of a "great industrial struggle," he said. "There are other things to consider besides property and other things to consider besides bloodshed."[26]

It might be hard to imagine in our current political climate, but a century ago, most Americans who were left of center, including those who would go on to found the ACLU, did not believe in reformist change through our current governmental system. They believed in class warfare. The ACLU was founded after a reorganization of the National Civil Liberties Bureau, an organization that helped legally defend dissenters during World War I. The ACLU's leaders wanted to go beyond the mission of the NCLB: not just legal defense, but agitation for a better world.[27] As law professor Laura Weinrib writes in her in-depth history of the ACLU during the early and mid-twentieth century, progressives of the era "sought to counter the consolidation of capital with organized power of their own. And in order to advance that broader project, they crafted a conceptualization of civil liberties that extended to concerted economic activity as well as expression."[28] To the labor leaders and their allies of the early 1900s, the Constitution was not protective of liberty, but a way to stifle it at the behest of property owners. Civil liberties were inextricable from economic power: the only way to guarantee liberty for all was for everyone to be on the same economic footing. When the early civil libertarians called for free speech, they meant not only free *speech*, but the freedom to organize, and even to overthrow the capitalist class. "In fact," Weinrib wrote, "the right of agitation was the conceptual ground in which modern civil liberties were rooted."[29]

The founders of the ACLU were outright and proud communists and people with close ties to communists. They believed in a class-based vision of revolution, and thought individual liberty was a code word for property ownership, not true freedom for the masses. When William Pickens, an NAACP field secretary, wrote to the ACLU shortly after its founding that lynching was not only a racial tool but one to keep black people economically depressed, ACLU cofounder Roger Baldwin bluntly agreed: "The race issue at bottom is the labor issue . . . and the master class of the south knows it."[30] In other words, Baldwin believed that racism (and virtually every other issue in the United States) was a tool to enshrine an unequal class system. Free speech, and particularly the right of labor to agitate, was the only way to fight against it.

The Industrial Workers of the World, the most radical of the large unions in the early 1900s, saw free speech as inherently disruptive (and therefore an effective political and organizing tool), and mounted dozens of "free speech fights," in which IWW members (known as Wobblies) would participate in civil disobedience and get arrested, then use the arrests to call attention to their view that the government always worked at the behest of industry and against workers.[31] A large part of the left thought that free speech, if it was defined as just speech, was pointless. They believed that "what was necessary was not advocacy, but action; not expression but economic power," Weinrib writes.[32] "Such activity might be accomplished through words, but it was not speech in its conventional legal sense." The court's view on free speech in the early 1900s was not dissimilar to its view today: speaking and distributing flyers was often okay, but direct advocacy for mass action against the government or corporations often led to arrests and other forms of suppression.

The founders of the ACLU in large part agreed with the IWW. Leftist intellectuals and labor leaders at the time thought that the court system would only ever maintain private property rights, and would suppress any rights that threatened the owning class. Thus, the way to change society was not to work through the courts, but to show how inherently biased they were, thereby invalidating their usefulness.[33] Clarence Darrow argued that even equal protection in the eyes of the law was virtually useless in an economically unequal society: the rich had little reason to trespass, to strike, to loiter on the streets, to steal to feed themselves or their families. Laws were, in his view, set up to burden the poor.[34]

Out of this radical moment, two main theories about how to equalize labor's power emerged: put free speech and the freedom to agitate above all other rights, so that it would trump the right even to private property, and so that workers could strike, and possibly even destroy factories, without legal consequence; or invalidate the courts completely as arbiters of free speech and agitation, showing them to be a farce that would always favor property owners, and instead leave the work of building a just society to labor and the few elected officials it found common ground with.[35]

Although the mainstream press regularly steamrolled over these labor-utopian ideas (the *Washington Post*, for example, celebrated the 1919 and 1920 arrests of thousands of leftists, including anarchist Emma Goldman, saying there was "no time to waste on hair-splitting over infringement of liberty when the enemy is using liberty's weapons for the assassination of liberty"), the ideas weren't fringe by any means.[36] In 1912, Congress established the Commission on Industrial Relations, and in a report issued by the body in 1916, its director of research and investigation, Basil Manly, endorsed many leftist ideas about speech and labor, including the belief that courts were essentially allowing the rights of property owners to trump the rights of all others.

Free speech and the right to organize, Manly suggested, needed much greater protection in the United States. It was critical for the future of economic equality.[37] The National Civil Liberties Bureau, the direct precursor to the ACLU, stated that its main mission was to protect the rights of labor to agitate, and argued that the main purpose of fighting for free speech was to allow for laborers to pamphlet, organize, and strike.[38]

As leftists pushed a labor-centric vision of free speech, they were met with an intense and violent backlash. Politicians directly sanctioned conservative vigilante groups whose members would attack union members and raid the offices of leftist organizations. In 1917, hundreds of US marshals raided the offices of the IWW across the country, and took with them five tons of documents and other materials. Ultimately, one hundred Wobblies, including the head of the IWW, "Big Bill" Haywood, were convicted on conspiracy charges for advocating for antigovernment action during wartime.[39]

The fact that so many could be jailed for nothing more than organizing reaffirmed the NCLB's contention (and later that of the ACLU) that agitation was the most important right for transforming the relationship between labor and capital.[40] Even as the ACLU became a more prominent force in free speech and strike cases through the 1920s, its purpose remained radical: its leaders knew most of the cases they took on would lose in the Supreme Court, but that was their tactic—invalidating the legitimacy of the Court by proving just how many times it would rule in favor of industrial capitalists.[41] Their goal, at least back then, was to transform the United States, not to support an abstract form of free speech.

"I feel myself just one protest in a great revolt surging up from among the people—the struggle of the masses against the rule of the world by a few," Roger Baldwin, who served as ACLU director until 1950, told a courtroom in 1918 after being sentenced to one year in prison for refusing to register for military service. "It is a struggle against the political state itself, against exploitation, militarism, imperialism, authority in all its forms."

"Most of us," Baldwin told the judge, do not fear jail, because we are "prepared even to die for our faith" in an equal future.[42] Civil liberties, as Weinrib writes, were a means to an end: "The early ACLU believed the class struggle was inevitable. Civil liberties, however, could minimize the bloodshed. The right of agitation might advance the economic status of the working class by peaceful means. The only alternative was violent revolution."[43]

It's hard to imagine the ACLU of today calling for the overthrow of the capitalist, imperialist class. Its website describes the organization as a "guardian of liberty" working to "preserve the individual rights and liberties that the Constitution and the laws of the United States guarantee everyone in this country."[44] The national branch and its state affiliates regularly defend Nazis in court, and it supported *Citizens United*, the Supreme Court case that opened the floodgates of corporate spending on political races. The organization justified this decision by arguing that limiting money spent on campaigns would effectively ban speech.

This is not to say the ACLU has become a conservative organization. But its view on free speech has changed substantially. To the ACLU of the early and mid-1900s, speech could not be considered free unless people were equally free to speak and transform the world through that speech—i.e., if people had the same amount of economic and political power. To today's ACLU, speech is speech, and it is separate from economic and political power. Billionaires and fast-food workers have the same right to it. The ACLU still mainly represents progressive causes. When it does choose to represent despicable people, it does so with the intent to prevent courts from setting dangerous precedents: if, for example, Charlottesville was allowed to ban Nazis from gathering in its city center, any city could block leftists from doing the same.[45] But, as has happened with many leftist-turned-progressive causes, the central question of power—who has it and therefore who controls the conversation—has been dropped.

What's more, by dropping economic and racial analysis from its definition of free speech, the ACLU might be bolstering the system it fights against. In the same way that race-blind college admissions end up favoring those with more money, access, and expertise on how to game the system, an agnostic view on free speech benefits those who know how to use the legal system to their advantage, and who have the money to buy the PR necessary to get their message across. On paper, the Koch brothers and the average American have the same right to free speech, but it's only the Kochs who can fight their way through the courts, buy ad time for their messaging, and influence national debates by funding research and purchasing professorships at universities. If the ACLU views both as legitimate victims of free speech suppression, the organization might waste resources it could use fighting battles for those less fortunate. By removing a class and racial analysis from its mission, the ACLU also further obfuscates what the point of free speech might be: the Kochs do not want to speak simply for the sake of it, but to advocate for lower taxes and less environmental regulation. Most speech is similarly motivated. Unless we are talking about purely religious or artistic expression, the purpose of speech—from protests to political campaigns—is to change the material conditions of the world.

The ACLU's turn from militancy to milquetoast progressivism was the result of both government repression and the organization's own success. After local, state, and federal officers arrested so many labor leaders and leftists through the 1920s, the ACLU's leaders began to fracture over how best to represent the interests of labor—whether they could successfully delegitimize the courts, which proved a more daunting task than its idealistic founders had realized, or simply protect people from the courts as repression grew.

Gradually, the organization began representing cases that had little to do with collective labor and more to do with individual liberty and academic freedom—perhaps most famously in the 1925 *Scopes* case, in which the ACLU represented a Tennessee teacher who wanted to teach evolution to his students. The ACLU lost the case, but it cemented the organization's status as more than a radical labor organization.[46]

After the *Scopes* case, wealthy donors to the ACLU who were more concerned with the cause of academic freedom than with communist revolution began pressuring the organization to take less radical stances. They wanted the ACLU to fight for the right of laborers to speak, *not* for the future they spoke of. One leader of the ACLU wrote in 1926 that while he was sympathetic to the cause of leftist organizers, he did not think the ACLU should "give out the overthrow of the capitalist system as one of the aims about which this organization is concerned."[47]

Slowly, the communist influence over the ACLU dwindled, mirroring organized labor's pull toward reformism. Gone were the days of blowing up factories and newspapers to advocate for class revolution, replaced by campaigns for workers' rights and higher wages. By 1937, the organization had professed to have no interest in economic change, only in the "maintenance of democratic rights," and said it would defend the rights of anyone—laborers, conservatives, and even anti-union workers. The organization's chairman, Harry Ward, who led the ACLU until 1940, said that its goal was not revolution, but "orderly social advance."[48]

In 1940, when the National Labor Relations Board challenged Henry Ford's right to distribute anti-union propaganda to his workers, the ACLU, after much internal debate, took the side of Ford. Employers, in its view, had free speech rights too. The ACLU would no longer just defend laborers; now it supported anyone whose free speech rights it felt were being impinged.[49] That decision, followed by the McCarthy era—during which the ACLU bought into the anticommunist hysteria as much as anyone, banishing many of its outwardly communist members—solidified the organization as no longer radical and no longer pro-labor. Instead, the ACLU became agnostic to the politics and power behind people's speech, as long as the speech itself was protected.

It would be easy to blame the ACLU for caving to moderates, or for abandoning its radical roots. But that would be unfair, because almost every leftist organization, from the biggest unions in the country to local nonprofits, had to face an impossible choice as the US government cracked down on anticapitalist organizations: reform or die. The ACLU might be less radical today, but it survived while many other organizations perished in the face of police raids, vigilante mobs, and McCarthy-era blacklists. So did the AFL-CIO, which took a less radical path than other unions, like the IWW. The IWW is still around, but it is much less influential than it once was, largely because its members were pummeled into submission by local, state, and federal governments.

One lesson from the history of the ACLU is not about reformism versus radicalism, but that government suppression is incredibly effective at turning anticapitalist movements into more reformist ones, and killing off (sometimes literally) those who do not conform.

What we've lost with the end of the ACLU's radical vision is a materialist view of free speech politics. The organization fights for something with much lower stakes now: the ability to say what you believe in, without the organizational ability (i.e., labor power) to act on your beliefs. Detached from materialist politics that interrogate who actually has the power to change things, free speech does little to give those without power more of it.

There are some on the left who are beginning to challenge this more centrist-liberal view. They have been called uniquely hostile to free speech by the press and conservatives, as if their ideas and tactics are born out of some newfangled politics. But I would posit that this new group of radicals, who are sick of the centrist, agnostic view of speech, actually hark back to an older understanding of speech. They hold the same views as the early ACLU, and hundreds of thousands of laborers who fought alongside it. The people who believe in this classic and resurgent definition of speech are most often referred to as antifa.

In March 2018, conservative provocateur Milo Yiannopoulos was supposed to give his first scheduled appearance in months, in Scottsdale, Arizona. A few days earlier, a talk he'd been scheduled to deliver at UCLA entitled "10 Things I Hate About Mexico" had been canceled amid protests from students and faculty.[50]

Yiannopoulos had had a hard few years: protesters had greeted him nearly everywhere he went, most infamously at UC Berkeley, where students and others had blocked the entrance to his talk and scuffled with police and his supporters.[51] His book had also been dropped by his publisher, Simon & Schuster, after comments Yiannopoulos had made supporting pedophilia resurfaced.[52]

In Arizona, Milo knew he had to take a different approach: instead of a public talk at a college or university, he'd speak at a private venue, where fans could purchase tickets for $45 or more if they wanted a VIP meet-and-greet package. He wouldn't announce the venue until twenty-four hours before the event. Still, Antifa Action Phoenix was determined to shut him down. To the group's members, Milo's visit was the latest in a long line of direct threats to vulnerable Arizonans. In years prior, white nationalists had rallied outside a mosque, and harassed immigrants near Phoenix.[53] Yes, AFAPHX members disagreed with Milo on political grounds, but they also saw him as part of that direct threat. Students at Berkeley had protested against a Milo talk because they said they had evidence he would out undocumented immigrants on campus.[54] In a 2016 talk at the University of Wisconsin-Milwaukee, he had publicly named a trans student and mocked her, projecting an image of her early in her transition.[55]

The group didn't want another Berkeley on its hands, partly because Arizona is a concealed-carry state, and after Charlottesville, members worried about the chance of deadly violence. But AFAPHX members also didn't think such a direct confrontation was necessary. The media portrays most antifa work as street-level direct action, but to a lot of people who participate in antifa actions, that's a last resort. "We never completely ruled out direct action, but we were really, really pushing for this to get shut down and never see the light of day," Emily, an AFAPHX member, told me. "Your last line of defense is to do the Berkeley thing to Milo."

Instead, the group began piecing together who had invited Milo to Phoenix, who was promoting the event on Facebook and other social networks, and what venues might host him. Members contacted anyone who was connected to the event, publicly shamed the promoters on social media, and called dozens of venues in the Phoenix area until they found one, The Venue Scottsdale, that admitted it was hosting Milo. Facing a growing chorus of concern on social media stoked by AFAPHX, The Venue backed out. Twenty-four hours before Milo was scheduled to speak, his promotions team emailed ticket holders telling them the event was postponed. It was never rescheduled. AFAPHX successfully kept Milo out, without any of the public demonstrations or subsequent public scorn from free speech worriers.

"No-platforming is something that antifascists have done for quite a long time," Eric, an AFAPHX member, told me. "And there's a lot of evidence that it works. The more often they're not allowed to speak, the more often they're kicked off Twitter or PayPal or college campuses, that proves to them they're not able to get their message out."

Milo likely wouldn't admit it, but the strategy does seem to be working: he has barely toured since losing his book deal and since several of his talks were canceled in 2018. Maybe the problem is that he can no longer draw a crowd, or maybe it's that the cost-benefit analysis of those hosting him has shifted, like it did in Phoenix. Richard Spencer, another white nationalist provocateur, said as much when he canceled his college tour shortly after the Milo event was canceled in Phoenix. "I really hate to say this, and I definitely hesitate to say this," Spencer said. "Antifa is winning to the extent that they're willing to go further than anyone else, in the sense that they will do things in terms of just violence, intimidating, and general nastiness."[56]

Antifa is not an organization. It has few core beliefs—antifa members are leftists, but they are not united in their vision for a future economic or political system. They are anticapitalists, anarchists, communists, and socialists. As many who participate in antifascist activity will point out, at its base, antifa is simply a reaction to fascism. The controversy over antifa in the United States, I would posit, comes less from the idea of a group battling fascism (most Americans would agree fascism is bad, right?) than from the debate over what fascism actually is. Does the line start and end at obvious genocide like the Holocaust? Or is it, as many antifa members would argue, the more subtle and less often condemned (or condemned only in hindsight) forms of violence, something that needs to be spotted and stomped out before it turns into a full-blown genocide?

The historian Mark Bray argues in his book *Antifa: The Anti-Fascist Handbook*, probably the most complete history on the movement, that while there's no central top-down philosophy guiding antifascists, the vast majority would disagree with the liberal principle of "I disapprove of what you say, but I will defend to the death your right to say it." Instead, they believe that not only Nazis, but anyone whose political philosophy involves the oppression of others, does not deserve a right to speak.[57] The kind of antifascist action we recognize today can be traced back to Western Europe at the turn of the twentieth century, but Bray and others argue that American antifascism actually predates that, with movements that developed as a reaction to the Ku Klux Klan. In the 1890s, Ida B. Wells advocated for armed self-defense among African Americans through her newspaper, the *Memphis Free Speech*. After a lynching in a Kentucky town, a group of African Americans set fire to many of the town's buildings, and Wells wrote in response, "Not until the Negro rises in his might and takes a hand resenting such cold-blooded murderers, if he has to burn up whole towns, will a halt be called in wholesale lynching."[58]

But before there could be something called antifascism, there had to be something called fascism: the formation of the Fasci Italiani di Combattimento in 1919, following Mussolini's rise to power in Italy, is the first known use of the term "fascism" in modern history. The word derives from a Roman symbol called *fasces*, representing a bundle of sticks placed around an ax. Two years later, the first modern antifascist group was born, called Arditi del Popolo (the People's Daring Ones). The group was able to push back against many of Mussolini's murderous campaigns against leftists.[59] As fascism grew in Western Europe, so did the proliferation of antifascist groups. The KDP (Communist Party of Germany) advocated for "proletarian mass-terror" against fascism in the 1920s, but as fascism encroached, it became clear to some that the masses would never mobilize in time to stop it. "In my opinion, mass-terror is a sheer impossibility," one KDP member said. "Fascism can only be held down by [individual] terror now, and if that fails, in the long run everything will be lost."[60]

In one famous instance, in 1936, thousands of anti-Semites encountered tens of thousands of counterprotesters as they marched through the majority-Jewish London neighborhood of East End. Police attempted to protect the proto-Nazis' assembly, but counterdemonstrators began throwing bricks at the police and the fascists, and emptying chamber pots from their apartment windows. As the fascists, led by Oswald

Mosley under the banner of "Blackshirts," retreated, they shouted, "We want free speech!"[61]

Bray estimates that during World War II, there were around 35,000 antifascists organized in fifty-three countries.[62] Antifascists were, of course, unable to stop the atrocities of the Holocaust, but Bray argues it's important to remember that's what the stakes were. "When we speak about fascism we must not drift too far away from thinking about the people who collected the hair, the gold teeth, the shoes of those they exterminated," he writes. "When we speak about anti-fascism, we must not forget that, for many, survival was the physical embodiment of anti-fascism."[63]

For decades, antifascists have had a more nuanced take on free speech and tactics for fighting fascism than most mainstream media accounts suggest today. Writing in 1945, one antifascist organizer argued that racist and anti-Semitic speakers were not simply crackpots who could be ignored, but instead that "Fascists advance a program which is carefully and methodically worked out, stupid as it may appear, to rally demagogically a crisis-torn middle class to be used as the props of big business."[64] It would be one thing if fascists could simply speak with little repercussion, if the masses would never be swayed by them, but as Word War II proved, that isn't the case. Fascism tends to become appealing, especially to the white middle class, in times of economic crisis. And the powers that be, as history suggests, usually let it grow.

Nearly seventy-five years later, many antifa activists I've spoken with hold similar views. They don't see people like Milo Yiannopoulos as just provocateurs, and they don't see the attendees of his talks as people committed to hearing out both sides. They see history as evidence that fascism does not stop because people ask it to. And they see American politics, and especially the election of Donald Trump, as evidence that the state will not stop it for us.

"There are people who are directly threatened by the rise of Nazis and white supremacists," one young woman who participates in antifa work in Philadelphia told me. Immigrants are being deported, and white nationalist violence is rising.[65] "By going and physically showing up and protesting white supremacists, you are saying that they are not welcome in your town. You are showing real, tangible support to those vulnerable minority groups." The idea of free speech, she said, means nothing to those who are deported, arrested, or killed.

Leah, a young, trans antifascist organizer in Berkeley who demonstrated against Milo's visit to campus, made a similar point. If we are debating the free speech rights of people like Milo, whom are we ignoring? What about the free speech rights of the people he is recommending we deport or imprison? "I think about the threats against people's bodies and lives," she said. "This is not something to be debated away."

# PART 2

# WHERE WE'RE GOING

## chapter six

# THE SHADOW CAMPUS

B Y THE MID-2010S, THERE APPEARED TO BE A CONSENSUS WITHIN THE mainstream press that speech, specifically conservative speech, was under attack, especially on college campuses. From op-ed pages to cable news networks to the stages of college commencements and graduations, American cultural and political leaders preached tolerance for right-wing views.

The idea of liberals blocking conservative views from their lives became so mainstream that *South Park* made a viral music video in which Cartman and several social-justice-warrior-looking characters tried to prevent a devious-looking figure named Reality from encroaching on their bully-proof safe space, where, in the words of one character, "you might call me a pussy, but I won't hear you."[1]

Unlike during the free speech panic of the 1990s, conservatives were no longer the only ones raising the alarm. In February 2017, Van Jones, the CNN commentator and former Obama administration official, spoke to an audience at the University of Chicago and ripped the idea of safe spaces, claiming that liberal college students just wanted to "feel good all the time." Safe spaces create a kind of liberalism that is, "not just useless," he said, but "obnoxious and dangerous."[2]

Even Obama himself weighed in, using his 2016 commencement address at Howard University to say, "Don't try to shut folks out . . . no matter how much you might disagree with them. There's been a trend around the country of trying to get colleges to disinvite speakers with a different point of view, or disrupt a politician's rally. Don't do that—no matter how ridiculous or offensive you might find the things that come out of their mouths."[3]

It's safe to say the number of times shutdowns or disinvitations of speakers were mentioned by publications and politicians in the mid-2010s far exceeded the actual use of the tactics on campuses. Adam Johnson, a media analyst at Fairness and Accuracy in Reporting, found that the *New York Times* published at least twenty-one op-eds about conservatives being silenced on college campuses in an eighteen-month period from 2016 to 2018.[4] The narrative persisted in other publications as well, perhaps most dramatically in February 2018, when Andrew Sullivan published a piece in *New York* magazine titled "We All Live on Campus Now," in which he proclaimed that the discourse of safe spaces and social justice on campus was so powerful that it was threatening the entire bedrock of American democracy. "The whole concept of an individual who exists apart from group identity is slipping from the discourse," he wrote.[5]

The Trump administration and other conservative legislators took the media's apparent consensus that there was a legitimate free speech crisis on college campuses and ran with it. The Justice Department announced in 2018 that it would support lawsuits against universities that prevented controversial speakers from setting foot on campus.[6] In 2018, the department filed a brief in support of Speech First, a group with ties to the Koch brothers that advocates against campus free speech restrictions, over the University of Michigan's speech code, which attempts to prevent harassment against people of color and LGBTQ students.[7] And Evergreen's Bret Weinstein, Middlebury's Allison Stanger, and a few others, including a representative from the Alliance Defending Freedom (which the Southern Poverty Law Center identifies as a hate group), were invited to testify in front of Congress about the dangers faced because of anti-free-speech zealots on college campuses.[8]

UC Berkeley proclaimed its 2017–2018 academic year Free Speech Year in response to the protests surrounding Milo Yiannopoulos, and several other schools followed suit. The University of Florida launched a website and press package discussing its rationale for hosting controversial speakers, after students announced plans to disrupt a talk being given by Richard Spencer, a neo-Nazi. The University of Chicago redoubled its commitment to free speech, with the dean of students going as far as sending all incoming students a letter saying the university did not condone safe spaces (the letter did not mention that the university already had an LGBTQ inclusivity program literally called Safe Space).[9]

To call the many alarm bells sounded about free speech on campus in the 2010s an overreaction would be an understatement. One survey by Gallup in 2016 found that four out of five college students supported free speech, and that 80 percent approved of hearing diverse opinions on their campus.[10] Another survey found that instead of pushing students into safe spaces, colleges actually acted as moderators of opposing viewpoints: after one year of college, conservative and liberal students had an equally "better attitude" toward each other.[11]

The Foundation for Individual Rights in Education (FIRE), a conservative-funded free speech organization, tallied the number of times speakers had been disinvited from college campuses in the United States in 2017, but could only catalog 36 disruptions at the 4,700 universities and colleges in the United States.[12] (Despite the low number in its own tally, FIRE President Greg Lukianoff is one of the most prominent free-speech-on-campus worriers—coauthor of the hyper-viral *Atlantic* article "The Coddling of the American Mind" and author of several books about how college campuses are threatening American liberty.) And according to one analysis of FIRE's data, while left-leaning students *did* participate in the disruption and disinvitation of speakers more than right-wing students, the right had done its fair share of disruption too, particularly around pro-abortion speakers. The analysis found that when they did disrupt, right-wingers were actually more successful in getting colleges to disinvite speakers than their left-wing counterparts.[13]

It's not a coincidence that the media and politicians began to publicly worry about campus free speech around the same time. The narrative had been building slowly, mostly behind the scenes. By the time America declared its free speech crisis in the 2010s, powerful conservative activists and the billionaires who fund them had been working for years, and in some cases decades, to drum up sympathy for the idea that conservative speech was being oppressed—all while obfuscating the fact that leftists and others had been subjugated to the same attacks (often at the behest of those same activists and billionaires).

The crisis, in other words, was the result of a carefully manufactured narrative pushed by right-wing organizations. These organizations, many of which were funded by the usual suspects of right-wingers like the Koch brothers, were well known for affecting other arenas of American life—electoral politics, the environment, corporate taxes—but they have largely been left out of the narrative about free speech on campus. And the mainstream media, usually so critical of these organizations' encroachments into other facets of American life, instead took their word when it came to free speech.

This sleight of hand has allowed a small cadre of conservative activists and billionaires to accomplish something quite remarkable: assaulting the free speech of those they disagree with—from leftists to abortion activists to Israel critics—all while convincing the rest of the world that they are the true victims.

In 2016, Simona Sharoni, then a professor of gender studies at SUNY Plattsburgh in upstate New York, gave an interview to an online magazine in which she talked about the need to connect feminism and gender to the movement for Palestinian rights.[14] The interview wasn't out of the ordinary for Sharoni. She'd made her critiques of Israel public many times in the past. And Sharoni is accustomed to receiving emails in response to her talks and public comments—being open to opposing viewpoints is part of being an academic. But this time, something was different.

Shortly after her interview, several articles proclaiming her an anti-Semite or "shill" surfaced on the web.[15] She began receiving rape and death threats via email and social media. Then, nineteen public requests were filed for Sharoni's records at SUNY Plattsburgh (freedom of information laws apply to professors at public universities). One request, filed by a nonprofit called StandWithUs, demanded seventeen forms of records, including lists of Sharoni's membership in professional organizations; donations made to her department; a list of every event she had ever attended, including rallies, talks, and faculty meetings; a list of her requests for sabbatical leave; all records that would correspond to her teaching load; and every email ever sent by any member of SUNY Plattsburgh's staff and faculty related to any of those records. If a professor had sent Sharoni an email about one of her talks six months or six years ago, StandWithUs wanted to see it.

The response to the request totaled many thousands of pages—documents laying out every detail of Sharoni's teaching life. It's hard to know exactly how all this information could potentially be used by StandWithUs, but the requests for records related to travel authorizations, time off, and teaching loads seem to suggest that StandWithUs was looking for any improprieties or technicalities that could lead to her tenure being revoked. StandWithUs bills itself as having close ties to the Israeli government: it worked with Israel on a public diplomacy campaign and received $250,000 for the effort.[16] Most of the group's work is similar to that of other right-wing campus groups, but focused almost solely on promoting Israel: training students on how to portray Israel, funding campus ambassadors, and sharing its views on social media.[17] The organization did not respond to several requests for comment.

SUNY Plattsburgh's administrators, Sharoni said, admitted that the public records requests seemed designed to intimidate the administration into taking action against her, yet they declined to issue a public statement denouncing the attacks, instead issuing an internal campus email about its commitment to free speech that did not mention the specifics of Sharoni's situation.

"While the attacks were going on, I was dealing with unbearable anxiety," she said. "I felt like I couldn't function, which is what these groups want."

Sharoni knows her views are controversial. What has riled up Israel supporters most is her linking of violence against Palestinians to the rape and sexual assault crisis on college campuses. Sharoni believes that both forms of violence are similar, and that gender and sexual violence is under-discussed when people talk about Palestine. She also posited that the way people disregard the testimonies of Palestinians who say Israel is hurting them is similar to the ways in which sexual assault survivors are often not believed when they come forward on college campuses.[18] Because of her views, she told me, she wasn't surprised, or even angry, when pro-Israel groups began harassing her. But she felt like the college had utterly failed to protect her academic freedom. How could she produce scholarship under a barrage of constant threats?

"I'm not pissed off at these groups—they're doing a hell of a good job at fighting a war," Sharoni told me. "I'm pissed off at these institutions, like my school. No one even checked in with me or asked about my well-being. There was no reply when I told them about the threats. Finally the dean said to me, 'We had a tough balancing act—alumni and community members were asking for you to be fired.' He wanted me to be grateful that they didn't fire me."

Sharoni began feeling nervous around campus. A doctor diagnosed her with adjustment disorder and post-traumatic stress disorder. She has moved on, and now teaches at Merrimack College in Massachusetts. But if you search for her name online, you'll see the results are littered with hit pieces on her from groups like Campus Watch and Canary Mission, two organizations with an explicitly racist outlook on anti-Israel activists, both of which are known for regularly posting personal information about their targets online.[19]

While the free speech debate has raged on in national newspapers, little attention has been paid to the stories of people like Sharoni. This is a shame, because stories like hers signal something new and scary in the free speech wars: unlike the student-led protests against Milo Yiannopoulos at Berkeley, or the faculty- and student-led protests at Evergreen against Bret Weinstein, increasingly, well-funded and secretive organizations tied to multimillionaires, billionaires, and even governments are waging battles against professors and students. The campaigns of harassment against these professors and students go beyond the usual forms of campus debate. They are full-frontal attacks that attempt to call into question students' true motivations for learning or discussing hot-button issues, ruin people's reputations, get professors fired for their beliefs, and make them subjects of mass harassment online.

The battles waged by pro-Israel groups against campus protesters are perhaps the best examples, or at least the most well documented instances, of large organizations using their power in an attempt to silence dissent. When pro-Israel groups target a professor or student, the point, it seems, is not to engage in a debate about Israel, but to make engaging in a debate about Israel so dangerous to one's career and mental health that engagement becomes unworthy.

Those being targeted are not politicians, or even public figures, but professors most people have not heard of and students who rarely have influence beyond their own campuses. And the level of sophistication and persistence of the attacks against these people suggests there's coordination behind them, either by well-funded pro-Israel nonprofits, or by the Israeli government, or both.

While the issue may seem niche, only potentially affecting those who work on Israel-related activism, it's becoming clear that what pro-Israel nonprofits pioneered—harassing leftist professors and students who critique Israel into silence (or at least attempting to)—is now being used as a playbook by conservative groups across the United States. President Trump has even suggested that schools should lose federal grants and research dollars if they don't ensure conservatives have unrestricted access to speak on campus.[20]

Right-wing pro-Israel groups, along with other right-wing groups, have descended onto college campuses as part of a larger strategy of intellectual domination: by funding student groups, fellows, events, and increasingly professorships and entire programs at colleges, conservatives are attempting to build an intellectual ecosystem friendly to their ideas. Students influenced by these groups go on to produce scholarship, write for news outlets, and become paid experts on television. This is not a secret mission, but something stated with pride by many of these organizations. On its website, StandWithUs, for example, used to proclaim that it has "a sizeable team of campus professionals and lay leaders who are dedicated to supporting students' efforts to promote and defend Israel amid the virulent anti-Israel movement."[21]

But often the techniques used by these groups go beyond simple education or activist training into something more akin to harassment.

By my count, there are at least a dozen nonprofits fighting professors and students critical of Israel. The organizations' tactics range from relatively milquetoast to militant. On one end of the spectrum are groups like the Anti-Defamation League, which most people have likely seen quoted in mainstream news reports about anti-Semitism and racism. It's a respectable nonprofit, its leaders' advice is sought after by journalists, and it's considered an unbiased source, but the organization is also staunchly pro-Israel: it tends to view any criticism of Israel and its treatment of Palestinians as anti-Semitic, and has supported bills to prevent the US government from working with any contractors that support the Boycott, Divestment, and Sanctions (BDS) movement, which seeks to pressure Israel and the United States to change their policies toward Palestinians.[22] In the wake of the massacre at a synagogue in Pittsburgh in October 2018, the ADL's director, Jonathan Greenblatt, suggested that leftist anti-Israel activists were complicit in the violent attack against Jews in the United States, writing, "If your allies in a range of social justice causes . . . justify demonizing the Jewish state of Israel and its existence, then they need to know that they can no longer be your ally."[23] The group also monitors "anti-Israel" activity on campuses, and signs on to letters expressing concern over courses with material critical of Israel or professors with anti-Israel stances.[24]

On the other end of the spectrum are groups like Canary Mission, which essentially provides a playbook for harassment. The Canary Mission website, which prominently displays its slogan, "If you're racist, the world should know," contains profiles and multiple photos of the people it targets; the site often includes targets' personal contact information. Many of those targeted are not affiliated with any university but are simply people of Arab descent who have expressed sympathy for Palestinian people. It's not clear how people are selected to be featured in the website's searchable database—people like Sharoni are on there, but so are some students who may have attended as little as one event about the crisis in Palestine.

Until recently, the website was run anonymously, and did a great job covering up its paper trail. Several journalistic investigations into Canary Mission led nowhere, but finally in 2018, the *Forward* newspaper began to reveal its apparent backers. Money for Canary Mission is funneled through a nonprofit that seems to do nothing except fund Canary Mission and has only one location: a padlocked and seemingly abandoned office in a dilapidated strip mall outside Jerusalem.[25] Its humble digs belie how much money the website pulls in: the *Forward* and the Israeli newspaper *Haaretz* found that two of the United States' largest and most mainstream Jewish nonprofits—the Jewish Community Foundation of Los Angeles and the Jewish Community Federation of San Francisco—both had contributed hundreds of thousands of dollars that went to Canary Mission (both organizations said they would stop funding the site once the media reported the connection between the organizations). It's unclear if the site is also officially linked to the Israeli government, but there is evidence that the government uses information from the site to determine whom to detain at its border crossings.[26]

Many of the other campus-focused nonprofits work behind the scenes, putting pressure on professors and college administrations without a public call to arms. That makes their work hard, but not impossible, to trace. The fingerprints of StandWithUs, for example, can been seen in the public records requests filed against Sharoni and others. StandWithUs has a budget of millions of dollars a year, and close ties to Israel. Its funders include conservative millionaires like Victoria's Secret heiress Susan Wexner, and Sandra and Lawrence Post, who also donate to a Christian organization that believes the Holocaust was God's way of encouraging Jews to return to Israel. [27]

Often, the groups appear to coordinate to varying degrees, with some sending messages to administrations petitioning for professors to be fired, others filing public records requests for their information, and others, like Canary Mission, providing resources for online mobs to do the rest. It's rare for a professor or student to be targeted by only one group. If you run afoul of one, you get the wrath of many.

Jasbir Puar, a professor of women's and gender studies at Rutgers University, was targeted by several groups after she gave a talk at Vassar College in February 2016 during which she spoke about a recent trip she'd made to the West Bank to conduct ethnographic research on the effects of Israeli military violence on Palestinians. Puar is accustomed to receiving criticism for her Israel-related work, but she'd never experienced the persistence and viciousness of what came next.

There was the op-ed in the *Wall Street Journal* by two prominent pro-Israel academics, who called Puar an anti-Semite. Then, over the next few weeks, dozens of articles were posted on pro-Israel websites in the United States and Israel about her, some containing statements she said she never made. Her biographical information was compiled on Canary Mission alongside a photo of her, and she began receiving a deluge of unsolicited emails. Some contained death and rape threats.

After Rutgers administrators showed police some of the threats, the university decided that only one was specific enough to suggest it could turn into real-life violence. The school building where Puar works was sent extra security. Administrators received letters asking for her to be fired. Her Wikipedia page seemed to be under constant monitoring; if she or one of her students tried to change something, it would be immediately flagged for review. She got an alert from a security website that people had been searching for her home address online. Thankfully, Puar said, Rutgers and her faculty union stood by her side. But she still worried college administrations wouldn't readily come to the defense of others, especially women and faculty of color who are less established than she is.

Puar's and Sharoni's cases were relatively run-of-the-mill for professors who have criticized Israel: hundreds have their names, contact information, and photos posted on Canary Mission, and everyone I've talked to has received harassing and threatening emails. But some campaigns go much deeper, and their origins remain more secretive.

In April 2016, three websites appeared that all targeted Purdue University American studies professor Bill Mullen, an outspoken critic of Israel who has worked with the university's pro-Palestine student group, Students for Justice in Palestine. One website criticized Mullen's academic achievements; another lambasted him for not supporting his university's administration; the third claimed to be run by an anonymous female student who said that Mullen had a track record of sexual harassment. An investigation by the *Electronic Intifada*, a pro-Palestinian news site, found that each of the three websites targeting Mullen were purchased through the same hosting provider and that its creator (or creators) shared an IP address.[28]

Other websites set up to target students involved with Students for Justice in Palestine in Indiana were linked to the same domains, including several that accused a Muslim student activist of betraying her faith by making out with her classmates at a party. That student, whom I'll call Sarah (she did not want her name used for fear it would further affect her reputation online), said the creation of the websites coincided with several phone calls from blocked or unknown numbers. The callers would hang up when she picked up, except for one, who said, *"As-salaam alaikum"* before hanging up. Sarah's brother also received an email from a person who claimed to be a sympathizer with Students for Justice in Palestine, but the email contained details of Sarah's life that made her suspect it was from someone who had investigated her online.

"I felt violated," Sarah said. "Like they were going into my life."

Sarah said she had to begin laying low, participating less frequently in activism because she feared the harassment would increase. A fellow member of her SJP chapter quit out of fear of being targeted as well. Sarah's parents suggested she do the same.

"I know I'm standing up for the truth and doing the right thing," Sarah said. "When my parents told me to quit, I was like, 'But then they're going to win.'"

Mullen and many of his colleagues voted for the American Studies Association to boycott Israel—for example, by refusing to have any academic conferences there—in order to take a stand against apartheid. They were sued by a pro-Israel nonprofit called the Brandeis Center, which accused BDS supporters of infiltrating the ASA and taking it over.[29] Though the lawsuit was thrown out, Mullen believes it succeeded at scaring other academics into silence.

On June 7, 2018, the leader of the Brandeis Center, Kenneth Marcus, was confirmed by the Senate and became assistant secretary for civil rights at the Department of Education.

The nonprofits that have been accused of being behind these harassment campaigns are not officially linked, but they have many of the same funders, according to a report by the nonprofit Palestine Legal.[30] Hundreds of millions of dollars have been spent by prominent conservative Americans on monitoring and attacking professors and students critical of Israel. Sheldon Adelson, the casino owner and fervent Trump supporter, has said he will spend at least $20 million fighting the BDS movement, which is primarily based on college campuses. And in 2013, the *Forward* reported that the Jewish Agency for Israel, a nonprofit that advocates for Israel-friendly policy and coordinates closely with the Israeli government, said it would spend $300 million from rich donors in the United States and the Israeli government to "create what is likely to be the most expensive pro-Israel campaign ever." Part of the money was earmarked for US college campuses and for sending US students to Israeli institutions.[31]

It's also impossible to know to what extent the Israeli government is involved in the harassment—for example, whether government officials are choosing which professors and students to target, or helping the

US nonprofits coordinate. Some argue that simply providing funds to nonprofits without any strings attached or knowledge of how that money might be used is tantamount to subsidizing the harassment.

What is known is that at least since 2010, a think tank named the Reut Institute, founded by a former advisor to the Israeli government, has been working on a "delegitimization" campaign meant to call into question anyone who criticizes the existence of Israel.[32] And in 2015 the Israeli government got even more directly involved, spending $25 million to set up a new task force dedicated to combating what Israeli officials saw as a growing threat posed by the BDS movement.

"We have failed to produce a solution to stop this movement," one member of Israel's Knesset said when the task force was created.[33] "With time, the pressure exerted on Israel [against the BDS movement] will steadily increase."

The effort has been led by former military captain Gilad Erdan and keeps a relatively tight lid on its activities, but Erdan told an Israeli newspaper that the agency participated in "black ops"—covertly waging smear campaigns against critics of Israel and directing online attacks against them.[34]

One clue to just how directly involved Erdan's force is in battles on US college campuses comes from what happened to a student-created course at UC Berkeley in the fall of 2016. UC Berkeley allows students to create their own courses overseen by a faculty advisor. Berkeley senior Paul Hadweh, who was raised as a teen in the West Bank, submitted a course called "Palestine: A Settler Colonial Analysis." The course was approved by the school's administration, and a faculty advisor was assigned. Then in late August, news sites based in the United States like the conservative outlet Campus Reform began to draw attention to the course.[35] It was the first time Hadweh had heard about controversy over it, and he was confused about how something that had generated no controversy on his campus or in surrounding Berkeley could all of a sudden be worth the attention of several newspapers and television stations nationwide.

Details that would eventually provide the answers to Hadweh's questions began emerging: a letter-writing campaign coordinated by

AMCHA, one of the larger pro-Israel nonprofits in the United States, and signed by forty other pro-Israel nonprofits, asked UC Berkeley administrators to cancel the class. And then, with no warning to Hadweh, the class was canceled. (AMCHA did not respond to several requests for comment.)

As the controversy over the course and its cancellation brewed at Berkeley, Hadweh was contacted by one of his friends in Israel, who said he'd seen Hadweh's course mentioned on Israeli news: a reporter for a local Israeli TV station had interviewed Gilad Erdan. The report said Erdan and his agency had covertly put pressure on UC Berkeley to cancel the course.[36] UC Berkeley communications officer Dan Mogulof told me the school did not receive any direct communications from the Israeli government, but did receive many emails from pro-Israel nonprofits. Put together, this is what Hadweh (and I) believed happened: someone local was alerted to the course, a pro-Israel nonprofit was then made aware of it, that nonprofit reached out to the Israeli government, which then pushed a coordination campaign through the dozens of nonprofits it donates to or maintains close ties with.

After weeks of protests from Berkeley students, the course was reinstated. But the full repercussions of the cancellation have yet to shake out: Hadweh is Christian, and when he is back in the West Bank for the holidays, he and his family usually cross into Jerusalem for Christmas, which requires a permit sponsored by a Jerusalem-based church. In 2016, for the first time in Hadweh's life, his permit to cross was denied by the Israeli government.

The consequences of these kinds of campaigns against critics of Israel stretch beyond college campuses. Talking to the people who have gone through them, I got the sense that it can be a uniquely isolating event. With the world turned against you, your career in jeopardy, and college administrations staying silent, it can feel like you're in it alone—you against a multimillion-dollar machine intent on taking you down.

Rabab Abdulhadi, a professor of ethnic, race, and resistance studies at San Francisco State University, has been battling pro-Israel groups for years. The harassment reached its peak in 2014, after she took a research trip to the Middle East and met with a few people that far-right groups like AMCHA consider terrorists. AMCHA and several other groups claimed that Abdulhadi's trip was a misuse of state funds and called for her to be fired.[37] After months of controversy, her school came to her defense. But Abdulhadi said she feels scarred by the years of emails, threats, and campaigns against her.

"If you want to speak out, they're going to make your life hell," she said. "There's a cost for everything. And the cost is very high. They want the cost to be high enough that you just shut up."

Local and federal governments in the United States have taken several steps recently to legitimize the tactics used by pro-Israel groups to harass professors and students. In response to a wave of anti-Semitic violence and vandalism in 2016, the Senate passed a bill that did little to end anti-Semitism, and instead directed the Department of Education to take any speech that "delegitimizes," "demonizes," or "applies a double standard to Israel" into consideration when investigating schools for discrimination (the effort died in the House).[38] And in the summer of 2016, New York Governor Andrew Cuomo signed a first-of-its-kind executive order meant to punish any groups or companies that support the BDS movement by barring the state from doing business with them. Civil rights groups called it a McCarthyesque blacklist. That didn't stop other states from adopting similar measures. By 2019, twenty-seven states had anti-BDS bills on their books, and fourteen more were considering them. Several of those bills require that states maintain a blacklist of companies and organizations that boycott Israel.[39]

Israel may be one of the most extreme cases of conservative funders and governments working in tandem to discourage speech and dissent on campuses, but the practice of using nonprofits with right-wing ties has become increasingly popular. Colleges are often seen as political bubbles, immune from the forces that affect politics everywhere else, but today college life and national politics are inextricable, largely thanks to the work of a few conservative billionaires.

The offices for the Foundation for Individual Rights in Education are tucked away on the twelfth floor of a glass-and-concrete skyscraper across from the Liberty Bell in Philadelphia. The organization has a relatively small national profile (for comparison, the ACLU is googled at an average rate roughly six times that of FIRE) and a relatively modest budget of $11 million, which supports about forty staffers.[40] Yet it is one of the biggest influencers over speech on college campuses.

FIRE's stated mission is to ensure that everyone on college campuses gets to speak their mind, regardless of their political background. And its employees do take on and publicize cases from across the political spectrum—for example, they've represented Students for Justice in Palestine. But a very large portion of FIRE's money (representatives wouldn't tell me exactly how much) comes from just a few donors: the Charles G. Koch Charitable Foundation, the giving arm of ultraconservative billionaire Charles Koch; the Lynde and Harry Bradley Foundation, another conservative megadonor group; the Dick and Betsy DeVos Family Foundation (the charity of the family of the US Secretary of Education under Donald Trump); the Sarah Scaife Foundation (another big conservative donor); and two organizations called DonorsTrust and Donors Capital Fund, which pool money from conservative donors and anonymize them—though several investigations have linked the two organizations back to many of the above donors, most prominently the Kochs.[41]

I interviewed two employees of FIRE in 2018: Samantha Harris, vice president for procedural advocacy, and Will Creeley, senior vice president of legal and public advocacy. Both told me that the money from their largely conservative donors in no way affected their work.

"I just think an objective look at our casework speaks for itself," Creeley said. "We have nothing to hide."

Both pointed to the wide variety of cases they'd taken on, from supporting radical rapper and moviemaker Boots Riley's trips to college campuses to advocating for Students for Bernie at Georgetown Law, as proof of their apolitical nature.

"But when it's Milo Yiannopoulos coming to Berkeley, that's what generates all the headlines," Creeley said. "I started a joke like, 'Campus free speech is a full employment plan for pundits.'"

FIRE does get a lot of flak from progressives over its funders. It gets even more over its stance against parts of Title IX, the US law that is meant to protect women and minorities on college campuses from harassment, sexual and otherwise, which FIRE sees as a way to skirt legal due process.[42]

In fairness, I believed Creeley and Harris when they told me their donors don't influence their cases. If FIRE was purely a conservative front group, its liberal caseload would likely be cursory, not robust, which it is. But that makes the organization all the more intriguing: why are so many conservatives donating millions to an ostensibly nonpartisan organization? The Kochs' other donations are in some ways investments: they donate to anti-environmental organizations so that their companies can keep polluting; they donate to conservative politicians who will pass laws to lessen their tax burden. What's the return on investment on FIRE?

One clue might come from the group's founders and leaders: President Greg Lukianoff spends much of his time traveling the country giving speeches at colleges and universities, often sponsored by conservative programs or professors. Although he does not get overtly political, he's wont to use phrases linked with the kind of free-market thinking favored by the Kochs, like the "marketplace of ideas."[43] His treatise on speech on campuses was published by Encounter Books, which only publishes conservative titles and is funded largely by the Bradley Foundation (which also funded Charles Murray's *The Bell Curve*).

FIRE's board of directors has at points included ultraconservatives like George Will and T. Kenneth Cribb, who worked in the Reagan administration and who ran the Intercollegiate Studies Institute, another campus group with a more explicitly conservative agenda. FIRE's founders, Alan Charles Kors and Harvey Silverglate, have also railed against political correctness as a destructive force on college campuses and beyond.[44] Kors has also contributed to the libertarian publication *Reason*.[45]

Although the cases FIRE takes on are a mix of liberal and conservative, its general messaging—from its president's books about the dangers of safe spaces and PC culture, to its founders' campus lectures about the need to listen to all voices, no matter how controversial—presents a more libertarian, if not outright conservative, view. As one of the most prominent campus speech groups in the country, FIRE is able to set the terms for debate with its messaging: all voices matter. And with those terms set, other groups are able to come in and do the more nefarious work.

The largest donors to conservative causes on college campuses are, by and large, the same ones that fund FIRE. The Leadership Institute has been around since 1979, training conservative students on how to massage their messages so that they will be more palatable to liberal audiences. Even in 2001, the Leadership Institute's primary strategy was to convince its audience and its donors that there was a liberal conspiracy to silence conservative voices. "Liberal media bias is out of control," one letter to donors read. "It's time you and I did something about it."[46] Now the group boasts nearly 2,000 campus chapters advocating for "limited government, the free market, traditional values and national defense."

In 2009, the Leadership Institute launched Campus Reform, a website with the sole mission of chronicling perceived injustices against conservative students and deriding anyone its authors see as overly liberal (including trans students who insist on people using their correct gender pronouns). Campus Reform has been central to the media outrage machine surrounding essentially every campus free speech fight. The site has hundreds of stories on the Evergreen controversy, hundreds on the fight at Middlebury, and *thousands* on protests over Milo Yiannopoulos. It's impossible to identify all the donors to the Leadership Institute and Campus Reform, but some of its main donors are the Charles Koch Foundation, the Lynde and Harry Bradley Foundation, Donors Capital Fund, and DonorsTrust.[47]

The College Fix, another prominent site in the free speech wars— which described Evergreen's Day of Absence / Day of Presence as a "no whites allowed" day, and which posts articles that are routinely shared online by tens of thousands of people and cited by mainstream networks like Fox News—also keeps its donors close to the chest.[48] But investigations have found that its parent organization, the Student Free Press Association, gets funding from DonorsTrust and Donors Capital Fund. The site repeatedly praised Betsy DeVos in the lead-up to her Secretary of Education confirmation. Afterward, reporters discovered that her son sat on the board of SFPA.[49] The DeVos family is second only to the Kochs in their influence on college campuses. They've sent more than $8 million to the Intercollegiate Studies Institute, the sixty-five-year-old organization formerly run by prominent conservative William F. Buckley Jr. with a fifty-year goal of reviving ultraconservatism by "implanting the idea in the minds of the coming generations."[50]

There are dozens of other groups geared toward campuses, like Students for Liberty and Young America's Foundation, and others, like the American Enterprise Institute (which invited Charles Murray to Middlebury), that focus only in part on the campus free speech wars. But the one with arguably the biggest media platform is Turning Point USA, which attempts to appeal to millennials through viral videos and slogans like "big government sucks." TPUSA boasts a presence on hundreds of campuses (though this number is in dispute as some, even fellow conservatives, say TPUSA inflates its numbers to attract donor money), and often financially sponsors the firebrands who get media attention for their speeches—Milo Yiannopoulos, Ann Coulter, Ben Shapiro.[51] But the organization also acts in the shadows of college campuses: for example, documents leaked to the Ohio State University publication *The Lantern* showed that TPUSA was quietly funding campaigns for student government races for conservative students across the country.[52]

Charlie Kirk, the boyish and brash face of Turning Point, and his colleagues at the organization have focused much of their messaging in recent years on the idea that conservative college students are being oppressed on campus—to mixed success. They produce viral videos of Kirk's speeches relatively often (with headlines like "TRIGGER WARNING! Charlie Kirk DESTROYS Safe Spaces and Anti-Free Speech Culture on College Campuses! #BigGovSucks"), but they also get routinely mocked for their more . . . creative . . . approaches to marketing their message (like when they dressed their members in diapers and had them suck on pacifiers on college campuses to illustrate that "safe spaces are for children").[53]

TPUSA does not disclose most of its funding, but much of it comes from the same roster of millionaires and billionaires who fund the major conservative campus groups, along with a few others who are in the "fossil-fuel space," as Kirk put it in an interview with *The New Yorker*.[54]

The attention around free speech on college campuses in recent years has circulated among very few people—mainly conservatives with large followings and controversial views like Milo Yiannopoulos, Charles Murray, and Ann Coulter. The media often presents them as popular because of their firebrand ways, but they too are given a big boost by the same nonprofits that fund campus groups like Turning Point and Young Americans for Liberty, which often help organize their entire college campus tours.[55] These controversial tours, which seem engineered to create backlash, are then extensively covered by the media.

To give one succinct example, self-described "factual feminist" Christina Hoff Sommers attempted to give a talk at Lewis & Clark Law School in March 2018, where she was disrupted by a few students. *New York Times* columnist Bari Weiss used the disruption in a piece a few days later called "We're All Fascists Now" to show that progressives were beginning to turn on their own (Sommers is a feminist, after all!). David Brooks followed up with a piece of his own in which he described the protesters as "student mobbists" and implored them to consider that yelling leads to revolution, and revolution is bloody, and therefore civilized behavior is a virtue.[56] Nowhere in either piece was it mentioned that Sommers is a paid employee of the American Enterprise Institute, which helps cover her costs for her speaking tours.[57] Brooks's piece neglected to mention that her talk was paid for by the Federalist Society, another group funded by the Kochs and other right-wing billionaires.[58]

Similarly, Milo Yiannopoulos didn't just make money from his books or campus tour fees: he's also been bankrolled by wealthy conservatives. In an investigative piece for *BuzzFeed News*, Joseph Bernstein found that Yiannopoulos and the news outlet he was once associated with, *Breitbart News*, were both funded by hedge fund billionaire Robert Mercer, who, along with Steve Bannon, gave directives to Yiannopoulos on what to cover for *Breitbart*, including stories on perceived persecution of conservatives on college campuses.[59]

None of this is organic or unplanned. Most coverage conceives of the campus free speech debates as a bottom-up phenomenon stemming from changing attitudes on college campuses. In this version of events, students are more liberal, less willing to hear other sides of an argument, and more concerned with political correctness than education. Conservative speakers are just trying to get their points across to an increasingly hostile audience.

In fact, these debates were carefully constructed, a play made by wealthy conservative donors to sow outrage. When students at Berkeley protested Milo, they, like their counterparts at dozens of other schools, were not (only) campus disruptors, but actors in a well-tested process they had very little control over: conservative groups were funded and strengthened by a select few billionaires, who then cosponsored events with headliners funded by those same billionaires, which were then sometimes disrupted by students, leading to an endless barrage of "news" from websites funded by those same billionaires and talk show circuits frequented by people like Charlie Kirk, who are on the payroll of those same billionaires.

It's a set of actions with predictable outcomes that has been performed over and over again at great expense (maybe free speech isn't cheap?). The question is: Why bother to go through it? If we take conservatives at their word, and agree that college campuses are nearly impenetrable fortresses of liberalism, then maybe the only way to infiltrate—and in turn reshape—colleges is under the cover of so-called liberal ideas.

If a billionaire said outright that he wanted to infiltrate college campuses and take them over, reshaping their curriculums to support conservative and free-market viewpoints, I would argue that it would cause too much of a ruckus. The mainstream media would be less likely to write breathlessly in his defense. Free speech *sounds* much better. And history shows it's a cause people can get behind: after the ACLU's retreat from leftist radicalism, the organization, and liberals writ large, appeared to believe that free speech was an ideal worth defending, regardless of the politics behind it. If a venerated and ostensibly liberal organization could defend Nazis and Henry Ford's union-busting, why would liberals question the motives of the free speech fights waged by the Kochs and their brethren?

It's a genius strategy: not only fight the enemy (liberals), but get many of your enemies to defend you while you battle. And it has worked well for conservatives. You're very unlikely to see an op-ed defending the poor Koch brothers caught red-handed trying to influence global warming policy, yet liberal pundits run to their defense when they spend their money trying to influence college campuses through their chosen campus groups, speakers, pundits, and media outlets.

Drexel University sociology professor Robert Brulle studied the dark money from the Kochs and other billionaires funding the climate denial movement and wrote, "Like a play on Broadway, the countermovement has stars in the spotlight—often prominent contrarian scientists or conservative politicians—but behind the stars is an organizational structure of directors, script writers and producers."[60] Is the free speech fight not similar?

The Kochs and other billionaires don't donate to places like the anti-global-warming-science Heartland Institute because they are charitable, but because they are investors in the fossil fuel industry looking for a return. We should think of the current free speech movement in a similar way. Organizations like Turning Point and Young Americans for Liberty give them influence; organizations like FIRE give them legitimacy. Yes, there is a debate over what should or should not be taught, said, and deemed acceptable on college campuses, but one side of the debate is vastly outfunded, and so far outmaneuvered, by the other.

But frequently, the conservative side of that debate will show what it's actually after: control of the university, and further control of the economic system that is already skewed toward their advantage. Charlie Kirk, for example, has no problem proclaiming the importance of free speech while simultaneously advocating for leftist professors to get fired.[61] The same organizations that are pushing for free speech on college campuses also spend their vast resources on pushing for, in the words of TPUSA, "the principles of fiscal responsibility, free markets, and limited government."[62] It's not surprising that conservative billionaires would fund a movement like this—because as the University of Chicago's economics department elucidates, influencing universities is a good investment in the future: those trained by conservative groups on college campuses go on to work for senators and presidents, large banks and lobbying firms.

What *is* surprising is that so many liberals have gone along for the ride, providing cover for conservatives as they attempt to take over the country's higher education system, accepting at face value the proposition that what they care about is a diversity of viewpoints, and not simply a furtherance of their own cause and their own wealth. With that cover, conservatives have been able to push further into campus life than ever before.

For more than thirty years, until 2015, a man named Richard Fink advised the Koch brothers on how to spend their billions to influence the world. His official title was executive vice president at Koch Industries, but he was really more of a hired political theorist who has been preaching the need to control the intellectual class of the United States for decades.[63] In a 1996 piece for *Philanthropy Magazine*, Fink compared his strategy to the economic theories of free-market-loving economist Friedrich Hayek, a favorite academic among billionaires, largely because he believed that society benefits when the rich get richer. Just like fictional character Robinson Crusoe can only fish and hunt with his hands until he "hoards enough food to sustain himself while he fashions a fishing net," Fink argued that social change can only happen once there is enough intellectual raw material for intellectuals to produce new theories of social change:

> At the higher stages we have the investment in the intellectual raw materials, that is, the exploration and production of abstract concepts and theories. In the public policy arena, these still come primarily (though not exclusively) from the research done by scholars at our universities. . . . To have consequences, ideas need to be transformed into a more practical or useable form. In the middle stages, ideas are applied to a relevant context and molded into needed solutions for real-world problems. This is the work of the think tanks and policy institutions.
>
> But while the think tanks excel at developing new policy and articulating its benefits, they are less able to implement change. Citizen

activist or implementation groups are needed in the final stage to take the policy ideas from the think tanks and translate them into proposals that citizens can understand and act upon. These groups are also able to build diverse coalitions of individual citizens and special interest groups needed to press for the implementation of policy change.[64]

For the past thirty years, the Kochs and the billionaires they influence have been implementing this strategy to a T, funding universities, think tanks, and "grassroots" movements like the Tea Party to get closer to their ultimate goal of increasing their own power and lowering their own taxes.

At a 1976 conference for conservative activists, Charles Koch told an audience that the right could no longer rely on ideas working on their own, arguing that they needed to be funded—through schools and youth programs—to have influence. At the same conference, a Koch loyalist named Leonard Liggio suggested modeling their program after the Nazis' work with Hitler Youth.[65]

But Koch and other right-wingers knew that this influence strategy had to be as much about PR as legitimate ideas. They knew that just coming out and saying they wanted lower taxes and less regulation wouldn't win people over. Instead, they had to convince people that their pursuits were noble, scholarly, and meant to increase the well-being of others. In 1950 Hayek said it was okay, even necessary, to be disingenuous to achieve these goals, and the Kochs agreed.[66]

That battle of ideas began in earnest in 1971, as part of a conservative backlash to the progress of the 1960s, when Lewis Powell, one of the most conservative Supreme Court Justices ever appointed, argued forcefully on the Court and in letters to places like the US Chamber of Commerce that restrictions on business were equivalent to the suppression of free speech, and that a "market" of ideas was needed to save democracy. He criticized places like the *New York Times* as being too liberal, disdainful of right-wing voices, and therefore antidemocratic, and in response the *Times* and other newspapers rushed to add a slew of conservative columnists to their pages. (Sound familiar?)[67]

Shortly after Lewis's clarion call, the Kochs opened the Cato Institute, an influential libertarian think tank that began funding and supporting the work of dozens of antigovernment scholars and pundits.[68]

From the beginning of their intellectual war to influence American minds, the Kochs and other billionaires saw the university as their main target. John Olin, the late executive of one of the world's largest ammunition companies, was motivated to action in 1969, when armed black students took over a building on Cornell University's campus to demand more diversity and the hiring of black professors (they weren't originally armed, but they took up guns when a white fraternity at the school attempted to forcefully eject them).[69] Olin wrote that he "saw very clearly that students at Cornell, like those at most major universities, were hostile to businessmen and to business enterprise, and indeed had begun to question the ideals of the nation itself."[70] He founded the Olin Foundation, which set about funding far-right causes, especially professorships and conservative law schools.

In 1978, William Simon, then president of the Olin Foundation, wrote, "Ideas are weapons—indeed the only weapons with which other ideas can be fought . . . [and] capitalism has no duty to subsidize [the ideas of] its enemies." To that end, Simon said, the right had to fund as many scholars, writers, and social scientists as possible. "They must be given grants, grants, and more grants, in exchange for books, books, and more books," he wrote.[71] Olin Foundation leaders developed a "beachhead theory" of change—quietly infiltrating college campuses by funding professors, conservative centers, and sometimes students directly to influence all of campus culture. The Olin Foundation subsidized Dinesh D'Souza's *Illiberal Education*, Allan Bloom's *The Closing of the American Mind*, and dozens of other books. One foundation official likened the organization's funding of professors and authors to amassing a "wine collection" that would accrue value for its owners over time.[72]

By the 2000s, the DeVoses, Kochs, and Olin had spent billions on infiltrating universities, subsidizing hundreds of professors, creating conservative student newspapers, and even funding entire centers dedicated to free speech. By 2015, the Kochs alone had subsidized programs in at least 307 higher education institutions, including Brown University's Political Theory Project and the Mercatus Center at George Mason University (which attracted students so conservative that professors there had to use machines to screen applications for how many times "Ayn Rand" and "Milton Friedman" were used).[73] The DeVos family alone has spent more than $200 million funding conservative causes at universities and think thanks, and helped found the James Madison Center for Free Speech, the think tank that laid the groundwork for *Citizens United*.[74]

But funding was only part of the battle. The Kochs and their fellow billionaires also had to make universities desperate for the money so that they would be more reliant on the tainted cash. Today, we can see the result of their war: in states where Koch-backed politicians have been elected, university budgets have been slashed, while billionaire money further influences the hiring decisions and curricula of schools. In Virginia, for example, the Kochs had a direct say in the hiring and firing of professors at the state's largest public university.[75]

The effects of this double-sided attack—defunding and refunding with tainted cash—is obvious if you look at state universities across the country. With the help of Koch-backed legislators at the state and federal level, nearly every state has slashed taxes and subsequently made up its budget shortfall by cutting down college and university funding by an average of 16 percent over the last decade. In some states, the cuts are over 30 percent.[76]

The Kochs and the other billionaires whose funds they bundle through DonorsTrust and Donors Capital Fund are now infiltrating public grade schools as well, spending millions to give cash-strapped social studies and history teachers free revisionist materials that tout the benefits of capitalism and even present slavery as a necessary evil to secure the freedom the country enjoys today.[77]

Now they are trying to codify into law their campus mission by sponsoring a slate of bills that would in effect criminalize protest on campus.

In 2017, the American Legislative Exchange Council (ALEC) and the Goldwater Institute, each of which has received millions directly from the Kochs and billionaire bundling groups DonorsTrust and Donor Capital

Fund, and millions more from other ultraconservative foundations (often the same ones that sponsor campus talks for people like Milo Yiannopoulos and Christina Hoff Sommers) introduced two pieces of model legislation—one called the Campus Free Speech Act and one called the Forming Open and Robust University Minds (FORUM) Act. The bills propose making it illegal for administrators to disinvite speakers who have been invited by campus groups, and set up a disciplinary process for disruptive students. Similar policies have already been adopted in Wisconsin, which now has a "three strikes" policy on its college and university campuses—anyone who disrupts a speaker or student three times can be immediately expelled. As of February 2018, fifteen states were considering thirty-three pieces of legislation modeled on the ALEC and Goldwater Institute bills.[78]

In 2018, a new group called Speech First opened up shop in Washington, DC, and almost immediately sued the University of Michigan over its harassment policy, which is meant to protect minority students, saying it hindered free speech on campus. The organization has a snazzy website with the text of the First Amendment in italics atop its About page, where it lists Nicole Neily as the organization's president.[79] Before heading up Speech First, Neily was the executive director of the Kochs' Independent Women's Forum.

The progressive responses to these attacks on the independence of higher learning have been at the very least inadequate. Instead of recognizing the true purpose of conservatives' current obsession over free speech—domination of the university—progressives have gone out of their way to defend them, with UC Berkeley announcing Free Speech Year in response to its campus protests, Middlebury's Allison Stanger going on a nationwide free speech tour, and ostensibly progressive commentators, and even leftists like Noam Chomsky, defending the speech rights of the campus infiltrators over those who protest them.[80]

This is partially because conservatives have been good at cloaking their true agendas in the language of free speech—smuggling in their controversial views under the guise of academic freedom. But it also speaks to an inherent flaw in the liberal understanding of power: in the same way that the ACLU's center-ward turn disadvantaged laborers, liberals' insistence on free speech equality for all ignores that we are already starting from a very uneven playing field. By downplaying the role of power in free speech, liberals allow those who already have it to continue having it, leaving those without it to continue living without it. There is no such thing as universal free speech, and, to paraphrase Stanley Fish, the only way to fight discrimination is with alternative forms of discrimination—against ideologies that perpetuate racism, classism, and all the rest. Until we acknowledge that, we'll have ceded to conservatives not only the free speech game, but the entire design of the field on which it is played.

What will campuses look like in twenty years? If you believe the mainstream media, colleges are at risk of becoming cultlike bubbles of progressive thought, intolerant to anything that falls outside a dogmatic set of values and rules. In this view, students, despite their large debt loads, their wobbly job prospects, and the fact that they are temporary residents of the campuses they inhabit, have the power to radically shift America away from a culture of free speech and democracy. Left out of this narrative, like most narratives surrounding free speech, are those who actually hold power in these situations: administrators, politicians, professors (though to a lesser extent), and the billionaires who support and influence them.

The free speech prognosticators who fill our op-ed columns aren't necessarily wrong: there *is* a student-led movement against many forms of conservatism on college campuses. But there has been for decades. That's not new. The tactics haven't changed—students were participating in sit-ins and disrupting talks in the 1960s too. The targets haven't changed—students throughout American history haven't only protested Nazis or blatant white supremacists, but also people they felt were responsible for war, poverty, and other social ills. What has changed is the balance of power: as state budgets are gutted, college is becoming more expensive, and as job opportunities and wages remain relatively stagnant, students have less power than ever. Meanwhile, billionaires have amassed nearly all newly created wealth in the United States in the past several decades, and they are using their money to subtly yet profoundly change what is taught and to dictate what is acceptable on college campuses.[81] Students aren't just battling against Milo and Charles Murray. They're battling an entire system that's increasingly rigged against them, from who pays the speakers they disagree with, to who is responsible for making their tuition more expensive, to who influences their curricula. No wonder they've taken to the streets.

## chapter seven

# SPEECH AND THE STREETS

A T THE CORNER OF NEW YORK AVENUE NW AND 13TH STREET IN downtown Washington, DC, sits a McDonald's with big glass windows wrapping around its brick façade. All the windows are tinted to nearly pitch black, except for one—a clear pane that hints at a hasty replacement job. A minor thing, barely noticeable unless you're looking for it, and the only remaining evidence of one of the largest crime scenes in recent history. The crime behind the hasty window replacement job could have netted its alleged perpetrators a combined 14,000 years in prison.

The crime? Not a mass murder or an international drug conspiracy, but a protest against the inauguration of Donald J. Trump, during which things got a bit rowdy: a few small fires set (including, most memorably, a stretch limousine), a few windows broken (Starbucks, Bank of America, McDonald's). The tactics and scale of the protests on January 20, 2017—a day that would come to be known as J20 among activists around the world, synonymous with prosecutorial zeal and the risk leftists face when they stand up for what they believe in—were nothing out of the ordinary. As liberal protesters marched with anti-Trump signs, shouting slogans about democracy and their displeasure with the new president, more militant factions were drawn to direct action, believing that if the United States really wanted to stop a relatively extremist president, relatively extreme measures had to be taken.

By anarchist standards, the protest was tame. The 1999 anti–World Trade Organization protests in Seattle, for example, lasted far longer and caused more property damage than J20: from November to December, somewhere around 50,000 people participated in the protests, which were met with intense police backlash. By the end of the demonstrations, protesters had damaged about $20 million worth of property, thousands had been tear-gassed, dozens beaten, and hundreds arrested by police.[1] Furthermore, no one was injured by the J20 protesters. The only damage was to property. From the start to the time police wrapped portable plastic fencing and metal barricades around a group of hundreds of people, essentially stopping the protest in its tracks, about twenty-five minutes had elapsed.

Dylan Petrohilos, a young graphic designer, overslept that morning. He arrived at the demonstration fifteen minutes later than he had wanted to. By that time, the police kettle had already formed, with his friends and fellow activists trapped inside. Those fifteen minutes saved him from arrest that day—which made it all the more confusing when, three months later, Petrohilos found himself on the floor of his apartment in nothing but his underwear and handcuffs while eight police officers ransacked his house, looking for evidence that he was one of the masterminds behind the protest, which would turn into a sprawling and legally unprecedented court case against hundreds of defendants.

In 2018, a video that circulated around alt-right message boards used the slogan "Jobs Not Mobs," interspersing footage of leftist protesters with cable news hosts calling the demonstrators mobs. The slogan quickly grew in popularity, ricocheting across the internet, from Reddit to Facebook to Twitter, until it was eventually picked up by mainstream conservative outlets like *Breitbart*.[2] After about two weeks of viral growth, President Trump tweeted a video in which he claimed the Democrats were a far-left "mob," accompanied by the hashtag #jobsnotmobs.[3]

The slogan was not only a case study in how far-right talking points are disseminated into the mainstream, but a peek into how this free speech battle line is fought over in real time. The same factions of the right that have claimed free speech is under constant threat were now equating protests with the actions of a violent mob. In doing so, they exposed the conundrum at the center of free speech logic: what is and is not free speech is in the eye of the beholder. And those in power will use the malleability of free speech to their political advantage.

When we talk about the politics of speech, we're already starting from a severely limited perspective. In general, the speech that we allow does not challenge power, does not challenge private property, and does not challenge capitalism. If it does, it's often met with intense backlash, as it was when unionists and the ACLU fought for a revolutionary definition of speech in the early 1900s.

How we define speech, protest, dissent, expression—how we define the line between speech and illegal or impermissible action (stealing, vandalism, fireable offense, permissible protest, nonpermissible tweet, unpublished op-ed)—that's where the battle lies.

It's because these are the places where normal people are challenging powerful interests: the Kochs, right-wing politicians, white nationalism. And so these are the areas where the powerful have decided to push back, hoping to hold the line—the ability to defend the meaning of free speech to their advantage—no matter the cost.

Dylan Petrohilos was sitting with some friends in the Black Cat Bar near Logan Circle on Election Day as he saw Hillary Clinton lose Ohio, Michigan, and Pennsylvania—states experts had predicted she'd easily carry. He'd been involved with activism for years. Petrohilos is half Latino and grew up in a predominantly black neighborhood in nearby Frederick, Maryland. Before that he lived on Long Island, and in both places he had seen white people's animosity toward people of color firsthand. In the early 2010s he helped organize protests against several white nationalist events. In 2011, he protested as the National Press Club—a prestigious group that represents DC's journalists—hosted a press conference for the National Policy Institute, a white supremacist think tank run by Richard Spencer. The fact that the mainstream press would host something so abhorrent made it clear to Petrohilos that fascism was more mainstream than most Americans believed. So on Election Night, he didn't think a Trump victory was a long shot. Still, when the official verdict finally came in, Petrohilos felt a bit shocked.

"I was just like, 'Oh, my fucking God,'" he recounted to me at a cafe about a mile north from where the J20 protests took place. "I just remember a kind of feeling of dread. And wanting and needing to do something. A bunch of us at the bar felt like, "Shit, the fascists are here. They're one step away from power—and if we don't act with some urgency, all the social movements that developed under Obama and before that are going to be in danger. Our communities are going to be in danger."

Over the next few days, DC activists began planning protests. There were a few in the immediate aftermath of the election—including some that caused minor property damage. But Petrohilos could tell something was different as Inauguration Day, which activists had dubbed J20, approached. The far right appeared to be emboldened by Trump's election. When one of Petrohilos's tweets asking people to come to planning meetings for J20 went semi-viral, hundreds of threats were sent to those who retweeted it. At a large planning meeting a few weeks before the protest, an operative from Project Veritas, a Koch-funded right-wing nonprofit that uses selectively edited, secretly recorded videos to take down progressive and left-wing causes, showed up and tried to get participants to say they planned on pursuing violent strategies on J20.[4]

There were no such strategies discussed. The closest Petrohilos ever got to discussing violence was during a meeting when he said that there should be a family-friendly part of the protest with no window-breaking, in addition to a more militant protest, where people dress in all black (often referred to as "black bloc"). Prosecutors would later try to use Petrohilos's insistence that no one break windows at the family-friendly side of the protest as evidence that he encouraged violence on the other side.[5]

For legal reasons, Petrohilos can't talk in too much detail about what happened on January 20, 2017. But he said he wanted to go because he was sick of waiting. "There's no point waiting for a revolution," he told me. "We are living in a crisis. Climate change is about to destroy the planet. And the far right is on the rise. So for me, it's about figuring out where the boundaries of social struggle are, and how do we get out of those current bounds and become forces that could actually exert power over society?"

Petrohilos's words reminded me of that dividing line we constantly are fighting over—the line between speech and action. For him, it was clear the line does not really exist, or that it doesn't matter. But what Petrohilos and others deemed an appropriate and deeply necessary protest was, to others, worth decades in prison. Still, Petrohilos felt morally obligated to participate in the J20 protests.

That sentiment was echoed by other defendants I spoke with. "I personally felt like it was important to set the tone for what the next four years of resistance would look like," one said. "A proto-fascist regime was coming to power in the US, and so it was important to show what they were up against."

But Petrohilos and the other J20 protesters didn't realize how hard the government was willing to hold their line. "We thought, 'Let's be reasonable: the policing protocols of the Bush and Obama eras are not going to change overnight,'" a demonstrator told me. "And then that's exactly what happened."

Fifteen minutes after arriving to the protest on January 20, Petrohilos was fleeing a cloud of pepper spray as he watched his friends and comrades get arrested by the dozens, placed into police vans and carted off to jail. In the police kettle, hundreds of activists huddled together in the cold. The police kept people kettled there for nearly nine hours and wouldn't let anyone leave to use the bathroom or eat. Isaac Dalto, a scruffy UPS worker and seasoned activist from Baltimore, had taken an Imodium pill so he could make it through the day without going to the bathroom. Others weren't so lucky. They passed the time singing songs like "Bohemian Rhapsody." And then, finally, the police slowly removed the group via paddy wagon. At the police station, Dalto couldn't hold it anymore. He shit himself as the cop dragged him, handcuffed, out of the van and into his cell.

"I took off my pants and smeared the walls of my cell with shit, like an IRA hunger striker during the Troubles or something," Dalto recounted when we met at a Panera Bread in a Baltimore suburb. He was laughing, along with a fellow former J20 defendant who had come with him named Riv. It was a good war story. "Then I gave myself a bird bath in the toilet to clean off, forgetting, of course, that my hands were drenched in pepper spray. My face and eyes and nose and anus are just drenched in fucking pepper spray. And I remember thinking, 'This is it. This is Day One of Trump's America. This is just what life's going to be like from now on.'"

One by one, the activists were released. They knew they weren't exactly free, but they had no idea what was to come next.

Four months later, eight police officers smashed through Dylan Petrohilos's apartment door, handcuffed him and his roommate, and took his computers and cellphone. A few days later, as Petrohilos was having lunch with a friend at a nearby restaurant, he got a call. His friend told him he would be indicted for conspiring to plan the J20 protests and faced up to seventy-five years in prison. Panicking, Petrohilos walked out of the restaurant and down the street to a park. His mind started reeling. Why was he being targeted? He wasn't even at the protest.

For several hours, Petrohilos thought he was the only one—he'd be taking the blame for a relatively run-of-the-mill protest that he couldn't even reach. For attending a few meetings, Petrohilos thought he was facing decades in prison. Then he got another call. It wasn't only going to be him. Prosecutors were going to charge all of his friends and anyone else they could identify that day with felony rioting and a host of other crimes. They'd *all* potentially face decades in prison. Petrohilos felt a strange sense of relief—at least it wasn't just him going up against the court system and police, but an entire movement. But he wasn't sure which was worse: possibly doing seventy-five years alone, or spending decades in prison together with 200 others, most of whom had done nothing more than walk down the street and chant at a permitted march.

◇◇◇

The prosecution of J20 activists was audacious and unprecedented. Lawyers for the defense, along with lawyers who had nothing to do with the case, were flabbergasted at the barrage of charges and the evidence prosecutors used to back them up. "In my over thirty years of practicing law, I've never seen anything like this," Mark Goldstone, a high-profile attorney in DC, said at the time.[6]

Mass arrests of protesters are relatively common (see: nearly every Democratic or Republican National Convention over the past few decades), but most often only a few demonstrators—for example, the ones police can prove are responsible for property damage or blocking traffic—are charged with serious crimes. Slapping anyone with felony riot charges—defined as a group of five or more people using "tumultuous and violent conduct or the threat thereof" to cause "serious bodily harm"—is rare these days.[7] Yet DC prosecutors decided to charge everyone they could identify in the vicinity of the broken McDonald's windows with felony rioting. Being there, anywhere near the blocks where a few activists had broken a few windows, and wearing black clothes, was enough evidence. In fact, video of you there and in black was the *main* evidence prosecutors used against most of the J20 defendants.

Led by Assistant US Attorney Jennifer Kerkhoff, the government prosecution attempted to persuade each J20 defendant to take a plea deal in exchange for testifying against their fellow arrestees or, if they wanted to go to court, to go in individual trials as opposed to collectively as one big group. All but a few defendants refused to be tried individually. If one was going to prison, they all were. If one was let go, they'd all be.

Several organizations, including the ACLU, helped the J20 defense. But still, with the mounds of paperwork the prosecution was throwing at them, the lawyers were overwhelmed. Defendants turned themselves into legal experts overnight by necessity. Elizabeth Lagesse, a thirty-one-year-old defendant, put her job search on hold, assuming she wouldn't find one anyway with seventy-five years hanging over her head, and started researching late into the night most weeks. Eventually she discovered that one of the videos the prosecution was relying on to prove that defendants had conspired to riot came, already edited, from Project Veritas. The prosecution was using right-wing videos as unbiased proof of defendants' guilt. The prosecutors had also introduced videos into evidence that were taken straight from right-wing conspiracy YouTube accounts, including one produced by the white nationalist Oath Keepers and one called "IN-SANE Protests Riots compilation."[8] The police, too, seemed ready to work with the alt-right—activists found that Rachel Schaerr, an employee of the DC Metropolitan Police Department, handed a spreadsheet with the names of all 231 arrestees to a right-wing conspiracy news website.[9]

Judge Lynn Leibovitz too seemed inclined to accept the prosecution's claims finding that a photojournalist named Alexei Wood could be considered part of a conspiracy to riot because Wood "played a role that furthered the purposes both of the conspiracy and of the riot itself, which was to advertise it, to broadcast it, to live-stream it such that others could be recruited to join it."[10]

Even with their legal defense paid for through donations, protesters had to upend their lives to participate in the trial. Dalto recounted going through every single text, social media post, and photo he'd taken in the past year with his lawyer, seeing which he could ask to redact from the prosecution because they were irrelevant and personal—photos of him and his girlfriend, for example. Kerkhoff wouldn't allow it. She attempted to pit people in relationships against each other. Some of the few plea deals taken by J20 defendants were from couples who were told they could get little or reduced time, but only if their partners agreed to the same deal. If they didn't, they'd be threatening the freedom of their significant others too.

Other protesters lost thousands in income, or their jobs, and spent much of their own money traveling back and forth to DC. Over the course of the next year, the trials, which were split up into several small groups of defendants, began to appear unwinnable for the prosecution. Defense lawyers found that the prosecution not only used right-wing videos but concealed sixty-nine other audio and video recordings that could have potentially helped exonerate defendants—a violation of the Brady rule, which says that prosecutors must present all evidence, including exculpatory evidence, to the defense in a criminal trial. Judge Leibovitz also admonished the prosecution for trying to pin an unrelated incident on the protesters being tried—a limousine was set on fire much later in the day, after all the defendants had been arrested—and told the jury to disregard Kerkhoff's insinuations to the contrary.[11] Leibovitz then prevented Kerkhoff from using the defendants' decision to wear black clothing as evidence that they intended to riot.[12] Dalto remembers thinking that the whole idea of freedom of expression had to be bullshit if prosecutors could jail people based on the color of the clothes they were wearing. Leibovitz, at least, seemed to agree.

Slowly, the state's case began to crumble as jurors dismissed the charges or the state dropped the cases right before the trials began. They petered out. On July 6, 2018, the last thirty-nine defendants' charges were dropped.[13] An anticlimactic end to a year and a half of upheaval. It felt, strangely, disappointing to some.

"We wanted to hammer them with evidence that they'd committed so much prosecutorial misconduct," Lagesse told me. "We wanted to nail them to the wall. And then they dropped my case two days before the hearing was scheduled, after eighteen months of me waiting. I had to go through eighteen months of bullshit, and I never had my say in court."

Eventually, charges were dropped for every person who decided to take part in the combined trial. Only one person, who took a plea deal early on, was sentenced to jail—receiving a four-month term.[14] But after a year and a half of stress, of not knowing what their lives would look like, the damage was already done. They were free, but in some ways they had been broken by the event. Several former J20 defendants told me they believed the state had won for that reason: their calculus was, either they were going to actually win the trial and set a new precedent against protest or lose the trial but scare 200 activists off the streets of DC, and possibly scare protesters across the country into thinking twice before heading down to any march.

Isaac Dalto compared it to many copyright lawsuits: "The goal is not necessarily to win. Winning's nice. Winning's a bonus," but the real point, he said, is to tire people out, drain them of their resources until they give up.

"I have not really gone out in the streets, so to speak, since this happened," Lagesse told me. "My activism now mostly happens at a computer in a dark room at one in the morning. That's maybe more effective, but in a way it's what they want."

The trial also changed how Lagesse thinks about the American government, and about dissent in general. She said she never really believed that the US government always has people's best interests at heart, but her opinion of it is even lower now.

"Those people who are like, 'Dissent is patriotic' or whatever—I don't think the leaders of our government have believed that for fifty years at least," she said.

Riv, the friend of Isaac Dalto's from Baltimore who had joined us at Panera, said he and others have struggled with symptoms of PTSD since being acquitted. He has friends who wake up thinking they're in jail, or on trial. He couldn't talk to his fiancée for the duration of the trial because he was afraid she'd be subpoenaed. She found a counselor through their insurance so she could have someone to talk to who legally wasn't allowed to reveal anything.

Riv also hasn't been to many protests since. "I feel like a dog with its tail between its legs," he said.

After keeping a strong face for the duration of the trial, photojournalist Alexei Wood broke down too. The state was still holding on to his camera equipment as evidence. He'd given up his apartment in San Antonio, Texas, so he could afford to be in DC for all his hearing dates. As soon as his charges were dismissed, he started bawling. And then he felt like he crashed—drinking heavily, smoking too much weed. He could barely leave bed for weeks.

"I didn't have control over my physical body," he told me. "My emotions, my mind, my body. It was a somatic experience."

I visited Wood in San Antonio, where he grew up and eventually returned after the trial. He's now living out of a box truck, parked on the street a few blocks from where he's taken up apprenticeship work for an artist. His small dog accompanies him everywhere. "I'm struggling. I'm barely getting the fuck through," he told me, sitting by the small stream that meanders through the city, where he frequently bathes himself. It was months after the trial. Wood said he felt better than he had felt right after the trial, but he still felt beaten down by the ordeal. He used to rush into action—to photograph protests and conflict and whatever else he could. Now he couldn't bring himself to do it.

"I haven't taken a fucking photograph since the trial," he said. "That whole focus I've had for nearly two decades, I won't even touch it now. I'm not even interested in taking a fucking photograph."

He planned on driving back up to DC in a few weeks to finally get his equipment back from the police lockup. Until then, it had been stashed away as evidence of his supposed rioting. Maybe he'd start to take photos again, but he wasn't sure if his equipment still worked. The last time he saw his camera, it was drenched in pepper spray.

America has a way of forgetting. Like my friend had told me on the way down to Charlottesville, the country is depressingly unique in its lack of reconciliation with its violent past. South Africa had the Truth and Reconciliation Commission. Germany paid reparations to Holocaust victims (including my grandparents). Reparations for slavery in the United States at this point are a political nonstarter, considering many public schools in the country still downplay the very existence of slavery and its contribution to the Civil War.[15] Does "hindsight is twenty-twenty" work if our glasses are always rose-tinted?

Our current dialogue about free speech—the ongoing insistence by politicians, journalists, and many Americans that we must uphold it as a value central to an American way of life—is only possible because of our penchant for historical amnesia, or at least historical misremembering.

From slavery, to the struggle for civil rights, to today, the government has proffered the rights of truly free speech and dissent on some and not others. And we don't need to look very far back to know that free speech is a conditional freedom in this country, and that those conditions are nearly always defined by those in power.

Imagine downloading a song off the internet from your office computer, maybe from a politically vocal artist. You listen to it on your way home and on your way to work the next day. When you enter your office, the entire staff is there, waiting for you. There's a chair for you to sit in. Your colleagues want to question your loyalty to the United States. If they're dissatisfied, you're fired, and possibly jailed. This was the reality for many leftists in the United States in the 1940s and '50s.

"McCarthyism" is still a household word. Schoolkids are taught the dangers of a fanatical man with too much power. The term is bandied about by politicians who accuse anyone who criticizes them of being a McCarthyist. But McCarthyism is also a misnomer. Yes, Wisconsin Senator Joseph McCarthy was one of the biggest proponents of investigating, questioning, and sometimes imprisoning communists, leftists, and others whose politics he did not perceive to serve the interests of the American government. But we remember McCarthyism as the aberrant and abhorrent acts of one man because it's an easier pill to swallow than the truth: McCarthyism was a nationwide phenomenon that the majority of Americans supported. It was backed by the founding director of the FBI, J. Edgar Hoover, and though President Dwight Eisenhower privately disagreed with McCarthy, he never fully denounced McCarthy's actions. His predecessor, Harry Truman, was more publicly critical, but he also went along with most of Hoover's McCarthy-inspired leadership.[16] Our misremembering of McCarthy fits in well with how we remember many things in America: slavery as a one-off mistake as opposed to a system based on a legacy of racial violence and oppression, the Salem witch trials as a population gone inexplicably mad as opposed to one of countless examples of women being persecuted as they fought for greater freedoms.[17]

The true lesson of McCarthyism isn't to keep a lookout for political zealots intent on increasing their power through persecution (though we should probably also be on the lookout for them); it's that powerful interests—namely corporations and politicians—can easily sow a fear so powerful in the American psyche that it takes on a life of its own, until people no longer need someone telling them to persecute and silence others because they'll do it themselves. The trials conducted by McCarthy himself were responsible for only a fraction of the damage done by the era of antileftist sentiment. Far more people's lives were ruined not by the federal government itself, but by the American public's willingness to do the government's bidding.

That's what happened to Anne Hale, a well-liked teacher in Wayland, Massachusetts, who had once been a member of the US Communist Party. One day in 1954, even though she had left the party years earlier, she sat facing 700 teachers, parents, and children in her high school's auditorium and learned that her neighbors had been secretly documenting her every move for years. One neighbor had informed the FBI that "a colored lady who appeared to be advanced educationally" resided with Hale part-time. Another neighbor had dug through her trash looking for "subversive" materials. A teacher she was close with had become afraid of associating with her, and so she too had ratted to the FBI, telling agents that Hale wasn't scared of living in poor neighborhoods and associated with "persons in these areas," which, apparently to the FBI, was a sign she could be a communist. One informant had told the FBI that she had purchased two Pete Seeger songbooks. The FBI kept Hale on a watchlist, but the Bureau had bigger fish to fry and told the school to act on its own—which it did, peppering Hale with questions about her loyalty in a pseudo-hearing, and ultimately firing her.

She was placed on landlord blacklists and fired from nearly every job she got afterward because her name was now known in Massachusetts—she couldn't even hold down a job as a dog kennel cleaner once her bosses found out who she was. She wasn't allowed to say goodbye to her students. So instead, she wrote each a letter: "Your family will tell you that different people have different ideas about how the country should be run. I have been working for a long time in the best way I knew to make sure that the 'liberty and justice for all' of which we speak every morning is always with us and that it will grow better. Those who don't agree with me may say harsh things. Just remember these things, which I am sure you know—I love my country and I love you."[18]

Hale's story is known partly because journalists at the *Boston Globe* took the time to file information requests with the federal government and retrieve all the documents related to Hale. But her story is typical. She's one of tens of thousands of Americans whose lives were ruined during the McCarthy era.

As historian Ellen Schrecker writes in her comprehensive history of McCarthyism, *Many Are the Crimes*, both the supposed threat the government was responding to (communists) and the actual response were relatively contained. The Communist Party peaked at 82,000 members in the United States in 1938, or about one out of every 1,600 Americans.[19] Only two people—Julius and Ethel Rosenberg, two Soviet spies—were killed during the era. A few hundred went to prison, and a little more than 10,000 lost their jobs.[20] And yet, despite the relatively small numbers involved, Schrecker writes that, "if nothing else, McCarthyism destroyed the left," and wiped an entire generation of political activism "off the stage of history," because the government had made clear, with relatively little effort, that if you were politically active on the left, your life *could* be destroyed. The government did not have to prosecute an entire movement, because it could simply scare the movement out of existence.[21]

By the end of the Great Depression, American leftists had made inroads into mainstream politics and unions because they were doing something about people's dire living and working conditions: organizing against mandatory military service on college campuses, preventing homelessness by setting up neighborhood groups that would help people move their furniture back into their houses after they were evicted.[22] Nearly 3,000 American leftists traveled to Spain after the outbreak of war in 1936 to fight off a fascist coup, and were greeted with cheers when they came back home.[23] Communists were active in organizing the United Automobile Workers union, and they participated in sit-ins and picketed segregated restaurants in the 1940s and '50s.

Though the economic crisis of the 1930s helped balloon the Communist Party USA's membership, the actual party was never that large.

Rather, the real threat perceived by conservatives was in the broad coalition of leftists (including communists but not limited to them), unions, progressive politicians, and black and Latino power groups that seemed to hold an ever-greater sway over American life and were increasingly organizing together.

The right, and the business leaders who funded it, needed a counternarrative to disprove the burgeoning thesis that America's economic system was fragile, unfair, and producing fewer and fewer returns for the average American. As Schrecker writes, "Americans have never suffered from a shortage of scapegoated aliens," whether it was Native Americans and slaves, who newspapers said during the era of chattel slavery would "possess themselves of the whole Country" and carry out white genocide if allowed to be free, or Catholic immigrants in the 1840s. By the turn of the twentieth century, the catchall term became "radicals"—which could mean black people, immigrants, or anyone else who could be conveniently demonized by the right. And by the 1940s, "radicals" had been joined by "communists," as the scapegoat, a threat supposedly so big a former FBI agent told a federal security council that the nation "need not worry about any other threat to the internal security of the nation, because it is not impossible that there will be no nation" if communism was allowed to spread.[24] (Though less dramatic, today's pundits strike a similar tone when they claim that if there are too many college protests, or too many NFL players kneeling during the national anthem, we'll end up ruining all of what America stands for.)

The initial fearmongering against communism came not during the Great Depression, but after World War I, when big business and conservative veterans feared that soldiers would return from Europe harboring socialist ideals. To prevent that from happening, they created the American Legion, which was explicitly anticommunist at its inception. Much like today's right (see: the Tea Party), the Legion presented itself as grassroots but in reality was funded by large corporations, mainly J. P. Morgan and other Wall Street banks. Many Legion members would physically assault radicals and pro-union operatives. The more respectable side of the Legion lobbied Congress for anticommunist legislation and hired staff to comb through public school curricula and textbooks to make sure they were sufficiently anticommunist.[25] The less respectable side acted as a roving street gang, beating up suspected communists. The ACLU counted fifty incidents of American Legion anticommunist violence in 1919 alone.[26]

The Sedition Act of 1918, as it's commonly called (it was actually a set of amendments to the 1917 Espionage Act, not a separate act), allowed police to arrest thousands of workers for striking under the ruse that they were encouraging Americans to be disloyal or advocating the overthrow of the US government. Though the act was repealed a few years later, that didn't stop laborers from being persecuted. By one estimate, 18,000 workers were arrested for striking between 1934 and 1936 alone, and a dozen states put their own Sedition Act–style laws on the books.[27] (You can still technically be fired for being a communist in several states that never removed the laws from their books, and the green card application still asks if you've been a member of the Communist Party.[28])

The media helped in the government and big businesses' propaganda efforts. The papers of the Hearst Corporation, which is still one of the largest media companies in the United States, lauded the efforts to arrest any labor leader or suspected communist from the 1930s through the end of the McCarthy era.[29] From World War I until the end of the McCarthy era, communism was as much an anti-right-wing branding opportunity as it was an actual threat to the United States. Businesses called anything and everything that threatened their bottom line "communist." It was easier to convince the American public that, for example, striking farmworkers in California wanted to ruin everyone's American way of life than it was to convince people that they did not deserve higher wages.[30]

By the time Franklin Delano Roosevelt's New Deal programs were in full swing, many politicians had realized "communism" was a great way to attack anything they did not like. In 1938, the majority of the House of Representatives (including many Democrats) voted to authorize the creation of the House Un-American Activities Committee (HUAC). Its leader, Texas Democrat Martin Dies, used the committee to probe every agency funded or created by the New Deal and root out "communists." Though few were ever found, the committee's activities were front-page news across America, and received widespread support from newspaper editorial boards and the American public. Progressives, instead of challenging the charges, attempted to appease the right. Roosevelt fired several staff members, and his National Labor Relations Board was purged. Of course, these purges served to legitimize the charges more than dissuade right-wing attacks on America's quasi-socialist New Deal policies.[31]

Then, in 1940, the prosecutions began. First up was Earl Browder, the head of the Communist Party USA, who admitted to accidentally making a false statement on his passport in front of the HUAC, and was sentenced to an unheard-of four years in prison.[32] The Supreme Court upheld the decision and his sentence. Fearing that leftists of all kinds would hamper World War II efforts by striking at weapons and transportation manufacturing plants, the Roosevelt administration ramped up its support for the HUAC and its related activities. The FBI went on a hiring spree, growing from 850 agents in 1939 to 4,600 in 1943, almost all of them there just to investigate communists.[33] The US Army compiled a list of 250,000 informants, and the FBI maintained a list of another 80,000. That worked out to about one out of every fifty Americans being a government informant, far exceeding the actual membership of the Communist Party.[34]

During World War II, Congress passed the Smith Act, a law similar to the Sedition Act, which again made it illegal to advocate for anything that could be perceived as encouraging the overthrow of the US government. Hundreds were prosecuted under the act, and the Supreme Court again deemed those prosecutions constitutional. It wasn't until 1957 that the act was again reviewed by the Court, which limited its applicability, though the law still technically remains on the books today.[35]

Though the number of actual legal prosecutions paled in comparison to the number of people accused of being communists, the anticommunist fervor worked to quell much leftist dissent during the 1940s and 1950s, and to pull semi-leftist organizations toward the center or right. The witch hunt also fell on predictable racial lines: black actors were targeted as outside threats to US sovereignty, and the activist and actor Paul Robeson had his passport revoked.[36] W. E. B. Du Bois, who helped found the NAACP and had communist sympathies, was accused of being

a Soviet agent, and was later succeeded by Walter White, a more con-
ciliatory leader who supported President Harry Truman.[37] The ACLU
and other civil liberties organizations fractured over defending communists. Newspapers fired anyone who might taint their image.[38] Hollywood
pushed out leftist and progressive actors, producers, and writers—though
Hollywood was liberal, the owners of studios were by and large in favor of
McCarthyism.

Corporations and the antileftist groups they funded used anticom-
munism, especially anti-Soviet fearmongering, as an excuse to launch
a massive antilabor public relations campaign. In one particularly odd
Canadair magazine advertisement, for example, parents were warned
in text, under a picture of a typical American classroom, that "in the
eyes of Communism, a child is simply something to be warped into one
shape: godless, ignorant of moral responsibility, devoid of intellectual
honesty."[39] How any of that related to Canadair's main pursuit—airplane
manufacturing—went unmentioned.

By the 1950s, paranoia was so widespread that nearly everything was
tainted by fear of communist infiltration. If you wanted a fishing permit in New York State, for example, you had to sign a loyalty oath to the
United States.[40]

Joseph McCarthy was an unremarkable senator from Wisconsin who
would have likely faded into obscurity if he hadn't figured out that anti-
communism was a great way to scare Americans into a renewed round of
panic, and boost his own image in the process. He had been accused of
campaign finance violations, had praised and defended the SS at various
points in his career, and wasn't known to be a particularly effective legis-
lator.[41] But he realized that the media would lap up his accusations about
communism.

What McCarthy excelled at was furthering the anticommunist paranoia and directing it toward the government itself, insisting that it wasn't
only labor unions, but each and every federal agency and department that
was lousy with communists. Though McCarthy received lots of press attention, and was successful in prosecuting some alleged communists, it's
odd that the movement came to be named after him. Anticommunist

fervor had started decades before McCarthy, and lasted only a few years after his fame peaked in the early 1950s. The press quickly became more skeptical of the prosecutions and of McCarthy's claims.[42] Politicians began challenging McCarthy, including fellow Republican Margaret Chase Smith (the first woman to serve in both the House and Senate), who in 1950 delivered a well-received speech in which she told McCarthy and his supporters that they were being un-American by accusing everyone they disagreed with of communism.[43]

McCarthyism died down as the civil rights era began. But the government's hatred of leftist movements didn't go away; it simply transformed into programs harder to spot and criticize, which required much less public political fervor. Trials, press attention, and popular support were no longer needed to quell antiracist and anticapitalist action, because now it was mostly being done in secret. McCarthyism was over, but the monitoring, prosecution, and demonization of activists was just getting started.

## chapter eight

# WHOSE SPEECH MATTERS?

R ATTLER, THE NAME GIVEN TO HIM BECAUSE HE ONCE KILLED AN AG-gressive rattlesnake with his bare hands, stood in the middle of the low-slung, concrete Unitarian Universalist Church in Bismarck, North Dakota, a building that looked barely different from the hundreds of big-box stores surrounding it. He was joined by what he called his family—none of them biological—a mix of Native American spiritual and community leaders, lawyers, local white people who had brought bland vegan food to the event, and old-school bikers in leather jackets who had parked their Harleys outside. His partner, Olive, who is two-spirit, stood next to him. The disparate group, one hundred or so strong, was a testament to the strength and compassion of and for Rattler, a large man with a beard and a Harley, who was one of the friendliest and most talkative people I'd ever met. He was there to say goodbye. The next day I'd watch him stand before a judge and get sentenced to three years in prison for his role in the Dakota Access Pipeline protests in 2016.

The world's attention has moved on since the protests, at which hundreds of local, state, and federal authorities used pepper spray, sound cannons, tanks, and handcuffs to break up the Standing Rock camp on the border of North and South Dakota. There aren't dozens of TV cameras and national news reporters in North Dakota anymore. There wasn't even a local TV news crew at Rattler's sentencing. But for hundreds of the activists who were most central to the fight, a cloud has hung over their heads for the past two years. North Dakota authorities charged nearly 850 people for a variety of offenses related to the protests at Standing Rock. Most of those cases—736, to be precise—have concluded, a significant number of them dismissed or given plea deals without much jail time. For a select few, though, including Rattler, the charges and potential consequences were much more severe: without coming to a plea deal, he faced up to fifteen years in prison for allegedly helping light fire to a barricade to prevent cops from coming into the camp and destroying it. The charge against him and several others—civil disorder—was used in the 1960s to limit the power of the black liberation movement.[1] When 200 American Indian Movement activists occupied the town of Wounded Knee in 1973 to call attention to the oppression still faced by Native Americans, they were also charged with civil disorder.[2]

Rattler only teared up at his goodbye event when Olive spoke. Otherwise he was calm. Ready. "I believe in what I did," he told me later. "That's why I done what I done. Because if you had been out there on the lines, I would have been protecting you too. That's what I was supposed to do."

I asked him if he felt angry, or resentful, that standing up for what he believed in would land him in prison for three years. "It was something I believe in, so, no," he said. "It was worth it as long as I kept people safe. And on October 27, I kept a lot of people safe."

Before October 27, 2016, Rattler had kept a lot of people safe too. He grew up on the Pine Ridge Reservation, about 250 miles south of Standing Rock. The per capita income in Oglala Lakota County, located on the Pine Ridge Reservation, is $8,768, the lowest in the United States. His childhood was rough. Rattler told me his mother drank and abused him and his siblings, and one night, when the abuse got to be too much and she broke Rattler's nose, he hit back. He ended up in prison on an assault charge; he was just fifteen. Since then, he has been living on his own. And after a few years bouncing around Pine Ridge, he got sober and became a leader of Sun Dances—traditional ceremonies common among Plains Indian tribes that often last up to four days. For Rattler, the Sun Dances were a way to keep himself humble and helpful to his community, and to connect to his spirit and his past. Sun Dances were outlawed by the US government when his mother was growing up as part of an attempt to forcibly assimilate Native Americans. Rattler wanted to reclaim his tradition.

Rattler made most of his money by transporting things, whatever needed to be transported, across the vast plains—mostly cattle and then, as hydraulic fracturing opened up huge swaths of the region to a new era of oil and natural gas drilling, fracking equipment. One day, a few years before Standing Rock, he dropped off some drilling equipment at a fracking site in North Dakota, where he could see that an oil company had dammed a stream in order to divert the water for its fracking operation. Fish wouldn't be able to swim down the stream and would die, he thought. The scene disgusted Rattler. The indifference of the workers there did too. He vowed never to work for the oil industry again. He returned to Pine Ridge, lived out of his truck and maintained a small garage on the reservation. Hardly anyone had money, or even a job. Still, Rattler wanted to help them. So he bartered for food and cigarettes in exchange for fixing people's cars, motorcycles, and trucks. He would still haul cattle on the side to bring in some cash.

A day after returning from a four-day Sun Dance in August 2016, Rattler was browsing Facebook and came across an article about how protests were starting to grow at Standing Rock, where Energy Transfer Partners and the Army Corps of Engineers had worked in tandem to push through approval of a massive pipeline capable of transferring 450,000 barrels of oil a day. The pipeline would pass right through an area populated by many Native Americans, including through burial grounds.[3]

"It was just spiritual," Rattler told me. The spirit "told me I had to go, so I was like, all right."

He packed his van with buffalo meat, potatoes, snacks, ketchup, salt and pepper, and blankets until he couldn't fit a square inch more. He would travel back and forth between Standing Rock and Pine Ridge every few days. But Rattler was away from the camp when, in early September 2016, private security guards released attack dogs on several protesters.[4] Rattler felt like he could have intervened if he had been there. He vowed never to leave again.

At their peak, the Standing Rock protesters numbered 10,000. They were meticulously organized on the sprawling plain, with medic tents, a food-and-water distribution operation, media teams that would stand on "Facebook Hill" (one of the only places at the camp with cellphone reception), and a security crew, which Rattler was part of, that helped to de-escalate internal conflicts and tried to prevent the pipeline company's private security teams, as well as local and state cops, from intervening.

From the start, police and private forces tried to disrupt the camp using pepper spray, rubber bullets, and military-style vehicles. One cold night, police used water cannons to push back hundreds of protesters, injuring over one hundred of them, according to protesters.[5] The legality of it all was complex: the camp moved several times, between private, public, and tribal lands. Protests were deemed legal, at least at first, on public lands, but not on land controlled by the Army Corps of Engineers or owned outright by the pipeline company. The varying legal status of the lands provided a good example of how the law is malleable, based on powerful interests' needs: private property here, as it does everywhere in the United States, trumped the right to free speech, but it didn't trump the rights of the pipeline company, which had state and federal government partners use eminent domain to push the line through.

It was never clear who had ultimate authority over the protesters—state police were intervening on tribal lands; private security forces were working on public lands. There was no clear jurisdiction, though the protesters made it clear they felt that *they* had ultimate say: the pipeline had the potential to ruin sacred land, and that, in and of itself, should have been enough to allow their presence. But the Army Corps of Engineers, police, and Energy Transfer Partners worked in tandem to push back and push out protesters wherever they were. They'd block public roads so that no one new could join the camp, and they'd close off camp entrances and exits so that protesters could not move.

While the tense standoffs between police and private security (who were often donning SWAT-style gear) and protesters made headlines, covert surveillance and infiltration of the camp played an arguably larger role in its repression.

Sitting inside a building in Bismarck, FBI officials, along with partners in local law enforcement, used the North Dakota State and Local Intelligence Center (also known as the Fusion Center) developed after September 11, 2001, to track activists. There, they'd monitor cameras around the camp and use flyover footage from helicopters owned by TigerSwan, the private security company hired by Energy Transfer Partners to track activists' every move.[6] They created flow charts to plot out prominent activists' ties to other movements like Black Lives Matter and Anonymous, with status markers next to them (spokesperson, leader, pepper spray buyer, arrested). Activists know there were FBI informants throughout the camp, but no one knew how many. The surveillance operations of the Department of Homeland Security, FBI, TigerSwan, and others also expanded their searches for potential threats beyond the confines of the camp, tracking activists in Chicago and elsewhere who had little to do with the Dakota Access Pipeline protests, but who were seen as leftists who could potentially influence the occupation.[7]

On October 27, the same day Rattler was arrested, police raided the camps. As they swept through, two officers tackled Red Fawn Fallis, an Oglala Sioux activist who was well known to police (she was on one of the Fusion Center charts). A gun went off. No one was hit. But the cops later claimed the gun belonged to Fallis, and that she had brandished it at them. Only later, during her trial, did the public find out that the gun had originally belonged to a man named Heath Harmon, a paid FBI informant who had pretended to be an activist at the camp, befriended Fallis, and become her lover.[8] She was sentenced to nearly five years in prison.

"They're doing this all the time to every movement," Molly Armour, one of Fallis's lawyers, told me. "They're in Black Lives Matter, they're everywhere. It just doesn't come out until there's something to reveal it-self. We don't know the full extent at Standing Rock or anywhere, but she's not the only one. It's just that her source got exposed."

October 27 saw the most intense police violence during the occupa-tion of Standing Rock, and the most intense pushback. Police rushed the camps from every side, making it difficult for protesters to move. Protest-ers, including Rattler, set up roadblocks made mostly out of wood to slow the police. That day, as police approached, the barricades were lit on fire. The fires likely posed no danger to police—they were relatively small. But police made no effort to put them out. They did not arrest anyone who built the fires on that day either. Instead, federal prosecutors waited until February to file charges—activists claim as a way to distract from their own use of rubber bullets, tear gas, sound cannons, and other aggressive policing tactics.[9]

In a report issued several months after the camp was dismantled, the Department of Homeland Security portrayed the protesters as violent, saying that Fallis had purposefully shot at police, a claim that had been discredited at her trial. The authors also claimed that Sophia Wilansky, a protester from Minnesota, had attempted to throw IEDs at police, which blew up prematurely, "resulting in the near amputation of her arm."[10] Multiple sworn witnesses said otherwise. Wilansky claimed she nearly lost her arm after police threw a concussion grenade toward the crowd.

By the end of the Standing Rock occupation, TigerSwan had gone full conspiracy theory against protesters, calling them jihadists and claiming that they were part of a vast operation funded by wealthy liberal billion-aires like Warren Buffett (TigerSwan did not mention that Buffett's com-pany, Berkshire Hathaway, was the largest investor in the energy company Phillips 66, which owned a 25 percent stake in the Dakota Access Pipe-line). Energy Transfer Partners then sued several environmental nonprof-its under the Racketeer Influenced and Corrupt Organizations (RICO) Act, which was established to help authorities take down the mafia. ETP claimed that by encouraging people to withdraw their business from banks that backed the pipeline, they were encouraging a form of crimi-nal racketeering. The lawsuit was dismissed, but it nonetheless put added financial and time pressure on activist groups, which many believed was the point.[11]

As winter progressed, some protesters left on their own accord—the temperature was often in the low tens overnight, and supplies, blocked by police, were dwindling. In January and February, only a few hundred remained at the camp. But after further police action, the numbers dwindled to the dozens. The camp was effectively cleared by March 2017.[12]

As hundreds of indictments came raining down from state and federal prosecutors in the months after the peak of the "NODAPL" protests, activists knew the deck was stacked against them. They were so extensively surveilled that every controversial action they participated in could be played in front of a jury, while their defense teams often only had the word of other activists to support them. Energy Transfer Partners had waged a PR campaign against the protesters, portraying them as unpatriotic and as outside agitators. By December 2016, two months before a grand jury handed down Rattler's charges, a survey found that about 75 percent of the jury-eligible population of the areas of North Dakota where pipeline protesters were being tried already thought the protesters were guilty.[13] But judges refused to move the trials to neighboring counties.

The weight of it all—the years behind bars, the surveillance, the fact that the nearly all-white population of Bismarck seemed to truly hate the protesters—was palpable in the Unitarian church the night before Rattler's sentencing. People tried to be happy, to have fun and share memories with Rattler. But it was hard. Many cried. Rattler seemed the calmest person there. In front of the crowd of his supporters, he spoke low and slow, about why this was all worth it:

> They tried to portray me as some kind of leader. I tell them I'm not. I'm a flea. I'm just a flea like everybody else. But if you want to irritate the dog, all the fleas have to get together. When all the fleas are together, that dog is gonna be irritated like crazy. And that's what happened out there. I irritated the dog. And there's more to come. So we got to get all the fleas together again, because fleas have one thing in mind: we gotta eat that dog.

After Rattler was sentenced, he and his friends had lunch together in a cafe in downtown Mandan, a small city next to Bismarck. He seemed in good spirits. I asked what his plans were between now and turning himself in, but he couldn't tell me: locals had threatened him and other NODAPL protesters. He had to protect himself. Likely he was just going to lay low.

The next day, I drove the hour down to Standing Rock, where the camps had once stood. If you didn't know where to look, you'd likely drive right by the remnants of the protests there. The only markers were a few signs warning people not to trespass. On a few fence posts were stickers imploring people to "Protect Our Water," with the hashtag #waterislife. Down a private road, on the private land of a woman who supported the protesters and allowed them to stay during the first weeks of the NODAPL campaign, is a ten-foot-tall statue of a Native American man painted red, looking out over a valley. It's called *Not Afraid to Look*, based on a traditional Lakota pipe carving from the nineteenth century called *Not Afraid to Look the Whiteman in the Face*.[14] But the largest monument to what transpired there is just down the road: a fifty-foot swath of brown, dead grass pushing out from a county road, over a hill, and beyond, as far as you can see—demarcating the place where, after the protests were disbanded by police, the pipeline went in.

At daybreak on December 4, 1969, fourteen police officers broke into a dilapidated two-story apartment at 2337 West Monroe Street, on Chicago's West Side. There were nine people inside the apartment, but the police were apparently after two: Black Panther members Fred Hampton and Mark Clark. Hampton was twenty-one; Clark, twenty-two. Both were shot dead as they slept. Four others were seriously injured.

Police said that the deaths were the unfortunate result of a firefight. The state's attorney issued a statement justifying the use of deadly force, claiming that the "violent and criminal reaction of the occupants . . . emphasizes the extreme viciousness of the Black Panther Party." The police allowed the *Chicago Tribune* to run a photo spread showing bullet holes fired from inside the apartment, supposedly toward the police. The officers involved in the raid even staged a reenactment for a local CBS television station, during which they claimed that as soon as they knocked, a shotgun blasted at them through the apartment door. But rival paper the *Chicago Sun-Times* found that the "bullet holes" were actually nail marks. There had been no firefight. The only two people killed had been sleeping. Later, a federal investigation found that one shot may have been fired by any of the nine occupants of the house. Police fired somewhere between eighty-three and ninety bullets.[15]

The Black Panthers in Chicago, and Hampton in particular, had been central to building cross-racial solidarity in the hyper-segregated city. Contrary to how they were described by the FBI, the Panthers, and Hampton in particular, were not just armed radicals. They believed in "revolutionary intercommunalism"—building educational programs, community centers, free clothing exchanges, free breakfast programs for kids, and more.[16] These programs, more than the guns they carried, is what scared the US government. In an FBI document outlining the mission to dismantle the Black Panthers, only one of four objectives mentions the risk of violence. The other three are about preventing pro-black groups from working together, building community bonds, and becoming well liked across the country. "In unity there is strength, a truism that is no less valid for all its triteness," the memo read.[17] The FBI was scared that the Black Panthers, communists, and other leftist groups, were effectively turning the country against the US government.

For years, leftists had been warning that a secretive force was infiltrating their movements, using informants to make arrests, purposefully sowing discord so that the movements would fracture, and even possibly carrying out assassinations. And for years much of the public had written these claims off as conspiracy theories. Hampton's assassination provided proof they weren't: the government was after leftists, especially the Black Panthers, and it appeared willing to go to extreme lengths to destroy them.[18]

◇◇◇

Just a year earlier, and a month before Martin Luther King Jr.'s assassination, FBI Director J. Edgar Hoover had sent a directive to the FBI, calling "an effective coalition" between black power groups, from King to the Black Panthers, "the first step toward a real 'Mau Mau'" in America (a reference to the black uprising against white colonizers in Kenya) and "the beginning of a true black revolution."[19] The FBI held a complete disdain for black radicals and anyone who sympathized with them.

In many ways Hoover's obsession with the black left, along with other factions of leftists, was just a more covert continuation of McCarthyism. After the setbacks Hoover and his allies faced once the public and courts began questioning the legality and morality of trying and/or imprisoning anyone suspected of being a communist, the FBI simply shifted its anti-activist activity underground. Although the post-McCarthy era produced fewer headlines, fewer firings, and fewer imprisonments, it was arguably just as effective in quelling free speech and dissent.

In March 1971, antiwar activists broke into an FBI field office in Media, Pennsylvania, a suburb of Philadelphia, and took with them hundreds of files the agency had compiled. The files suggested that the FBI had plans to place informants in essentially every black student union across the country, as well as in antiwar groups and pro-communist and socialist groups. The documents also contained a theretofore unknown word: COINTELPRO. The activists had no clue what it meant. After several Freedom of Information Act requests filed by an NBC reporter, the truth finally came out: the FBI had been running a sprawling surveillance operation that had infected every facet of the American left since 1956, right as the McCarthy era was ending.[20] Without the break-in, it's likely most Americans would have never heard of COINTELPRO. Which makes it likely that many more programs surveilling and discrediting activists existed then (and may still exist today), but have never been brought to light.

What activists and journalists eventually discovered was that COINTELPRO, which stands for Counter Intelligence Program, was not only a surveillance system but a new kind of war on dissent in the United States. Having learned their lessons from the McCarthy era, and from the even more blatant and violent repression of unions and anticapitalist activists after World War I, the FBI, other federal agencies, and their local law enforcement partners turned to less flashy tactics: instead of beatings, trials, and shootings, they'd try to make leftist and antiracist movements crumble from the inside.

COINTELPRO tracked thousands of people and carried out more than 2,000 operations ranging from the relatively straightforward (stake-outs, phone taps) to the truly bizarre. The leaders of COINTELPRO were explicit about the program's aims: to continue the persecution of people they perceived to be communists and others who threatened the dominant powers in America.

"To counteract a resurgence of Communist Party influence in the United States, we have a . . . program designed to intensify confusion and dissatisfaction among its members," Hoover wrote in a booklet to President Eisenhower in 1958. The booklet went on to describe how the FBI had infiltrated several Communist Party chapters with members who often rose high in the ranks, then collected information that led to more than 250 tax evasion cases being referred to the FBI. Hoover also bragged in the memo about the Bureau anonymously mailing anticommunist literature to select party members perceived to be susceptible to influence.[21] It's impossible to quantify the efficacy of this or really any COINTELPRO operation, but as historian Robert Justin Goldstein has noted, soon after COINTELPRO began going after the Communist Party—attending meetings, sowing discord and doubt—the party was "virtually destroyed by factional infighting."[22]

Still, even as party membership dwindled, the COINTELPRO program continued under the Kennedy and Johnson administrations, and grew more creative in its approach to sowing doubt and discord among members of the Communist Party and the public: FBI staff leaked to news media that one prominent party member's son had been arrested on drug charges; they publicized the purchase of a party leader's new car (apparently as a way to highlight the hypocrisy of a communist buying something); they planted a document in the car of one of New York's most prominent communists that made him look like he'd worked as an informant, a move that led to his expulsion from the party. The suspicion and infighting caused by the FBI's trickery helped fracture the left. By 1965, the FBI bragged in a memo, many places that used to donate space for the Communist Party's meetings no longer would, because they were no longer on friendly terms.[23]

With the Communist Party essentially destroyed, and leftist racial justice groups on the rise, the FBI turned its attention to the American Indian Movement; groups fighting for Puerto Rican independence; and other groups fighting for the rights of people of color, including the Student Nonviolent Coordinating Committee (SNCC), which was instrumental in the fight for civil rights.[24] But the Black Panthers became an obsession for COINTELPRO's leaders.

Anonymous letters were one of the favored methods of COINTELPRO agents: they'd send unsigned letters to activist groups' leaders in which supposed fellow leftists would complain about tactics or accuse one another of misdeeds. One FBI agent cheered that a letter to a Puerto Rican independence movement leader probably caused enough stress for him to have a heart attack: "It is clear . . . that our anonymous letter has seriously disrupted the ranks and created a climate of distrust and dissension from which it will take them some time to recover," the memo stated. The FBI used the same tactic against the Black Panthers, trying to pit gangs that were allied with the Panthers against it and claiming that Panther leaders, including Fred Hampton, had ordered hits on gang members. In one memo, they concluded that the anonymous letters had worked to create a "high degree of unrest," including shootings and stabbings in a black neighborhood of San Diego that were "directly attributable to this program." They also tried, unsuccessfully, to incite the American mafia to kill members of the Communist Party by writing anonymous leaflets claiming that the party was after the mob for its immoral activities.[25]

Keenly aware of the media's willingness to report whatever law enforcement fed it without much fact-checking, the FBI gave countless fake stories to the press—most of the time falsifying or exaggerating the sex lives and drug use of members of the Puerto Rican independence movement, the Black Panthers, and other targeted groups. It even created newspapers of its own, including one in St. Louis that claimed to be run by local black community members, which slandered local black leaders and activists—again revealing (often fake) details about their sex lives.

In one of the most infamous examples of the FBI and media's cozy relationship, COINTELPRO agents fed the *Los Angeles Times* a story about a young, anonymous actress who had donated money to the Black Panthers. The story claimed that the actress—the FBI, and subsequently the *Times*, gave enough detail for anyone to guess it was Jean Seberg—was pregnant (which was true), and that a Black Panther was the father (untrue). The story was syndicated in hundreds of papers. *Newsweek* printed Seberg's name. The actress was distraught at the accusation that she had cheated on her husband and at all the media attention she was receiving. The controversy essentially killed her career. Later, she attempted suicide, which may have resulted in her giving birth to a stillborn. At the funeral, she opened the casket to prove the baby was white, and therefore not fathered by a Black Panther. She never fully recovered, and at forty she made a final, fatal suicide attempt by overdosing on barbiturates.[26]

As illustrated by Seberg's story, the FBI's tactics were often eccentric and cruel. As COINTELPRO agents increasingly targeted black leaders, they zeroed in on Martin Luther King Jr. "We must mark [King] now, if we have not before, as the most dangerous Negro in the future of this Nation," one high-ranking FBI employee wrote in a memo. "It may be unrealistic to limit [our actions against King] to legalistic proofs that would stand up in court or before Congressional Committees."[27] To that end, COINTELPRO agents tapped King's phones, sent IRS agents after him, and compiled a tape of secret recordings of King, including information on alleged affairs he'd had.

In 1964, the FBI sent King a letter claiming to be from a black activist who supported the civil rights movement. The letter writer said he would release a secret tape of King that proved an affair if King did not kill himself. The FBI also sent the tape to King's wife, Coretta Scott, in an attempt to end their marriage. Coretta and Martin Luther both suspected the FBI was behind the stunt and disregarded it.[28]

Often, the ideas cooked up by COINTELPRO were so ridiculous it's hard to imagine anyone in the FBI could think them effective: in 1968, for example, noting that many leftists were into psychedelics, the FBI decided to send vague letters to leftist leaders with drawings of bugs and amphibians accompanied by sayings like, "BEWARE! The Siberian Beetle." The thinking, outlined in one FBI memo, was that leftists would go on a psychedelic trip and conclude that the notes were some kind of mysterious, spiritual intervention persuading them to leave their activism behind.[29] Another operation was hatched when the FBI learned that the Soviet Union planned to send a few expensive horses to the Communist Party USA as a gift. The FBI ordered a veterinarian to go to the dock where the horses were being unloaded and inject them with a chemical that would sterilize them.[30]

Though a letter to a leftist encouraging dissent from the party line may seem in itself insignificant, and the drugging of a horse ridiculous, the FBI was, by and large, not filled with idiots. The tactics were extremely effective. Sterilizing horses, planting stories about famous actresses, sending bizarre letters to leftists—even if the letters could easily be identified as coming from the FBI—all had a grand purpose: to make everyone participating in radical activism paranoid and stressed, unsure of who was or was not an agent, and unsure about how to proceed with the work they cared so deeply about. Each action had a point. The false gossip about Jean Seberg, for example, wasn't meant just to dissuade her alone from working with the Panthers, but to place a wedge between all of Hollywood, which funded a lot of Panther activity, and the Panthers, helping dry up the group's already-sparse funds.[31]

After COINTELPRO started, anyone could be an infiltrator, any legitimate disagreement a sign of FBI involvement. If you participated in activities viewed as suspicious by the government, your phones could be tapped, your life (or lies about your life) could be put on display for the entire country to see, your friends could start to believe you were ratting on them to the FBI. The genius of COINTELPRO was that it did not need the heavy hand of the McCarthy era. With relatively little effort, the government could make you distrust everything and exhaust your emotional capacities. If something as strange as your horse being sterilized could be the work of COINTELPRO, then anything could. Fear worked.

Of course, the FBI didn't stick just to secretive tricks. Agents continued their legacy of outright intimidation too: They broke in and stole documents from no less than ninety offices of the Socialist Workers Party; framed black activists for murdering or shooting at police; raided and shut down socialist and pro-black newspapers; jailed student organizers on frivolous charges until their organizations ran out of funds by paying for bail; and even funded violent right-wing groups to do their bidding for them, beating up black activists and vandalizing their offices.[32]

We only know about COINTELPRO because of the activists who broke into those suburban Pennsylvania FBI offices, and thanks to the thousands of hours of journalistic work that was done to follow up on those findings. But for many who were active in the COINTELPRO years, mystery still shrouds much of the program.

Dozens of Black Panthers were convicted for violent events against police in which evidence was planted or testimony falsified. Rumors spread about whether the FBI had a hand in Martin Luther King's death (Coretta Scott King insisted until her death that the government was involved, and even government evidence points to some sort of conspiracy, suggesting that King's assassination was not the work of only one man, but it's unclear who the other people involved could be).[33] Ditto for Malcolm X's assassination, where at the very least there is evidence that the NYPD and FBI understaffed the ballroom where he gave his final speech. Malcolm X rallies normally had up to two dozen police officers present. But this time, just a week after his house had been firebombed, only two police officers showed up, stationed in a separate room from the main event, while none guarded the door.[34] After his assassination, the crime scene was left unsecured and was quickly cleaned up so that a dance scheduled for later in the day could take place.[35] And on the Pine Ridge Reservation after the occupation of Wounded Knee in 1973, dozens of Native Americans were murdered or violently beaten. Many American Indian Movement members charged that the murders were the work of the FBI or the Guardians of the Oglala Nation, an armed group with links to the FBI.[36]

As Noam Chomsky pointed out in a 1975 essay, we can contrast America's reaction to COINTELPRO to that of another 1970s scandal—Watergate—to see where our country's priorities lay. Both Watergate and COINTELPRO involved illegal wiretapping, breaking into private offices, and stealing documents. But only Watergate ended in dozens of prosecutions, wall-to-wall media coverage, and several Hollywood movie renditions of the events. While COINTELPRO officially ended in 1971, its activities did not (the American Indian Movement controversies, for example, took place in the years after the program's supposed end). No government officials were prosecuted. Today, it's barely remembered, much less glorified on screen as an example of an injustice righted. Chomsky writes:

> The lesson. . . . is simple. American liberalism and the corporate media will defend themselves against attack. But their spirited acts of self-defense are not to be construed as a commitment to civil liberties or democratic principle, despite noble and self-serving rhetoric. Quite the contrary. They demonstrate a commitment to the principle that power must not be threatened or injured. The narrow "elites" that control the economy, political life, and the system of conventional doctrine must be immune to the means of harassment that are restricted, in the normal course of events, to those who raise a serious challenge to ruling ideology or state policy or established privilege. An "enemies list" that includes major corporate leaders, media figures, and government intellectuals is an obscenity that is seen as shaking the foundations of the republic. The involvement of the national political police in the assassination of Black Panther leaders, however, barely deserves comment in the national press.[37]

We can see a similar double standard play out today in our free speech debates. It's national news when someone like Charles Murray or Steve Bannon is not allowed to speak on a college campus. Their rights eclipse the rights of so many others in mainstream discourse: Dakota Access Pipeline protesters, or J20 defendants, or Black Lives Matter activists. Sure, they too get media coverage, but imagine if each J20 defendant got as much as Murray or Bannon. Imagine if Rattler's court case was covered by dozens of national media outlets.

Yes, these events are different. Just as different as Watergate was from a radical group advocating for the dissolution of the government.

But how we perceive that difference gets to the central fallacy of our conceptualization of free speech: We interpret some things as speech, and some things as action; and although speech is protected under the First Amendment, much action is not.

Yet when Milo Yiannopoulos is paid to speak on a college campus and lambastes trans people, those are actions. It involves him speaking, as well as the action of the college approving the speech, renting the space, cutting his check, the student group inviting him in the first place, travel on a plane and in a taxi, a stay at a hotel, and so on. Those actions have just as much power to influence others as a communist sending a letter through the US mail or a Black Panther providing free lunch to a hungry child, or a J20 defendant holding a sign and shouting against fascism.

How we define what speech is—that is totally and inescapably political. The fact that the mainstream media mourns the inability of some to speak but not others shows what we place value in. And if we apply the Chomsky quote to our current moment, we can see precisely where the dividing line is: we decide, as a society, that something counts as speech only if it upholds and protects those already in power. And as Chomsky so presciently wrote more than forty years ago, the reason elites, including the media, invoke civil liberties is most often not because they believe in their universal applicability—if they did, you would see them defend the rights of political prisoners and protesters as vigorously as right-wing provocateurs. Instead, they are protecting themselves and their power, and obfuscating what would otherwise be obvious: those with power are allowed to do and say what they want, and those without power, or those who choose to challenge the fundamental structures of that power, are judged by a different set of rules.

In true 2010s fashion, the best rebuttal to the idea of free speech I've seen comes from a blog, and it was written by an anonymous anarchist:

> There is no free speech in practice for those who live hand to mouth. There is no free speech in practice for those whose educational systems are funded by paltry tithes from their own already destitute communities. There is no free speech when police have been given free rein to

publicly execute minorities on the grounds that they are perceived as dangerous. Smoking a joint, playing with a toy gun, selling loose cigarettes, and owning a legal firearm have been upheld by our so-called justice system as grounds for murder.

The anarchist, writing on the anarchist site It's Going Down, concludes: "When you ask if I 'believe' in free speech, I view the question with the same regard that you would if I inquired as to your belief in unicorns. You do not stop and consider the question of whether unicorns would hypothetically be a force for good in the world. You don't ponder the potential morality of a world in which unicorns exist. You would scoff, and say no, because in all of your life experiences, you have encountered no evidence to support their existence."[38]

While the free speech worriers of the 2010s defended the rights of conservatives to speak wherever and whenever they wanted, the House Judiciary Committee introduced the Unmasking Antifa Bill, which would in effect make it illegal to wear a mask in public. A bill was introduced in the Senate that would make it a felony to boycott Israel. A bill was introduced in West Virginia that would allow any law enforcement officer to deem any assembly illegal, and arrest those present. Several states passed laws criminalizing protests that block road traffic with proposed prison sentences for offenders of up to one year. Missouri enacted a law that prohibits public employees from participating in strikes and picketing. Louisiana enacted a law that punishes anyone protesting around "critical infrastructure" (e.g., oil pipelines) with up to five years in prison. South Dakota passed a law that allows the governor to deem any protest on public land that might "damage public land" or interfere with someone else's use of that land as illegal. The attorney general of Texas backed a school district that expelled an eighteen-year-old girl for not standing for the Pledge of Allegiance. Georgia police used a law meant to limit the efficacy of the KKK to arrest dozens of antifa protesters. A forty-three-year-old woman named Crystal Mason was sentenced to five years in prison for accidentally casting a ballot in the 2016 presidential election without realizing she was prohibited from doing so because she had a previous charge on her record for tax fraud. The FBI raided the house of and arrested pro-black activist Christopher Daniels under the suspicion that he was a Black Identity Extremist, which legally places him in the same category as domestic terrorists. And an eighteen-year-old kid called Mapache, who was raised in the United States for nearly his entire life, attended a protest, was picked up by ICE, interrogated by the FBI, jailed for more than a month, deported, and told he would likely never be able to return.[39]

These events, combined, seemed to elicit less national press attention than the protest of Charles Murray at Middlebury College.

I first learned about Mapache through Alexei Wood, the J20 protester from San Antonio, Texas. When I flew down to San Antonio to meet Wood, he told me it was a shame I wouldn't get to meet Mapache, because he was so central to the activism scene in the city. Mapache, whose legal name is Sergio Salazar, had been deported a few months earlier. He had come to the United States with his family when he was two. His parents had settled in San Antonio. As Mapache entered his teen years, he began getting involved in activism; at eighteen, when Occupy ICE protests sprang up around the country, Mapache decided to join in. He knew he was at risk of deportation: not being born in the United States, even though he'd been here for nearly his entire life, meant that he was in a legal limbo. Mapache was a DACA (Deferred Action for Childhood Arrivals) recipient. But he felt there was no point to being in the United States, no point to life really, if he couldn't express what he wanted, and he felt that the treatment of immigrants across the country was unjust. More than that, he thought borders were unjust. Period.

So for weeks, Mapache camped out at an ICE facility in San Antonio, along with Wood and dozens of others. Mapache's DACA application was up for renewal in early August 2018, at the height of the occupation. The day after it was due to be renewed, as Mapache was walking away from the protest camp, an ICE van pulled up next to him. Another truck pulled up. An officer yelled that he was under arrest. Mapache was searched in the van and then taken to a detention center near San Antonio.

Mapache was interrogated for hours. He found out that his DACA renewal application had been denied because, in the words of one agent, he was a "bad person."[40] Agents searched his phone, looking for activist contacts, and told him he had to give up the names of those he organized with. He refused. They said they had evidence he was going to make a bomb (they never presented any such evidence—Mapache's best guess is that one of the protest songs he and his comrades were singing had the word "Molotov" in it). RAICES, one of the largest immigrants' rights groups in the country, assigned lawyers to Mapache's case. It was no use. After forty days, he decided he had no chance at being released, and his lawyers said his chances of facing a judge and winning back DACA would be slim. He opted to be deported. I filed a Freedom of Information Act request with the Department of Homeland Security to see the justification for detaining Mapache. His deportation file was barely longer than a page. The only explanation given: Nonimmigrant Overstay.

Mapache now lives in Monterrey, Mexico. He barely spoke Spanish when he arrived, but he's learning, and planning on attending film school. He's making some anarchist friends. He has a hamster and a cat, which I could hear meowing in the background as he spoke to me over the phone.

"I definitely have a connection to the people and this land. I like it here a lot," he told me. "But that doesn't mean I wasn't separated from my mom and my dad and my family. I wish I had the option to go back to the US. I wish I had the option to be able to visit my friends and my family there. I still miss the US. That's where I was raised. I still miss it. I don't know if that will ever change."

I wanted to talk to Mapache because his case made me think about the intrinsic limits of speech according to the US government, or really any government. In defining what private property is, we already limit free speech; in defining a line between speech and action, we limit it further; and in defining who is and is not a citizen, or what actions can revoke you of your status as an American, we limit it even further still. Free speech for those born on US soil, who did not make the error of tax fraud years ago, who do not wear masks, who do not advocate the overthrow of the US government, who are willing only to speak on public property, whose speech does not infringe on anyone's copyright—that's more of a mouthful than the First Amendment, but it's the true nature of speech in this country.

Despite the fact that he was only eighteen years old, Mapache was keenly aware of these contradictions. "The idea was created to defend a certain class," he told me. "The idea of free speech is completely incompatible with the idea of private property. If you're in somebody's establishment, if you're a worker, you can be fired for what you say. The idea that you have freedom to express yourself is completely incompatible with the government of the United States."

I believe there's also a flip side to all this: speech means nothing without someone to hear it. So it's not only about who is allowed to express themselves and who is not, or where people are allowed to express themselves and where they're not. Speech is about whom we are willing to listen to. Mapache's deportation was covered by one national leftist media outlet and two local news outlets. The arrest of Crystal Mason for voting was covered a bit more widely, but the story received nowhere near wall-to-wall coverage. Contrast that with the interrupted speeches of so many conservative campus speakers, and it becomes clear that the free speech rights of some in this country fall into the same category as everything else we'd rather not acknowledge: race, class, nationality, gender.

After talking with Mapache I thought back to that drive down to Charlottesville, when my friend said that the difference between the United States and so many other countries is that we've failed to reckon with our history here. I think that's true. We use free speech as a platitude to obfuscate the truth and rhetorically level a playing field that has not been level since the founding of this country. When we talk about free speech, we're really talking about everything else. And until we reckon with that everything else, there will be little point to talking about free speech at all. Until we acknowledge that poor people, women, people of color, and immigrants have less ability not only to speak, but to be heard, then free speech will remain elusive, a unicorn, a fantasy.

## chapter nine

# FREE SPEECH IN THE PANOPTICON

I N 2011, Earle Fisher, a young and charismatic man from Michi-gan, became the lead pastor at the Abyssinian Missionary Baptist Church in South Memphis, Tennessee. The area is majority black and mostly middle-class. It's quiet and residential, and the church is quiet too, drawing in just thirty to forty people most Sundays. But Pastor Fisher's sermons are fiery. He's proudly Afrocentric, and proudly oriented toward social justice. He rails against racism in his sermons. Until 2015, Fisher kept most of his opinions within the church walls, but on July 17, 2015, Darrius Stewart, a black nineteen-year-old, was shot and killed by a po-lice officer in Memphis. The police claimed there was a scuffle that re-quired the officer to use a gun, but Stewart was unarmed. It was the latest in a long line of deaths of unarmed black men and women at the hands of police, and it brought Memphis residents to the streets.

Fisher offered his church for activist meetings. He wanted to teach those who usually did not get involved in politics to push for reforms after Stewart's death. He also sent a letter to the city's district attorney, complaining that there was never any justice served for people who had experienced violence at the hands of police.

Then, Fisher started noticing little things: he'd receive calls from numbers he didn't recognize, and when he called back, he'd get a not-in-service message. Once, at his house, he opened his computer's Wi-Fi panel and saw "Tennessee Department of Homeland Security" as one of the listed networks. He took a picture of the drop-down menu with his phone. One Sunday morning, two police cars were in his church parking lot. Fisher asked the officers what they were doing there. They said they were just following a tip, and then drove away. After Fisher walked out of a panel discussion at a local college about Stewart's death, he noticed a police car on a hill, directly behind where he'd parked his car. Stewart began hearing similar, troubling things from his fellow activists.

In 2018, Shahidah Jones, another activist in the city, and her friend were talking inside Jones's house when she noticed a police car circling the block. Her friend left the house, pulled her car out slowly, and was immediately pulled over by the cop, supposedly for failure to signal. His car was searched. Nothing was found. A few days later, Jones entered a building in downtown Memphis for a work meeting. Part of the city's police department—the Memphis Real Time Crime Center, where officers monitor cameras and other surveillance—shared office space in the same building. As she got onto the elevator, Jones saw a familiar face: a man who had been in attendance at many of the same Black Lives Matter meetings she'd gone to. He was chatting with a group of uniformed police officers in the lobby.

At the same time that dozens of activists in Memphis were reporting similar incidences to one another, Nour Hantouli, the cofounder of a local feminist group called the 901 Memphis Feminist Collective, received a friend request on Facebook from a "Bob Smith." Smith's profile photo was of someone wearing the Guy Fawkes mask, a common symbol of anarchy that was popularized by the film *V for Vendetta* (though, as far as I know, not many actual anarchists wear the mask).

"Who are you?" Hantouli asked.

"Just a fellow protester," Smith responded.

Hantouli was suspicious, and asked Smith if he was a cop. Smith grew testy, accused Hantouli of being a cop, and then said that he was just exercising his right to free speech. Hantouli immediately unfriended him.

In 2018, the ACLU sued the City of Memphis on behalf of activists who belonged to Black Lives Matter and other progressive groups in the city, and the documents unearthed by the suit confirmed activists' suspicions. They weren't being paranoid. Cops were tracking them everywhere they went, driving by their homes, making contact trees to connect activists to one another, sending undercover agents to monitor their meetings, and using fake social media profiles to snoop into their personal lives.[1] "Bob Smith" was actually Memphis Police Department Sergeant Timothy Reynolds. In court, he admitted he'd friended more than 200 activists in an attempt to find information about protests that "could become unlawful."[2] After one activist who had accepted a request from Smith posted on Facebook that they liked a book written by the famed activist Saul Alinsky, Memphis police began monitoring not only the poster's activities, but collected the names of each of the fifty-eight people who had "liked" the post. Another activist noticed that as soon as the lawsuit started, her Facebook friend count dropped by about two dozen.

The ACLU won the court case, and Memphis police promised they wouldn't use the same surveillance tactics in the future, though activists say they're sure they're still being tracked. Activists say the surveillance has scared some off from meetings, and added stress to those who still attend.

"It's definitely part of disrupting our movement. It's a flex of power," Shahidah Jones told me. "It's a constant reminder of the reality that they can do whatever they want."

I asked every activist I spoke with in Memphis whether they thought our phone calls might be recorded, listened to by a cop somewhere deep in a Memphis Police Department building. All replied that, while they couldn't be sure, the assumption they now had to operate under was "yes."

It's impossible to know how common the tactics used in Memphis are, but there are countless anecdotal stories from across the country about infiltrators and surveillance in activist circles. We *do* know that the FBI carried out extensive surveillance on Black Lives Matter activists in recent years, tracking their cars and movements, and infiltrating some meetings, including in New York, where the NYPD kept troves of photographs of suspected Black Lives Matter leaders.[3] Between social media and real-world surveillance, most activists I know now assume they are being tracked at all times—if they're proven wrong, great, but history shows them they're most likely not being paranoid.

Thirty miles off Cuba's mainland, on La Isla de la Juventud (Isle of Youth), lie five five-story circular, domed buildings that, sixty years ago, held thousands of Cuban prisoners. Each building's walls are lined with tiny cells, and in the center of the otherwise empty dome is a concrete tower, where a guard would keep watch of each prisoner every day and night—a 360-degree view into each cell. These buildings are some of the last remaining in the world that were influenced by eighteenth-century English philosopher Jeremy Bentham.[4] He called his idea the Panopticon, and he believed his design would be the future of architecture not just for prisons, but for anywhere people needed to be watched.

"Morals reformed—health preserved—industry invigorated, instruction diffused—public burdens lightened . . . the gordian knot of the Poor-Laws are not cut, but untied—all by a simple idea in Architecture!" he wrote in his treatise on the idea in 1787.[5]

The idea behind the Panopticon was to surveil everyone in as economic a fashion as possible: with a central guard tower and open cells lining the walls, everyone could be watched by a centralized authority. But more ingenious was Bentham's idea that the tower should be darkened, so that no one knew *when* they were being watched. If you lived in the Panopticon, it didn't matter when you were actually surveilled, as long as you knew you could, at any point, be surveilled—that, in Bentham's view, would engender constant self-discipline and regulation.

The French philosopher Michel Foucault used the architecture of the Panopticon as a metaphor for modern, surveilled society in his 1975 book, *Discipline and Punish: The Birth of the Prison.* Foucault posited that those in power rarely had to show force to keep people in line: if we all know that at any point we *can* be watched and *can* be disciplined, we will do the enforcement ourselves.

"So to arrange things that the surveillance is permanent in its effects, even if it is discontinuous in its action; that the perfection of power should tend to render its actual exercise unnecessary; that this architectural apparatus should be a machine for creating and sustaining a power relation independent of the person who exercises it; in short, that the inmates should be caught up in a power situation of which they are themselves the bearers," Foucault wrote. "The inmate must never know whether he is being looked at at any one moment; but he must be sure that he may always be so."

Power, Foucault wrote, must be like the man inside the cloaked watchtower: visible, but unverifiable. You know it's there, but you can't quite pin it down. Just like COINTELPRO. Just like the Memphis Police Department.

What does free speech look like in a Panopticon? Outside your house are thousands of surveillance cameras, on the subway, on the way to work, at your workplace. There are 17,000 cameras on the streets of New York, 30,000 in Chicago, and an estimated 500,000 in London. The police don't need a warrant to track you between your house and a protest, or to intercept your cellphone signal, or to fly planes or helicopters overhead and take photos of you. Using a technology called Persistent Surveillance, they can monitor thirty square miles with one small plane.[6]

The photos they take are increasingly paired with facial recognition technology produced by Amazon and other large corporations. That means if you're photographed at more than one protest, you might have a profile assigned to you.[7] You might be watched more closely. We know it happens sometimes, as J20, NODAPL, Memphis, COINTELPRO, and so many other examples prove. We don't know all the times it happens. Visible, but unverifiable.

How free are we to say what we want, to act on our desires, to fight for a better future, with this eye upon us, the threat of punishment possibly only a few steps away? When some protests go fine and others end in mass arrest, how many of us will continue to protest, risking that any given protest might turn out like J20? How many will participate in activism knowing that Memphis police surveilled the moves of nonviolent antiracist organizers?

Maybe, increasingly, we'll stay home, in the confines of our privacy domes. Unfortunately, we're out of luck there too, because under the guise of increased connectivity and productivity, nearly every American has enabled their own personal panopticon, sitting right there on your desk and in the palm of your hand.

We've been told again and again that the internet is a free speech equalizer. With the advent of the web, suddenly anyone could say anything. *New York Times* columnist Thomas Friedman argued in his mega-bestselling book *The World Is Flat* that the internet would help erase inequality. Pundits since then have compared the spread of the internet to the fall of the Berlin wall. "Did Facebook Bring Down Mubarak?" a CNN headline pondered in 2011.[8] The internet would be "freedom's tipping point," *Wired* proclaimed in 1997. The 2010 mass protests in Iran were even called the "Twitter revolution" by many pundits.[9] In mainstream discourse, the internet is viewed as anywhere from benign to downright revolutionary. But that wasn't always the case.

On September 26, 1969, dozens of students at Harvard broke into the school's Center for International Affairs and attacked a few employees while shouting, "Fuck US imperialism!" Outside the building, hundreds more students protested.[10] They were there voicing their opposition to the Cambridge Project, a program developed by MIT and Harvard that would enable military analysts to keep deep dockets on any person of interest, including arrest files, welfare rolls, and financial transactions. The Cambridge Project was built on the Advanced Research Projects Agency Network (ARPANET or ARPA)—it was the world's first internet, funded by the Department of Defense for the purpose of monitoring and quashing dissent.[11]

William Godel, a US intelligence operative who was central to the creation of ARPA (which is still in existence, now known as DARPA, the Defense Advanced Research Projects Agency), explicitly wanted the network to be developed to defeat communism abroad.[12] The first computers developed by the military were rudimentary. For example, one early ARPA project involved placing thousands of microphones, motion and heat sensors, and urine detectors around the forests of Vietnam that would transmit signals back to a centralized computer in Thailand controlled by the US military. The project was a failure, as the Vietnamese quickly figured out how to create false alarms with tape-recorded sounds of trucks and bags of urine, leading the United States to drop dozens of bombs on no one. Still, the idea for a centralized surveillance monitoring system was considered a success, and it was brought back stateside to patrol the Mexican border.[13]

One of the biggest hopes for ARPA was that it could be applied to myriad issues back on US soil. With new technology, the military was able to compile unprecedented amounts of data on its enemies and nonfighting populations, and then use that data to try to predict uprisings and attacks, as well as to formulate plans of attack—demographics, location data, and even psychological data were used to microtarget areas. After the United States lost the Vietnam War, researchers working for a group called the American Institutes for Research, which often performed work for the CIA, came back to the United States to apply the same data-collection technologies to Americans. One of the researchers was none other than Charles Murray, who was tasked with figuring out how to use ARPA data collection techniques in American inner cities in an attempt to predict uprisings and pacify those living in poverty.[14]

The United States poured billions into developing networked computers throughout the 1960s and '70s, paying universities and their professors to turn their research labs into quasi-arms of the military. Many of the leaders behind the movement were invigorated by a philosophy called cybernetics: the idea that the entire world, from humans' nervous systems to global events like war, were parts of one interlocking machine. And just like with a machine, certain inputs would yield expected outcomes. The US military wanted total control of that machine. That's what the internet was for.

But as its network of data collection and analyzing spread, even the inventor of the term "cybernetics," Norbert Wiener, sounded the alarm. He warned that the United States was creating a "colossal state machine . . . for the purposes of combat and domination" that was "sufficiently extensive to include all civilian activities."[15] He also said that once computers were advanced enough, humans would have to compete economically with them, driving down wages to essentially slave labor and creating an economic depression like the world had never seen. After inventing the philosophy that inspired the US military to attempt to surveil the entire world, Wiener became so scared by its implications that he died a pariah among the military-friendly academics he had influenced, and was even added to McCarthy-era watchlists.[16]

The military was largely secretive about its computer work. But when information did leak out, it made front-page headlines and caused protests. In the 1960s, an ARPA-funded project called Methods for Predicting and Influencing Social Change and Internal War Potential (better known as Project Camelot) attempted to create a database that could monitor left-wing movements across the globe and predict revolutions before they started. When the public found out about it, the military was forced to, at least publicly, shut the project down. In reality, it was transferred to MIT and renamed the Cambridge Project. When MIT and Harvard students and professors, including Howard Zinn and Noam Chomsky, protested the project, the military rebranded it. Cambridge wasn't about counterinsurgency, officials insisted; it was about using data to help all the social sciences that rely on massive datasets. The project continued without much more fanfare.[17] Though the Cambridge Project no longer exists, MIT still works closely with, and gets much of its research funding from, the US military.[18]

Over the next three decades, between the invention and privatization of the internet, the military and other government agencies worked to apply the same counterinsurgency technology used abroad to US citizens. Police departments and the feds began compiling and centralizing massive amounts of data on Americans with the new technology. By 1970, the centralized US defense center had compiled 25 million files on Americans.[19] But Americans' suspicions again grew. Why was this new technology being used to surveil so much? There were magazine cover stories and in-depth investigations by TV news networks into the massive surveillance network being created by the military. But the network kept growing. Instead of curtailing the worldwide surveillance machine they were building, the leaders of this new surveillance age instead, again, re-branded it.

In 1993, *Wired* magazine published its first issue. The magazine was run by Louis Rossetto, who used its pages to frame the internet as a democra-tizing, even hippieish technology. But Rossetto was no hippie—he was a former College Republican and a steadfast Nixon supporter in his college years.[20] And his magazine was financially supported by Nicholas Negro-ponte, a wealthy businessman who had spent twenty years working for the military, helping to develop ARPA.[21]

*Wired* was one of many media properties in the newly burgeoning privatized internet field that melded the aesthetics of the hippies and the libertarian ideals of Ayn Rand. They gave a kind of hip, liberal sheen to military technology and corporate control. In its early days, *Wired* ex-tensively profiled telecom millionaires and conservative politicians like Newt Gingrich, who were waging a war against the government to privat-ize the internet and hand it over to a select few telecoms, framing them as rebels who wanted to liberate technology and democratize it.

This new brand of millionaire-backed techno-utopians were deeply influenced by a man named Stewart Brand, who published the *Whole Earth Catalog*, which advocated for self-sufficiency and a reliance on DIY culture—i.e., a life without government help. Brand inspired the creation of several techno-utopian communes where people adhered to the idea of cybernetics: specifically, that we are all individual parts of a machine, and the way to liberty is to allow those machine parts to function without in-tervention. To that end, no organizing or collective actions were allowed in the communes. Instead, people had to resolve conflicts through "connection sessions."

As Yasha Levine writes in his history of the internet, *Surveillance Valley*, the communes foretold the future of many internet spaces: they devolved into bullying, hazing, shaming, and exercises in control. Those with more power or standing took advantage of others, and dominated with fear.[22] Still, Brand maintained a big following. Rossetto, along with Apple cofounder Steve Jobs, were huge fans. Three multimillionaire Brand followers created the Electronic Frontier Foundation in 1990. Today, the nonprofit is associated with civil liberties in much the same way the ACLU is. But it was started to push for a privatized internet. "Life in cyberspace seems to be shaping up exactly like Thomas Jefferson would have wanted," one of the foundation's cofounders wrote in *Wired* in 1993. "Founded on the primacy of individual liberty and a commitment to pluralism, diversity, and community."[23]

For the libertarian-utopians who took a government surveillance and counterinsurgency technology and turned it into a wildly profitable omnipresent private one, the internet had the power to change everything. But then again, those who preached its virtues for liberation were the same who worked alongside the government agents who used it for surveillance, and who stood to reap billions off the technology's privatization. In 1995, Rossetto wrote in *Wired* that the internet would level the playing field of the entire world, giving everyone the same platform and power. "Everything we know will be different," he wrote. "Not just a change from LBJ to Nixon, but whether there will still be a President at all."[24]

Given the way things have shaken out, one has to wonder whether these people truly believed the ideals they espoused, or whether they were simply good at advertising, making a military weapon used to defeat anticapitalism around the globe sound fun and liberatory. Were they true believers, or good marketers? Maybe a little of both. Either way, we now live in a world that these men created, and the internet, far from becoming the liberatory technology they preached it would be, has instead become just another tool for surveillance and corporate control of speech that favors the powerful over the many.

◇◇◇

The internet is not a neutral machine. It was built by people (often people with a wonky techno-libertarian sensibility). If we are concerned about free speech, we must right off the bat recognize that the internet inherently privileges some people's speech over others'. After ARPA had amassed an astonishing amount of data on protesters, militant groups, and others, the military needed some way to comb through them, and so in the 1960s it began the Digital Library Initiative, paying universities to conduct research on search engines. The first widespread success was Lycos, born in 1994 from a DARPA-funded project at Carnegie Mellon University. Larry Page began researching search engines and algorithms at Stanford a year later, and published a research paper in 1998 that would become the basis for Google's search algorithm. The paper was funded in part by DARPA.[25]

What Page and his longtime friend Sergey Brin discovered in their research was that by using complex mathematical algorithms, web pages could be ranked by their trustworthiness and usefulness to the average searcher. Links from prominent news sites get more weight than links from a blog; links that many other websites have referenced get higher PageRank scores than links that few websites have referenced. Brin and Page creepily dubbed the system Backrub and gave it a logo of a hairy hand rubbing a smooth back.[26] But it was technologically revolutionary. With their algorithm, massive amounts of data on the internet could be sorted, and therefore became manageable to average people. PageRank and algorithms like it are why if you search, say, "Amazon," you're likely to get results about the large corporation and not someone's travelogue about backpacking through the rainforest. The web would likely be much more complicated to navigate without these sorting algorithms.

But built into every algorithm is bias: Google privileges well-established sources over unknown ones. That turns up more relevant sources a lot of the time, but, for example, if you want to learn about the US military's role in the creation of the internet and you search "DARPA," you'll get many results that portray DARPA positively, and a few that only superficially cover the agency's controversies, before you get to something truly critical, like Yasha Levine's *Surveillance Valley*. If you search "Chiquita banana," you'll likely get many results about buying bananas, listings for job openings at Chiquita Brands, and videos of early banana commercials, but very few in-depth explanations about how, with the help of the US government, Chiquita's corporate predecessor, the United Fruit Company, helped overthrow Latin American governments and killed thousands of people in order to produce its bananas.[27]

If I'm searching to buy headphones on Amazon, or for a job at Chiquita, Google is doing a good job for me. But it's also reinforcing what we think of as useful and suppressing what we think of as irrelevant to our daily lives and our average searches.

The algorithm is created largely by white men (Google is about 70 percent men and only 2.5 percent black).[28] As Safiya U. Noble, a professor of communications at USC Annenberg, has detailed in her book *Algorithms of Oppression: How Search Engines Reinforce Racism*, Google has been shown to, for example, show more sexually explicit results when you search "black girls" than "white girls" and suggest you search "gorillas" when you search for pictures of black people. As Noble writes, "It will become increasingly difficult for technology companies to separate their systematic and inequitable employment practices, and the far-right ideological bents of some of their employees, from the products they make for the public."[29]

Sandra Harding, a professor emeritus of education and gender studies at UCLA, was writing about epistemology in general when she said the following, but as Noble points out, the same could be said of Google: "Feminist challenges reveal that the questions that are asked—and, even more significantly, those that are not asked—are at least as determinative of the adequacy of our total picture as are any answers that we can discover. Defining what is in need of scientific explanation only from the perspective of bourgeois, white men's experiences leads to partial and even perverse understandings of social life."[30]

In other words, companies like Google, founded and run by white men, and set up to make large profits, will inherently bias the ways we find information. Even when they are proclaiming to be "unbiased" or "scientific," without explicitly correcting for their own backgrounds, they will reinforce the status quo—racism and all.

Is this a free speech issue? It depends on how you define free speech, but I would argue it is, in the same way that Reed College's decision to teach only books written by dead white men is, or in the same way that black students at Evergreen wanting more diversity on their campus is: without an analysis of power, race, and class, a free-for-all-approach to information is a sure way to let the status quo maintain relevancy and power over the oppressed. Is it a problem that Google is biased? In a vacuum, no. Every human construction is biased, and if I knew how to code and had a few billion dollars, I could create an equally useful (in my opinion) search engine that would privilege results about Chiquita's Banana Republic over its cute, antique advertisements featuring dancing bananas.

The problem is, a social-justice-based search engine would have no way of making as much money as Google, and therein lies a conundrum of free speech under capitalism: the speech that rises to the top is the speech that reinforces the system we live in. Even our current era of "woke" internet culture falls into this trap: our discourse is stuck on which TV shows produced by massive capitalist corporations are most and least problematic, which celebrities said the worst things. Recently, a meme went around queer internet circles after them.us, a website owned by multinational publisher Condé Nast, called Princess Diana a "queer icon," in which lots of queers joked that now anything could be queer.[31] The idea that a cis, straight, multimillionaire member of the royal family could be queer was funny, but it also pointed to something deeply sad: the internet, which was sold to us as a tool of liberation, has instead become more like cable TV—bland, run by the powerful, and with little meaningful critique to be found. Now, when I want deeper explanations of the world, I turn to books.

Remarkably, even more so than television, the internet is consolidating into a near-monopolistic power. I'm a journalist, and most of my friends are too, and in the past few years, about half of them have been laid off, as newspapers and news sites struggle to make a profit from advertising. That's largely thanks to Google and Facebook, which take in more than 60 percent of *all* internet ad revenue each year.[32] They maintain an effective duopoly over much of what people see on the internet, and thus everything—including what stories get written and what headlines they get—must bend to their proprietary algorithms. If most of the internet is controlled by just a few corporations (Facebook, which owns WhatsApp and Instagram, and Google, which owns YouTube, now control 70 percent of all internet traffic), we've essentially ceded control of the digital public square.[33] There is little public space online, and increasingly, thanks to these same companies, there's little public space in our physical lives too.

Google has become so ubiquitous, such a part of our daily lives, that former Google executive chairman Eric Schmidt once said that "eventually . . . we don't need you to type at all. . . . Because we know where you are. We know where you've been. We can more or less guess what you're thinking about."[34]

The next frontier for Google, Facebook, Amazon, and the other tech giants is turning governments into customers, and turning themselves into quasi-governments. Startups like Predpol, which contracts with police to identify people, tracks them using facial recognition, and stores their data on government-controlled servers, are backed by Google, Facebook, Amazon, eBay, and other tech giants.[35] Google runs the email and networks of hundreds of local governments in the United States; has contracts with the NSA, CIA, and FBI; and runs the apps that more than half of all US schoolchildren use in their classrooms.[36]

"The societal goal is our primary goal," Larry Page told the *Financial Times* in 2014. "Some of the most fundamental questions which people are not thinking about—there's the question of how do we organize people, how do we motivate people. It's really an interesting problem, how do we organize our democracies?"

Looking a century into the future, and imagining Google at its center, Page said, "We could probably solve a lot of the issues we have as humans."[37]

◇◇◇

The internet started as a government surveillance tool to quash communist dissent, then was privatized to profit a handful of telecoms, then captured by a few megacorporations, which then worked hand in hand with
the government to blur the line between the private and public, the state
and corporations. And yet I was still surprised at how swiftly a bill was
passed that caused many of my friends' social media accounts to be shut
down and livelihoods made more precarious, and how little friction there
was in doing it.

In the spring of 2018, Congress passed a set of bills collectively known
as FOSTA/SESTA—the Fight Online Sex Trafficking Act and the Stop
Enabling Sex Traffickers Act. The bills were supported by Democrats and
Republicans alike, and celebrities like Amy Schumer campaigned for
them. The bills, among other things, essentially reversed part of the Tele-
communications Reform Act of 1996, which stated no internet company
could be held accountable for the content published by third parties on
its platform.[38] The small bit of text was crucial to how the internet functions. If Facebook, Google, or any other company were held responsible
for everything posted on its platform, the companies might have to man-
ually approve every post. Entire websites could get shut down because
one person posted something illegal. But FOSTA/SESTA changed that:
now, when it comes to sex trafficking, which includes consensual adult
sex work, websites *can* be held accountable by the government for whatever is posted on them.[39]

Almost immediately, large internet companies fell in line. Two days
after SESTA was approved by the Senate, Craigslist shut down its entire
personals section, including all the parts not used for sex work. Several
friends and acquaintances who do sex work because they either like it and
it pays well, or because they need the money to survive, lost thousands
of dollars. Payment processors like PayPal and Venmo (which is owned
by PayPal) have shut down countless accounts, making it harder for sex
workers to earn a living. And there's evidence that instead of limiting sex
trafficking, all the bills have done is push sex workers onto the streets,
where they are at higher risk of violence.[40]

Countless people not involved in sex work were affected too. I talked to an acquaintance on Instagram named Justin Branch, an artist based in North Carolina. Branch grew up in a rural, swampy area of North Carolina where no one accepted his sexuality. Instagram became a refuge for him—he could find people who expressed themselves like he did, who weren't ashamed of their bodies.

"It was my little playground," he told me. "And then it got deleted."

The day after Craigslist shut down its personals section, Branch's account, which contained some pictures that toed the line on Instagram's nudity policy, was completely erased, with no way for Branch to recover it. It was a shock to Branch not only because he'd made so many friends via Instagram, but because he was making connections for his art through Instagram too. He had to start all over again.

Branch felt like his story was insignificant, but it struck me as deeply frightening in the wake of other news I'd heard: Facebook, which owns Instagram, had recently admitted to deleting accounts when asked to by the US and Israeli governments.[41] A few months later, Twitter suspended a popular antifascist account after some of its members protested in front of a Fox News host's house in Washington, DC.[42] Google was found to be rejiggering its algorithm to favor US-based news over RT, a Russian government-owned news site and television station. (Whatever you think of RT, it strikes me as hypocritical to push down RT in the algorithm, while leaving the algorithm untouched for, say, PBS, NPR, or Voice of America, a US government–backed news outlet.[43])

An Instagram deletion in and of itself is a small act, but the fact that Facebook and Google are allowed to control over half the internet, and that the line between the two companies and the government is ever more blurry, means that increasingly, people have nowhere else to turn to express themselves. Every company, every platform, will have a bias. But when just a few companies control so much, we must live with their biases, and hope for their leaders to remain benevolent.

◇◇◇

In the summer of 2018, I attended a protest against Immigration and Customs Enforcement in Philadelphia, and was keenly aware of all the ways I was likely being tracked. I woke up and checked my phone (an Android, made with Google's software), and knew I was already being followed by Google and Facebook, even when I left their websites. I knew certain news was kept out of my feeds by their algorithms, and certain news pushed up. I knew that all my emails were being read by Google's crawler to sell me ads on my Gmail account, and that if the police ever requested them, they could be handed right over. When I walked out the door, I knew my face was captured by dozens of cameras. My fellow activists had relied on Signal, an encrypted chat app, to organize the protest, but I knew that wasn't safe either—Signal relies on web servers owned by Amazon (as does about 40 percent of the cloud-based internet, including many of the news sites, shopping sites, and everything else we use on a daily basis), and there's circumstantial evidence suggesting that police can figure out when people are using Signal, and track them anyway.[44] At the protest I was photographed by police (Philadelphia's police department has a man whose job it is to videotape every single protester's face from a distance at every protest). Would my face be analyzed by Amazon's own facial recognition software, which Amazon has pitched to police departments across the country, including ICE?[45]

Even though I decided to try not to do anything that would get me arrested at the Occupy ICE protest (I was in the middle of writing a book, and I had a dog to take care of), I knew to keep most information off Facebook and Instagram because I'd had too many friends questioned by police for their social media postings that were critical of the government. And though I knew I was doing nothing illegal—standing outside a government building is still within our First Amendment rights for now—I wasn't convinced I wouldn't face the law. A day after Independence Day, police rammed into Occupy ICE protesters with bikes and took down the encampment. Several were arrested.

If I *were* arrested at that encampment, or at another protest, would the ACLU come to my defense, given their century-long turn toward centrism? It's not clear. The organization did defend J20 protesters, but they've also declined to take up cases in which leftists have been charged with things like environmental terrorism for blocking oil pipelines.

It's getting harder and harder to speak without risk—without being surveilled by Google and Amazon and the local police and the federal government. It's less clear than ever who will defend you if you do get arrested, and as uncertain as it ever has been in this country if the government will try to prosecute you: if participating at the J20 protest is a prosecutable offense, but the vast majority of what occurred in Charlottesville is not, finding the line between acceptable speech and illegal action seems impossible.

But there has never been speech without risk: unionists who fought for revolution, or even just for fair wages, were targeted, arrested, killed. So were civil rights leaders and Black Panthers. Free speech is defined by the state to benefit the state. In the early 1900s, when speech meant more than standing on a street corner but was inherently linked to the fight for workers' equality, the state and the progressives-turned-centrists who helped it watered down free speech so that it would operate within state-supported definitions. Speech as we currently conceptualize it still fits within those definitions: when the deportation of Mapache gets less press coverage than a protest over a talk by a white supremacist at a liberal arts school, we are reifying what counts as speech—who gets it and who doesn't.

If the mainstream definition of free speech is increasingly milquetoast—speech that does not disrupt, that does not lead to violence or to actions that break the law (even if the law is unjust)—and increasingly agreed-upon by progressives and conservatives alike, is that a definition worth defending?

What does standing on a sidewalk and following police orders not to block traffic get you besides a couple more data points about you and your face in your local police department's Amazon-run database? In an era when a few companies control most online expression, and governments increasingly surveil what you do online, the lane you must stay in to speak without risk gets narrower and narrower.

Free speech, to many progressives, once meant the freedom to change the world—as it did to the founders of the ACLU. Now it seems to mean the freedom to respectfully disagree with the world as it rapidly heads toward totalitarianism and climate catastrophe.

If our free speech is defined as speech on public property that does not interfere with traffic or police activity, that does not advocate for the overthrow of the government, that's tracked and watched by police and corporations like Google and Facebook, is it really free? And more important, given all those limiting factors, can it change anything? And if "free speech" *doesn't* change anything, then what's the point of it at all?

# TOWARD A SMARTER DEFINITION OF FREE SPEECH

In 2014, Princeton University professor Martin Gilens and Northwestern University Professor Benjamin Page released a study that compared thousands of public opinion surveys of Americans on specific policy issues with the outcome of those policies (were they voted into law, vetoed, did they win in a referendum, etc.). They found that Americans who did not have at least hundreds of thousands of dollars had effectively zero influence on the outcomes of our public policy decisions.

"Our analyses suggest that majorities of the American public actually have little influence over the policies our government adopts. . . . We believe that if policymaking is dominated by powerful business organizations and a small number of affluent Americans, then America's claims to being a democratic society are seriously threatened," the authors concluded.[1]

Throughout this book, I've argued not that free speech is bad, but that it simply does not mean much—it's an empty signifier that has been co-opted by every part of the political spectrum throughout American history. The Nazis who rallied in Charlottesville, shared memes encouraging the murder of protesters via motor vehicle, and ultimately murdered Heather Heyer rallied under the banner of free speech. Alt-right speakers like Milo Yiannopoulos get paid to speak on college campuses in the name of free speech, and their conservative backers further infiltrate college campuses with paid agitators, organizers, and professors who defend their actions with the claim of free speech. Those same conservatives successfully lobbied to dump a deluge of cash into American politics via *Citizens United* by arguing for their free speech. In the 1920s, leftists tried to create a classless society using the tactic of free speech, though their definition also, critically, included the right to agitation. And when protesters today are arrested for attempting to draw attention to fascism and racism, they defend themselves in court—often with the help of the ACLU—by invoking free speech. If all these things can fit under the umbrella of free speech, yet some are prosecuted and others defended, does free speech exist? Or does that umbrella obfuscate the state's support for fascist and white supremacist ideas and persecution of anything with the ability to change our world?

One might argue that free speech, while it does not exist in pure form, is an ideal to aspire to. But if you believe that, you must reckon with the US government's near-constant suppression of speech throughout our history, especially antiracist and leftist speech, beginning with the ratification of the First Amendment and continuing through the McCarthy era until today, when protesters are arrested for exercising their rights.

If you do believe free speech is an inherently American value, then I think you must also believe that it is in crisis. What does free speech mean when the average voter has no control over their political destiny, when so many congressional districts have been so thoroughly gerrymandered that Democrats regularly win the popular vote at the state level but lose by wide margins in most recent elections? The entire concept of the US Senate means that rural Americans' votes greatly outweigh those of urban residents.[2] And as the 2018 midterm elections showed, our electoral system is rife with voting "irregularities," voter purges, and outright election tampering.

To look at the thousands of examples in history of the US government repressing speech within its borders (not to mention the countless examples of US military intervention abroad that have limited the speech of non-US residents via military junta, dictatorship, and all-out war) and conclude that free speech is something this country truly values is, in my opinion, naïve. To appropriate a software saying, it's not a bug, but a feature. Under US capitalism, the powerful have more of a say, or more free speech, than the less powerful, and that is by design.

So why does the myth of free speech persist? For the same reason Americans perpetuate the myth that we've moved beyond racism, or the myth that our economy is in better shape than ever before: those who benefit from these myths have a vested interest in making sure we still believe them.

As Alex Carey highlights in his book *Taking the Risk Out of Democracy*, there has been a direct correlation between the expansion of democracy in this country—of free speech for the average American, workers' rights, rights for women and people of color, and the right to vote—and the proliferation of corporate and conservative propaganda that associates unions, leftism in general, and strong government with tyranny and oppression, and equates a "free enterprise system" with true freedom.[3]

It wasn't until the 1920s, when union drives were at their peak and Americans were questioning the validity of capitalism more than ever, that corporations began pouring hundreds of millions of dollars into advertising.[4] In 1933, a professor named Harold Lasswell, who was known as a preeminent expert on propaganda, and a big supporter of it, wrote that because Americans were by and large too stupid to make decisions for their own good, propaganda was necessary to sway them in the right direction. Propaganda, Lasswell wrote, "is the one means of mass mobilization which is cheaper than violence, bribery or other possible control techniques."[5] How do we keep believing in free speech, or even freedom, as the government deports thousands, imprisons hundreds of thousands, and cracks down on peaceful protest?

Historian Daniel Boorstin wrote the following in 1961, but I believe it's equally applicable today: "We [Americans] risk being the first people in history to have been able to make their illusions so vivid, so persuasive, so 'realistic' that they can live in them. We are the most illusioned people on earth. Yet we dare not become disillusioned, because our illusions are the very house in which we live; they are our news, our heroes . . . our very experience."[6]

I don't think it's a coincidence that a supposed free speech crisis has cropped up at this moment in American history. When six in ten Americans don't have $500 to their name, an ever-increasing number of jobs are part-time, health care can bankrupt anyone who is not wealthy, our electoral system is increasingly precarious, and global warming looms on the horizon, we have, instead of confronting our reality, retreated further into that American fantasy.[7] If only the college kids would be calm and let the old man speak, if only the protesters wouldn't protest so loudly and disrespectfully, then everything would be okay.

Free speech is not an ideal, but a thick layer of paint obfuscating many truths—about racism, our country's predilection for fascism, our increasingly unequal economy, and the fact that a few people and corporations control nearly every fiber of our lives. The more you peel the paint back, the more you reveal the reality, the deep rot of a country in unending crisis. It's our choice if we want to deal with that rot now, or keep painting and painting, making the layers thicker and thicker and thicker, until the paint is so thick, the smell of its coats so pungent, that it becomes obvious to all there's something we're trying to hide.

What happens if we start to peel back that paint—if we stop obfuscating the truth and instead deal with it? If we use free speech not to layer over the truth, but as a tool to pull back the layers? To do that, we have to move toward a more materialist definition of free speech, and work toward a positivist version of liberty—the idea that people are truly free only when they are materially equal. What we currently have is a theoretically (though not in practice) negativist definition of free speech: anyone is able to speak in the United States. There are (theoretically) no formal obstacles to that (though as I hope this book proves, that is not true). But in negativist liberty, although you, I, and the Koch brothers have a theoretically equal *right* to speak, we do not have the same ability to convey that speech, or the same guarantee that our speech will be heard. This is why freedom of speech must be tied to economic, gender, and racial inequality if it is to mean anything at all: if we truly deserve the same right to be heard, then we have to fight for everyone to have a level playing field. Only then, when an activist has the same ability to speak and influence policy as a billionaire, will free speech exist in this country. Of course, to get there, we have a lot of leveling to do. As of now, most people are not even on the same playing field as those with true power in our country. We're not even playing the same game. Realizing a meaningful definition of free speech—one that encompasses everyone, not just those with privilege who want to uphold our current system—will likely require massively overhauling our government through illegal actions, and perhaps violence. Only then will free speech apply to all. Until then, we should recognize that our current definition—given all its limitations, and the ways it replicates power while dissuading dissent—is at best inconsistent and flawed. More accurately, I believe, it is totally meaningless.

# ACKNOWLEDGMENTS

I couldn't have written this book without my supportive editor, Katy O'Donnell at Bold Type Books, nor without the support of my tenacious agent, Mackenzie Brady Watson.

Writing a manuscript while struggling with PTSD would not have been possible without the help of my friends and family, particularly (but not limited to) Sally Moskowitz, Michael Moskowitz, John Moskowitz, Christina Salway, Erin "Storm Chaser" Corbett, Harron Walker, David Haub, Eddie Wright, Edge Eugene, and Irene Rosenzweig. My psychologist Dennis Debiak deserves credit for helping keep me relatively sane through the process.

I'm eternally grateful to those who directly assisted with this book—the people I relied on for my reporting, analysis, and words of encouragement, especially Naima Lowe, Dylan Petrohilos, Alexei Wood, Mapache Salazar, Rattler, and Olive. They were brave and generous enough to tell their stories, and gave me, and hopefully you, a new perspective on the world.

# NOTES

## Introduction

1. Ian Carter, "Positive and Negative Liberty," Stanford Encyclopedia of Philosophy, https://plato.stanford.edu/entries/liberty-positive-negative/.

## Chapter 1: The Line

1. Hawes Spencer and Matt Stevens, "23 Arrested and Tear Gas Deployed After a K.K.K. Rally in Virginia," *New York Times*, July 8, 2017, www.nytimes.com/2017/07/08/us/kkk-rally-charlottesville-robert-e-lee-statue.html.

2. "Unite the Right Free Speech Rally—Charlottesville," Eventbu invite, https://us.eventbu.com/charlottesville/unite-right-free-speech-rally/3855389.

3. *Janus v. American Federation of State, County, and Municipal Employees Council 31, et al.*, 585 US __ (2018), www.supremecourt.gov/opinions/17pdf/16-1466_2b3j.pdf.

4. *Abood v. Detroit Board of Education*, 431 US 209 (1977), https://supreme.justia.com/cases/federal/us/431/209/.

5. Anna Sauerbrey, "How Germany Deals with Neo-Nazis," *New York Times*, August 23, 2017, www.nytimes.com/2017/08/23/opinion/germany-neo-nazis-charlottesville.html; "German Criminal Code," *Federal Law Gazette*, November 13, 1998, www.gesetze-im-internet.de/englisch_stgb/englisch_stgb.html#p1241.

6. "The Trial of Henry Wirz," Military Legal Resources, Library of Congress, May 4, 2016, www.loc.gov/rr/frd/Military_Law/Wirz_trial.html.

7. Joseph Bernstein, "Alt-White: How the Breitbart Machine Laundered Racist Hate," *BuzzFeed News*, October 5, 2017, www.buzzfeednews.com/article/josephbernstein/heres-how-breitbart-and-milo-smuggled-white-nationalism#.inq1rVA0D.

8. Spencer Ackerman and Betsy Woodruff, "Homeland Security Ignores White Terror, DHS Veterans Say," *Daily Beast*, October 31, 2018, www.thedailybeast.com/homeland-security-ignores-white-terror-dhs-veterans-say.

9. Peter Hermann, Joe Heim, and Ellie Silverman, "Police in Charlottesville Criticized for Slow Response to Violent Demonstrations," *Washington Post*, August 12,

2017, www.washingtonpost.com/local/public-safety/police-in-charlottesville-criticized
-for-slow-response-to-violent-demonstrations/2017/08/12/869720fc-7f84-11e7-a669-b4
00c5c7e1cc_story.html.

10. Sam Levin, "California Police Worked with Neo-Nazis to Pursue 'Anti-Racist' Activists, Documents Show," *Guardian*, February 9, 2018, www.theguardian.com /world/2018/feb/09/california-police-white-supremacists-counter-protest; Michael Hutchins, "Former Colbert Police Chief with Neo-Nazi Background Back in Law Enforcement," *Herald Democrat*, September 14, 2018, www.heralddemocrat.com/news/20180913 /former-colbert-police-chief-with-neo-nazi-background-back-in-law-enforcement; Jess Fournier, "Why Do the Cops Keep Protecting White Supremacists?" Feministing, September 2018, http://feministing.com/2018/09/12/why-do-the-cops-keep-protecting -white-supremacists/3; Jackson Landers, "A Leaked Message Board Shows What White Supremacists Think of the Police," *Rewire News*, March 9, 2018, https://rewire.news /article/2018/03/09/leaked-message-board-shows-white-supremacists-think-police/.

11. Henry Grabar, "'Run Them Down': Driving Into Crowds of Protesters Was a Right-Wing Fantasy Long Before the Violence in Charlottesville," *Slate*, August 14, 2017, www.slate.com/articles/business/metropolis/2017/08/driving_into_crowds _of_protesters_was_a_right_wing_fantasy_long_before_charlottesville.html; Steven Hsieh, "To Protect and Troll: Police Union Chief Under Investigation for Incendiary Posts," *Santa Fe Reporter*, February 20, 2017, www.sfreporter.com/news/2017/02/20/to -protect-and-troll/; Jasmine Turner, "Fields' Instagram Posts Depicting Car Running into Crowd to Be Shown," NBC 12 (Richmond), November 30, 2018, www.nbc12 .com/2018/11/30/fields-instagram-posts-depicting-car-running-into-crowd-allowed -trial/.

12. Henry Graff, "ACLU, Rutherford Institute Represent Kessler in Lawsuit Filed Against Charlottesville," NBC 29 (Charlottesville), August 10, 2017, www .nbc29.com/story/36112221/aclu-rutherford-institute-represent-kessler-in-lawsuit -filed-against-charlottesville.

13. Anthony Romero, "Equality, Justice and the First Amendment," Speak Freely (blog), ACLU, August 15, 2017, www.aclu.org/blog/free-speech/equality-justice-and -first-amendment.

14. Joe Palazzolo, "ACLU Will No Longer Defend Hate Groups Protesting with Firearms," *Wall Street Journal*, August 17, 2017, www.wsj.com/articles /aclu-changes-policy-on-defending-hate-groups-protesting-with-firearms-1503010167.

15. Adam Epstein, "'Blood and Soil': The Meaning of the Nazi Slogan Chanted by White Nationalists in Charlottesville," *Quartz*, August 13, 2017, https://qz.com/1052725 /the-definition-of-the-nazi-slogan-chanted-by-white-nationalists-in-charlottesville/.

16. Sean McElwee, Twitter post, January 28, 2018, https://twitter.com /SeanMcElwee/status/957741330192633856.

17. Bari Weiss, "We're All Fascists Now," *New York Times*, March 7, 2018, www .nytimes.com/2018/03/07/opinion/were-all-fascists-now.html.

18. Craig Schneider, "Wear a Mask? In Georgia, You Could Be Arrested," *Atlanta Journal-Constitution*, April 25, 2016, www.ajc.com/news/wear-mask-georgia" -you-could-arrested/tz4NZUFAgMROd42UTyfCpM/.

19. Adam Johnson, "In Month After Charlottesville, Papers Spent as Much Time Condemning Anti-Nazis as Nazis," Fairness and Accuracy in Reporting (website),

September 13, 2017, https://fair.org/home/in-month-after-charlottesville-papers-spent-as-much-time-condemning-anti-nazis-as-nazis/.

20. *City of Charlottesville, et al. v. Pennsylvania Light Foot Militia, et al.*, US District Court for the Western District of Virginia, filed October 27, 2017, at www.law.georgetown.edu/academics/centers-institutes/constitutional-advocacy-protection/upload/lawsuit-charlottesville.pdf.

21. "National Lawyers Guild Opposes 'Both Sides' Charlottesville Lawsuit, Supports Redneck Revolt and Socialist Rifle Association," Press Release, National Lawyers Guild (blog), February 9, 2018, www.nlg.org/nlg-opposes-both-sides-charlottesville-lawsuit-supports-redneck-revolt-and-socialist-rifle-association/.

## Chapter 2: Are We All Snowflakes?

1. Cathy Young, "How Campus Politics Hijacked American Politics," *Boston Globe*, January 26, 2018, www.bostonglobe.com/ideas/2018/01/26/how-campus-politics-hijacked-american-politics/GsJwJwG78lqq6LPYcKWERK/story.html.

2. Richard M. Aborn and Ashley D. Cannon, "Prisons: In Jail, but Not Sentenced," *Americas Quarterly*, Winter 2013, www.americasquarterly.org/aborn-prisons.

3. Donald Ratcliffe, "The Right to Vote and the Rise of Democracy, 1787–1828," *Journal of the Early Republic*, 33 (2013): 219, http://jer.pennpress.org/media/26167/sampleart22.pdf.

4. David S. Yassky, "Eras of the First Amendment," *Columbia Law Review* 91 (1991): 1,700.

5. "The Alien and Sedition Acts: Defining American Freedom," Constitutional Rights Foundation, www.crf-usa.org/america-responds-to-terrorism/the-alien-and-sedition-acts.html.

6. Yassky, "Eras of the First Amendment," 1,713.

7. Richard K. Crallé, ed., *Speeches of John C. Calhoun* (New York: D. Appleton, 1853), 517.

8. Yassky, "Eras of the First Amendment," 1,715.

9. *Ex parte Jackson*, 96, US 727 (1878), https://supreme.justia.com/cases/federal/us/96/727/.

10. *Gitlow v. New York*, 268, US 652 (1925), https://supreme.justia.com/cases/federal/us/268/652/.

11. Joshua Waimberg, "Schenck v. United States: Defining the Limits of Free Speech," Constitution Daily (blog), National Constitution Center, November 2, 2015, https://constitutioncenter.org/blog/schenck-v-united-states-defining-the-limits-of-free-speech/.

12. Jane Mayer, *Dark Money: The Hidden History of the Billionaires Behind the Rise of the Radical Right* (New York: Anchor Books, 2017), 97.

13. Allan Bloom, *The Closing of the American Mind* (New York: Simon and Schuster, 1987), 26.

14. Bloom, 26.

15. Bloom, 26.

16. Bloom, 28–29.

17. Donald Lazere, "'The Closing of the American Mind,' 20 Years Later," *Inside Higher Ed*, September 18, 2007.

18. Roger Kimball, "The Groves of Ignorance," *New York Times*, April 5, 1987, www
.nytimes.com/1987/04/05/books/the-groves-of-ignorance.html.

19. Lazere, "Closing."

20. Moira Weigel, "Political Correctness: How the Right Invented a Phantom Enemy," *Guardian*, November 30, 2016. www.theguardian.com/us-news/2016/nov/30
/political-correctness-how-the-right-invented-phantom-enemy-donald-trump.

21. Richard Bernstein, "The Rising Hegemony of the Politically Correct,"
*New York Times*, October 28, 1990, www.nytimes.com/1990/10/28/weekinreview
/ideas-trends-the-rising-hegemony-of-the-politically-correct.html?pagewanted=all.

22. Weigel, "Political Correctness."

23. Jerry Adler, Mark Starr, et al., "Taking Offense: Is This the New Enlightenment
on Campus or the New McCarthyism?" *Newsweek*, December 24, 1990; "In Memoriam:
Vincent Matthew Sarich," University of California Academic Senate (website), October 2012, https://senate.universityofcalifornia.edu/_files/inmemoriam/html/Vincent
MatthewSarich.html.

24. George H. W. Bush, speech to University of Michigan graduates, May 5,
1991, excerpted in *New York Times*, www.nytimes.com/1991/05/05/us/excerpts-from
-president-s-speech-to-university-of-michigan-graduates.html.

25. Greg Lukianoff and Jonathan Haidt, "The Coddling of the American Mind,"
*The Atlantic*, September 2015, www.theatlantic.com/magazine/archive/2015/09
/the-coddling-of-the-american-mind/399356/.

26. Frank Bruni, "I'm a White Man. Hear Me Out," *New York Times*, August 12,
2017, www.nytimes.com/2018/03/22/opinion/speaking-as-a-white-male.html.

## Chapter 3: Campus Wars—Middlebury

1. Bruce Caldwell, "The Chicago School, Hayek, and Neoliberalism," in *Building
Chicago Economics*, eds. Robert Van Horn, Philip Mirowski, and Thomas Stapleford
(New York: Cambridge University Press, 2011), 301–334.

2. Bill Kristol, Twitter post, March 3, 2017, https://twitter.com/billkristol/status
/837726862541365248?lang=en.

3. "Fall 2015 Reflections," Life as a Middlebury College Student (blog), December
30, 2015, http://middlife.tumblr.com/post/136299955717/fall-2015-reflections.

4. Tiffany Chang, "20 Thoughts from the Third Town Hall Discussion," Beyond the Green (blog), December 14, 2015, https://beyondthegreenmidd.wordpress
.com/2015/12/14/20-thoughts-from-the-third-town-hall-discussion/.

5. Dan Bauman, "Hate Crimes on Campuses Are Rising, New FBI Data Show,"
*Chronicle of Higher Education*, November 14, 2018, www.chronicle.com/article/Hate
-Crimes-on-Campuses-Are/245093; Megan Zahneis, "White-Supremacist Propaganda
on Campuses Rose 77 Percent Last Year," *Chronicle of Higher Education*, June 28, 2018,
www.chronicle.com/article/White-Supremacist-Propaganda/243786.

6. Minutes from Town Hall Discussion, Community Council at Middlebury
College, November 30, 2015, www.middlebury.edu/system/files/media/CC%20
Minutes%20Meeting%208%20Town%20Hall%20Discussion%2011.30.15.pdf.

7. "I'm Only Human," *Middlebury Campus*, February 17, 2016, https://middle
burycampus.com/34064/opinion/im-only-human-2/.

8. Taylor Gee, "How the Middlebury Riot Really Went Down," *Politico*, May 28, 2017, www.politico.com/magazine/story/2017/05/28/how-donald-trump-caused-the-middlebury-melee-215195.

9. Gee, "Middlebury."

10. Richard Herrnstein and Charles Murray, *The Bell Curve: Intelligence and Class Structure in American Life* (New York: The Free Press, 1994), 331.

11. Herrnstein and Murray, 548–49.

12. Daniel Bice, "Hacked Records Show Bradley Foundation Taking Its Conservative Wisconsin Model National," *Milwaukee Journal Sentinel*, May 5, 2017, https://projects.jsonline.com/news/2017/5/5/hacked-records-show-bradley-foundation-taking-wisconsin-model-national.html; Charles Murray profile, S.H.A.M.E. (website), updated April 9, 2014, at https://web.archive.org/web/20181116080102/https://shameproject.com/profile/charles-murray/; Eric Alterman, "The 'Right' Books and Big Ideas," *The Nation*, November 4, 1999, www.thenation.com/article/right-books-and-big-ideas; "Arkansas Project," The Encyclopedia of Arkansas History and Culture, February 21, 2018, www.encyclopediaofarkansas.net/encyclopedia/entry-detail.aspx?entryID=5378; Jim Naureckas, "Racism Resurgent," Fairness and Accuracy in Reporting, January 1, 1999, https://fair.org/home/racism-resurgent/; "The Bell Curve and the Pioneer Fund," *ABC World News Tonight*, November 22, 1994.

13. William Bennett and Peter Wehner, "Single Moms and Welfare: Cut 'Em Off," *Baltimore Sun*, February 6, 1994, at www.evernote.com/shard/s1/sh/4d73dad7-624c-4a29-8e16-937196550ef5/bd608a28f36b763453557d7a7700c50f.

14. Nicholas Confessore, "Tramps Like Them," *New York Times*, February 10, 2012, www.nytimes.com/2012/02/12/books/review/charles-murray-examines-the-white-working-class-in-coming-apart.html; David Brooks, "The Great Divorce," *New York Times*, January 30, 2012, www.nytimes.com/2012/01/31/opinion/brooks-the-great-divorce.html.

15. "Middlebury Students: College Administrator and Staff Assault Students, Endanger Lives After Murray Protest," Beyond the Green (blog), March 4, 2017, https://beyondthegreenmidd.wordpress.com/2017/03/04/middlebury-students-college-administrator-and-staff-assault-students-endanger-lives-after-murray-protest/.

16. "Three Months of Crisis: Chronology of Events," *California Monthly*, February 1965, at http://bancroft.berkeley.edu/FSM/chron.html.

17. Mark Reed Stoner, "The Free Speech Movement: A Case Study in the Rhetoric of Social Intervention" (PhD dissertation, Ohio State University, 1987), 47, https://etd.ohiolink.edu/!etd.send_file?accession=osu1487585645578684&disposition=inline.

18. Mark Edelman Boren, *Student Resistance* (New York: Routledge, 2001), 142–43; "Visual History: Free Speech Movement, 1964," University of California, Berkeley (website), https://fsm.berkeley.edu/free-speech-movement-timeline/.

19. Stoner, "Free Speech Movement," 6.

20. DeNeen Brown, "'Stained with Blood': The 1968 Campus Massacre of Black Protesters by South Carolina Police," *Washington Post*, February 8, 2018, www.washingtonpost.com/news/retropolis/wp/2018/02/08/bang-bang-bang-recalling-the-1968-campus-massacre-of-black-protesters-by-south-carolina-police/?utm_term=.54216afb6bcb.

21. Charles Hamilton, "Howard Students Continue Sit-In as University Seeks

Injunction," *Harvard Crimson*, March 22, 1968, www.thecrimson.com/article/1968/3/22/howard-students-continue-sit-in-as-university/.

22. Boren, *Student Resistance,* 174; Robert McFadden, "Remembering Columbia, 1968," *City Room* (blog), *New York Times*, April 25, 2008, https://cityroom.blogs.nytimes.com/2008/04/25/remembering-columbia-1968/.

23. Boren, 190.

24. Frank Bruni, "The Dangerous Safety of College," *New York Times*, March 11, 2017, www.nytimes.com/2017/03/11/opinion/sunday/the-dangerous-safety-of-college.html.

25. Danielle Allen, "Why Middlebury's Violent Response to Charles Murray Reminded Me of the Little Rock Nine," *Washington Post*, March 7, 2017, www.washingtonpost.com/opinions/why-middleburys-violent-response-to-charles-murray-reminded-me-of-the-little-rock-nine/2017/03/07/7c829e38-02b7-11e7-ad5b-d22680e18d10_story.html?utm_term=.4eb20ff1df0b.

26. Allison Stanger, "Understanding the Angry Mob at Middlebury That Gave Me a Concussion," *New York Times*, March 13, 2017, www.nytimes.com/2017/03/13/opinion/understanding-the-angry-mob-that-gave-me-a-concussion.html.

27. Sabine Poux, "Allison Stanger Appearances Show Faculty Rift," *Middlebury Campus*, March 14, 2018, https://middleburycampus.com/38046/news/stanger-appearances-show-faculty-rift/.

28. Charles Murray profile page, Speaker Booking Agency (website), https://speakerbookingagency.com/talent/charles-murray/.

29. Robby Soave, "The Craziest Demands of College Kids in 2016," *Daily Beast*, June 7, 2016, www.thedailybeast.com/the-craziest-demands-of-college-kids-in-2016.

30. "Broken Inquiry on Campus: A Response by a Collection of Middlebury Students," March 12, 2017, https://brokeninquiryblog.wordpress.com/2017/03/12/broken-inquiry-on-campus-a-response-by-a-collection-of-middlebury-students/.

31. Donations to the Leadership Institute compiled by Conservative Transparency, http://conservativetransparency.org/advanced-search/?adv=leadership+institute&donor=&recipient=&candidate=&min=&max=&yr=&yr1=&yr2=&order_by=&submit=; Chris Quintana, "A Campus-Politics Whodunit: Who Invited James O'Keefe to Speak at Middlebury?" *Chronicle of Higher Education*, December 13, 2017, www.chronicle.com/article/A-Campus-Politics-Whodunit-/242050.

32. William Kidder, "A High Target for 'Mismatch': Bogus Arguments about Affirmative Action," *LA Review of Books*, February 7, 2013, https://lareviewofbooks.org/article/a-high-target-for-mismatch-bogus-arguments-about-affirmative-action.

## Chapter 4: Campus Wars—Evergreen

1. Olympia Campus Census Statistics, Evergreen College, 2010–2017, www.evergreen.edu/sites/default/files/OlympiaDemographics1994-2017.pdf.

2. Alex Dobuzinskis, "White Supremacist Stabs Black Man in Olympia, Washington," Reuters, August 18, 2016, www.reuters.com/article/us-washington-hatecrime/white-supremacist-stabs-black-man-in-olympia-washington-idUSKCN10T21Z; Forest Hunt, "Protest Follows Year of Controversy over Racism at Evergreen," *Cooper*

*Point Journal*, October 12, 2016, www.cooperpointjournal.com/2016/10/12/protest-follows-year-of-controversy-over-racism-at-evergreen-contextualizing-bias-on-campus/.

3. 2010 Census Summary File 1, Race and Hispanic or Latino Origin: 2010, US Census Bureau, https://factfinder.census.gov/bkmk/table/1.0/en/DEC/10_SF1/QTP3/0500000US53067.

4. Eduardo Bonilla-Silva, "The Structure of Racism in Color-Blind, 'Post-Racial' America," *American Behavioral Scientist* 59, no. 11 (May 2015): 1358–76, https://journals.sagepub.com/doi/10.1177/0002764215586826.

5. Sean McElwee, "How America Can Fix the Racial Wealth Gap," *Salon*, December 7, 2014, www.salon.com/2014/12/07/how_america_can_fix_the_racial_wealth_gap.

6. Georgie Hicks, "Protests on Evergreen Campus," *Cooper Point Journal*, May 27, 2017, www.cooperpointjournal.com/2017/05/27/protests-on-evergreen-campus-students-challenge-racism-and-anti-blackness/.

7. Eric Weinstein, "What Scientific Term or Concept Ought to Be More Widely Known?" *Edge*, 2017, www.edge.org/response-detail/27181.

8. Amelia Dickson, "Demonstrators, Patriot Prayer and Troopers in Riot Gear Face Off at Evergreen," *Olympian*, June 15, 2017, www.theolympian.com/news/local/article156470379.html.

9. "New Jersey Man Accused of Threats That Closed Evergreen State College Last Month," *Seattle Times*, July 4, 2017, https://www.seattletimes.com/seattle-news/crime/new-jersey-man-accused-of-threats-that-closed-evergreen-state-college-last-month/.

10. Bret Weinstein, Twitter post, June 5, 2017, https://twitter.com/BretWeinstein/status/871864321629868033.

11. First-time, First-year Applicants, Admitted and Enrolled, Office of Institutional Research and Assessment, Evergreen State College, December 20, 2017, http://www.evergreen.edu/sites/default/files/FTFY_App_to_Enroll_2001-17.pdf.

12. Demands, Reedies Against Racism (website), updated November 5, 2017, http://reediesagainstracism.weebly.com/demands.html.

13. Chris Lydgate, "Taking a Fresh Look at Hum 110," *Reed Magazine*, April 20, 2017, www.reed.edu/reed-magazine/articles/2017/hum-110-fresh-look.html.

14. See, for example, Chris Bodenner, "The Surprising Revolt at the Most Liberal College in the Country," *The Atlantic* (online), November 2, 2017, https://www.theatlantic.com/education/archive/2017/11/the-surprising-revolt-at-reed/544682/.

15. Carol Jouzaitis, "NIU Split on Political Correctness," *Chicago Tribune*, October 24, 1991, http://articles.chicagotribune.com/1991-10-24/news/9104050808_1_diversity-policies-political-correctness-affirmative-action.

16. Stanley Fish, *There's No Such Thing as Free Speech . . . And It's a Good Thing, Too* (New York: Oxford University Press, 1994), 8.

17. Fish, 71.

18. Fish, 94–95.

19. "The Condition of Education 2018," National Center for Education Statistics, US Department of Education, https://nces.ed.gov/fastfacts/display.asp?id=61.

20. David Randall, "Beach Books 2017–2018," National Association of Scholars, https://www.nas.org/projects/beachbooks.

## Chapter 5: Pushing the Line

1. Douglas Kneeland, "72 Seized at Rally of Nazis in Chicago," *New York Times*, July 10, 1978, www.nytimes.com/1978/07/10/archives/72-seized-at-rally-of-nazis-in-chicago -police-keep-2000-under.html.

2. Steven J. Heyman, ed., *Hate Speech and the Constitution* (New York: Garland, 1996), 1,211.

3. Mike Royko, "Nazi March Solution Is Simple," *Chicago Sun-Times*, March 4, 1978, at Illinois Digital Archives, www.idaillinois.org/cdm/ref/collection/skokiepo001/id/41.

4. Marcia Kramer, "'Nazis Must Never Come . . . '; Skokie President Vows to Fight in Court," *Chicago Sun-Times*, March 26, 1978, at Illinois Digital Archives, www.idaillinois .org/cdm/ref/collection/skokiepo001/id/107.

5. Irving Louis Horowitz and Victoria Curtis Bramson, "Skokie, the ACLU and the Endurance of Democratic Theory," *Democratic Theory* 43, no. 2 (Spring 1979): 329, https://scholarship.law.duke.edu/cgi/viewcontent.cgi?article=3589&context=lcp.

6. "Overview of the Fundamental Right to Protest," ACLU of Illinois, April 24, 2012, www.aclu-il.org/en/news/overview-fundamental-right-protest.

7. *Nebraska Press Assn. v. Stuart*, 427 US 539 (1976), https://supreme.justia.com /cases/federal/us/427/539/case.html.

8. *Chaplinsky v. New Hampshire*, 315 US 568 (1942), https://supreme.justia.com /cases/federal/us/315/568/.

9. *Snyder v. Phelps*, Supreme Court Case, 562 US 443 (2011), https://supreme.justia .com/cases/federal/us/562/443/dissent.html.

10. Horowitz and Bramson, "Skokie," 330.

11. Horowitz and Bramson, 343.

12. Horowitz and Bramson, 343.

13. "Skokie Security Plans Canceled. No Demonstrations on Sunday," at Illinois Digital Archives, www.idaillinois.org/cdm/ref/collection/skokiepo001/id/425.

14. Philip Oltermann, "Tough New German Law Puts Tech Firms and Free Speech in Spotlight," *Guardian*, January 5, 2018, www.theguardian.com/world/2018 /jan/05/tough-new-german-law-puts-tech-firms-and-free-speech-in-spotlight; Angel- ique Chrisafis, "John Galliano Found Guilty of Racist and Antisemitic Abuse," *Guard- ian*, September 8, 2011, www.theguardian.com/world/2011/sep/08/john-galliano -guilty-racism-antisemitism; Editorial, "Speech and Anti-Semitism in France," *New York Times*, February 3, 2015, www.nytimes.com/2015/02/04/opinion/speech-and -anti-semitism-in-france.html; JTA, "BDS a Hate Crime? In France, Legal Vigilance Punishes Anti-Israel Activists," *Haaretz*, February 15, 2014, www.haaretz.com/jewish /the-french-law-that-battles-bds-1.5322519.

15. Editorial, "Nazis, Skokie and the ACLU," *New York Times*, January 1, 1978, www .nytimes.com/1978/01/01/archives/nazis-skokie-and-the-aclu.html.

16. "Editor's Mail: Readers Divided on Handling of Nazi Demonstrations," Lerner Communications, May 4, 1978, at Illinois Digital Archives, www.idaillinois.org/cdm /ref/collection/skokiepo001/id/21.

17. Horowitz and Bramson, "Skokie," 331; J. Anthony Lukas, "The ACLU Against Itself," *New York Times*, July 9, 1978, www.nytimes.com/1978/07/09/archives

/the-aclu-against-itself-aclu-aclu.html; Samuel Walker, *In Defense of American Liberties: A History of the ACLU* (Carbondale, IL: Southern Illinois University Press, 1999), 327; JTA, "ACLU Defends Representing Nazis at Free Speech Convocation," June 14, 1978, www.jta .org/1978/06/14/archive/aclu-defends-representing-nazis-at-free-speech-convocation.

18. Lukas, "ACLU Against Itself."

19. Lukas, "ACLU Against Itself."

20. Aryeh Neier, "Free Speech for All," *Index on Censorship*, August 1, 2008, www .indexoncensorship.org/wp-content/uploads/2008/12/neier_a_330850.pdf.

21. Ron Grossman, "'Swastika War': When the Neo-Nazis Fought in Court to March in Skokie," *Chicago Tribune*, March 10, 2017, http://www.chicagotribune.com/news /opinion/commentary/ct-neo-nazi-skokie-march-flashback-perspec-0312-20170310 -story.html.

22. "Jewish Defense League Braves Fire From All Sides," *Winnipeg Free Press*, September 28, 1972, https://newspaperarchive.com/winnipeg-free-press-sep-28-1972-p -80/.

23. Jesse Dukes, "The Nazis' Neighborhood," WBEZ (Chicago), April 23, 2017, http://interactive.wbez.org/curiouscity/chicagonazineighborhood/?utm_source =facebook.com&utm_medium=social&utm_campaign=npr&utm_term=nprnews &utm_content=20170507.

24. "Labor Must Drive Nazis Out of Chicago!," *Workers Vanguard*, June 30, 1978, www.marxists.org/history/etol/newspape/workersvanguard/1978/0210_30_06_1978 .pdf.

25. German Lopez, "There Are Huge Racial Disparities in How U.S. Police Use Force," *Vox*, November 14, 2018, www.vox.com/identities/2016/8/13/17938186 /police-shootings-killings-racism-racial-disparities.

26. Laura Weinrib, *The Taming of Free Speech* (Cambridge, MA: Harvard University Press, 2016), 19.

27. Samuel Walker, "The Founding of the American Civil Liberties Union, 1920," Mudd Manuscript Library (blog), Seely G. Mudd Manuscript Library, Princeton University, 2012, https://blogs.princeton.edu/mudd/2012/08 /the-founding-of-the-american-civil-liberties-union-1920.

28. Weinrib, *Taming of Free Speech*, 7.

29. Weinrib, 7.

30. Weinrib, 10–11.

31. Ross Rieder, "IWW Formally Begins Spokane Free-Speech Fight on November 2, 1909," The Free Encyclopedia of Washington State History, June 22, 2005, www .historylink.org/File/7357.

32. Weinrib, *Taming of Free Speech*, 31.

33. Weinrib, 40.

34. Weinrib, 43.

35. Weinrib, 47.

36. Weinrib, 117.

37. Final Report of the Commission on Industrial Relations, Washington Government Printing Office, 1916, 17–152.

38. Weinrib, *Taming of Free Speech*, 76.

39. Steven Parfitt, "The Justice Department Campaign Against the IWW, 1917–1920," IWW History Project, Unversity of Washington, 2016, http://depts.washington.edu/iww/justice_dept.shtml.

40. Weinrib, *Taming of Free Speech*, 84.

41. Weinrib, 114.

42. Roger Baldwin, statement in court, as published in "The Individual and the State: The Problem as Presented by the Sentencing of Roger N. Baldwin," 1918, https://catalog.hathitrust.org/Record/004008650.

43. Weinrib, *Taming of Free Speech*, 129.

44. ACLU (website), www.aclu.org/about-aclu.

45. Author interview with Ben Wizner, director of the ACLU's Speech, Privacy, and Technology Project, May 8, 2018.

46. Scott Bomboy, "The Scopes Monkey Trial and the Constitution," Constitution Daily (blog), National Constitution Center, July 21, 2018, https://constitutioncenter.org/blog/the-scopes-monkey-trial-and-the-constitution.

47. Weinrib, *Taming of Free Speech*, 181.

48. Weinrib, 291.

49. Samuel Walker, "Review: Rethinking the History of the American Civil Liberties Union: Donohue's *Politics of the American Civil Liberties Union*," *American Bar Foundation Research Journal* 11, no. 3 (Summer 1986): 547–55.

50. Katie Kilkenny, "Milo Yiannopoulos' UCLA Talk Canceled," *Hollywood Reporter*, February 14, 2018, www.hollywoodreporter.com/news/milo-yiannopoulos-ucla-talk-canceled-1085059.

51. Madison Park and Kyung Lah, "Berkeley Protests of Yiannopoulos Caused $100,000 in Damage," CNN, February 2, 2017, www.cnn.com/2017/02/01/us/milo-yiannopoulos-berkeley/index.html.

52. Sian Cain, "Milo Yiannopoulos Drops Lawsuit Over His Cancelled Book," *Guardian*, February 20, 2018, www.theguardian.com/books/2018/feb/20/milo-yiannopoulos-drops-lawsuit-over-his-cancelled-book.

53. Elizabeth Stuart, "Fights Erupt at Phoenix Mosque as People Attack and Defend Islam," *New Times* (Phoenix), October 10, 2015, www.phoenixnewtimes.com/news/fights-erupt-at-phoenix-mosque-as-people-attack-and-defend-islam-7734311.

54. Maya Oppenheim, "UC Berkeley Protests: Milo Yiannopoulos Planned to 'Publicly Name Undocumented Students' in Cancelled Talk," *The Independent*, February 3, 2017, https://www.independent.co.uk/news/world/americas/uc-berkely-protests-milo-yiannopoulos-publicly-name-undocumented-students-cancelled-talk-illegals-a7561321.html.

55. Diana Tourjée, "Trans Student Harassed by Milo Yiannopoulos Speaks Out," Broadly (*Vice*), January 3, 2017, https://broadly.vice.com/en_us/article/vb4e44/trans-student-harassed-by-milo-yiannopoulos-speaks-out.

56. Natasha Lennard, "Is Antifa Counterproductive? White Nationalist Richard Spencer Would Beg to Differ," *The Intercept*, March 17, 2018, https://theintercept.com/2018/03/17/richard-spencer-college-tour-antifa-alt-right/.

57. Mark Bray, *Antifa: The Anti-Fascist Handbook* (New York: Melville House, 2017), XV.

58. Bray, 6.

59. Bray, 12–13.

60. Bray, 21.

61. Bray, 30.

62. Bray, 35.

63. Bray, 37.

64. Martin Glaberman, "Does Freedom of Speech Include Fascists?" *New International* XI, no. 8 (November 1945): 241–43, http://libcom.org/library/does-freedom-speech-include-fascists.

65. Wesley Lowery, Kimberly Kindy, and Andrew Ba Tran, "In the United States, Right-Wing Violence Is on the Rise," *Washington Post*, November 25, 2018, www.washingtonpost.com/national/in-the-united-states-right-wing-violence-is-on-the-rise/2018/11/25/61f7f24a-deb4-11e8-85df-7a6b4d25cfbb_story.html.

## Chapter 6: The Shadow Campus

1. *South Park*, Season 19, ep. 5, "Safe Space," originally aired October 21, 2015, https://www.youtube.com/watch?v=sXQkXXBqj_U.

2. "Clip: Van Jones on Safe Spaces on College Campuses," Institute of Politics, University of Chicago, February 24, 2017, www.youtube.com/watch?time_continue=260&v=Zms3EqGbFOk.

3. Barack Obama, remarks at Howard University Commencement Ceremony, published on *Politico*, May 5, 2016, www.politico.com/story/2016/05/obamas-howard-commencement-transcript-222931.

4. Adam Johnson, "NYT's Campus Free Speech Coverage Focuses 7-to-1 on Plight of Right," Fairness and Accuracy in Reporting, November 15, 2017, https://fair.org/home/nyts-campus-free-speech-coverage-focuses-7-to-1-on-plight-of-right/.

5. Andrew Sullivan, "We All Live on Campus Now," *New York*, February 9, 2018, http://nymag.com/intelligencer/2018/02/we-all-live-on-campus-now.html.

6. Moriah Balingit, "DeVos, Sessions Warn of Deepening Free-Speech Crisis on College Campuses," *Washington Post*, September 17, 2017, www.washingtonpost.com/local/education/devos-sessions-warn-of-deepening-free-speech-crisis-on-college-campuses/2018/09/17/21c5f8c6-ba9b-11e8-a8aa-860695e7f3fc_story.html.

7. Statement of Interest by US Department of Justice in *Speech First, Inc. v. Mark Schlissel, et al.,* filed June 11, 2018, www.justice.gov/opa/press-release/file/1070601/download?utm_medium=email&utm_source=govdelivery.

8. Drew Millard, "The Intellectual Dark Web Goes to Washington," *The Outline*, May 27, 2018, https://theoutline.com/post/4717/the-intellectual-dark-web-goes-to-washington?utm_source=FB&zd=4&zi=p73gxfvu.

9. Osita Nwanevu, "When 'Free Speech' Is a Marketing Ploy," *Slate*, March 23, 2018, https://slate.com/news-and-politics/2018/03/when-campus-free-speech-is-a-marketing-ploy.html.

10. "Free Expression on Campus: A Survey of U.S. College Students and U.S. Adults," Gallup, 2016, www.knightfoundation.org/media/uploads/publication_pdfs/FreeSpeech_campus.pdf.

11. Matthew Mayhew et al., "Does College Turn People into Liberals?" *The Conversation*, February 2, 2018, https://theconversation.com/does-college-turn-people-into-liberals-90905.

12. Disinvitation Database, Foundation for Individual Rights in Education, www.thefire.org/resources/disinvitation-database/.

13. Jeffrey Sachs, Twitter posts, March 9, 2018, https://twitter.com/JeffreyASachs/status/972203477991673856.

14. Colleen Flaherty, "'Public' Information," *Inside Higher Ed*, September 13, 2016, www.insidehighered.com/news/2016/09/13/professor-who-advocates-israel-boycott-latest-face-demands-records-about-her-career.

15. Lee Kaplan, "Simona Shironi Shills for the Arabs Against Israel," DAFKA (website), www.dafka.org/news/index.php?pid=4&id=1572.

16. Itamar Bazz, "StandWithUs to Take Cash, Messaging from Israeli Government," *972 Magazine*, January 13, 2015, https://972mag.com/standwithus-to-take-cash-messaging-from-israeli-govt/101314/.

17. Judy Maltz, "The Commander Behind the Pro-Israel Student Troops on U.S. College Campuses," *Haaretz*, March 15, 2016, www.haaretz.com/jewish/.premium-leading-the-pro-israel-charge-on-u-s-college-campuses-1.5417981.

18. Aviva Stahl, "Why Feminists Should Care About the Israeli-Palestinian Conflict," *Alternet*, April 14, 2016, www.alternet.org/world/why-feminists-should-care-about-israeli-palestinian-conflict.

19. Hannah Broad, "NY Professor Says 'Israeli Apartheid' Akin to Campus Rape," *Jerusalem Post*, April 20, 2016, at www.meforum.org/campus-watch/articles/2016/ny-professor-says-israeli-apartheid-akin-to-camp; Simona Sharoni profile, Canary Mission (website), https://canarymission.org/professor/Simona_Sharoni.

20. Dave Boyer, "Trump to Hold Event with Kristan Hawkins for Free Speech on College Campuses, Sign Executive Order," *Washington Times*, March 18, 2019, https://www.washingtontimes.com/news/2019/mar/18/trump-hold-event-free-speech-college-campuses/.

21. "StandWithUs Campus," StandWithUs (website), www.standwithus.com/campus/college/.

22. Amir Tibon, "Anti-Defamation League Supports Controversial Anti-BDS Bill," *Haaretz*, August 10, 2017, www.haaretz.com/us-news/adl-supports-controversial-anti-bds-bill-act-won-t-limit-free-speech-1.5441786.

23. Jonathan Greenblatt, "When Hate Goes Mainstream," *New York Times*, October 28, 2018, www.nytimes.com/2018/10/28/opinion/synagogue-shooting-pittsburgh-anti-defamation-league.html.

24. Report on Anti-Israel Activity on Campus, 2014–2015, Anti-Defamation League, www.adl.org/news/article/anti-israel-activity-on-campus-2014-2015-trends-and-projections?referrer=https%3A//www.google.com/#.WGqR27bytZ0.

25. Josh Nathan-Kazis, "Revealed: Canary Mission Blacklist Is Secretly Bankrolled by Major Jewish Federation," *Jewish Daily Forward*, October 3, 2018, https://forward.com/news/national/411355/revealed-canary-mission-blacklist-is-secretly-bankrolled-by-major-jewish/.

26. Josh Nathan-Kazis, "Canary Mission's Threat Grows, from U.S. Campuses to the Israeli Border," *Jewish Daily Forward*, August 3, 2018, https://forward.com/news/national/407279/canary-missions-threat-grows-from-us-campuses-to-the-israeli-border/.

27. Nathan Guttman, "StandWithUs Draws Line on Israel," *Jewish Daily Forward*, November 27, 2011, http://forward.com/news/146821/standwithus-draws-line-on-israel/; Bazz, "StandWithUs to Take Cash"; Eli Clifton, "StandWithUs Money Trail Reveals Neocon Funders," *Electronic Intifada*, October 22, 2009, https://electronicintifada.net/content/standwithus-money-trail-reveals-neocon-funders/8503.

28. Whitney Webb, "Leaked Documentary Shows Israel Lobby Used Fake Sexual Assault Claims Against BDS Activists," Mint Press News, November 7, 2018, www.mintpressnews.com/leaked-documentary-shows-israel-lobby-used-fake-sexual-assault-claims-against-bds-activists/251605.

29. Bill Mullen, Heike Schotten, and Dabid Palumbo-Liu, "More Legal Warfare: How Critics of Israel Are Being Subjected to Aggressive Lawsuits," *Truthout*, December 18, 2017, https://truthout.org/articles/more-legal-warfare-how-critics-of-israel-are-being-subjected-to-aggressive-lawsuits/.

30. "The Palestine Exception to Free Speech," Palestine Legal report, September 2015, http://palestinelegal.org/the-palestine-exception/#chilling.

31. Josh Nathan-Kazis, "Jewish Agency Plans $300M-a-Year Push for Israel," *Jewish Daily Forward*, August 15, 2013, https://forward.com/news/israel/182354/jewish-agency-plans-300m-a-year-push-for-israel/?p=all&p=all.

32. "The Delegitimization Challenge: Creating a Firewall," Reut Institute, February 10, 2010, http://reut-institute.org/Publication.aspx?PublicationId=3769.

33. Doron Peskin, "Israel Commits $25 Million to New Anti-BDS Task Force, but What Exactly Will They Do?" *Al-Monitor*, December 23, 2015, www.al-monitor.com/pulse/originals/2015/12/boycott-bds-movement-israel-government-office-gilad-erdan.html.

34. Yossi Melman, "Defamation, Harassment and Threats: The Danger of 'Special Operations' Against BDS," *Maariv*, September 4, 2016 (translated from Hebrew), www.maariv.co.il/landedpages/printarticle.aspx?id=555835.

35. Celine Ryan, "Berkeley Students Teach Peers about 'Whiteness,' 'Decolonizing,'" Campus Reform (website), August 28, 2017, https://www.campusreform.org/?ID=11253.

36. "A New Course at Berkeley University Offers Ways to Expel Jews from Israel," News 13, September 11, 2016 (translated from Hebrew), http://news.nana10.co.il/Article/?ArticleID=1209136.

37. AMCHA and other organizations to SFSU President Leslie Wong, May 27, 2014, www.amchainitiative.org/amcha-write-sfsu-president-leslie-wong-regarding-sfsu-professor-of-ethnic-studies-rabab-abdulhadi-egregious-misuse-of-university-and-taxpayer-funds/.

38. Alex Emmons, "Senate Responds to Trump-Inspired Anti-Semitism by Targeting Students Who Criticize Israel," *The Intercept*, December 2, 2016, https://theintercept.com/2016/12/02/senate-responds-to-post-trump-anti-semitism-by-targeting-students-who-criticize-israel/.

39. "Anti-Palestinian Legislation," Palestine Legal, https://palestinelegal.org/righttoboycott/.

40. Google Web Search Trends, January 1, 2018, to December 31, 2018, https://trends.google.com/trends/explore?date=2018-01-01%202019-01-01&geo=US&q=American%20Civil%20Liberties%20Union,Foundation%20for%20individual%20rights%20in%20education; Foundation for Individual Rights in Education, 990 IRS return (2016), https://d28htnjz2elwuj.cloudfront.net/wp-content/uploads/2017/11/02133228/2016-17-form-990.pdf.

41. Andy Kroll, "Exposed: The Dark-Money ATM of the Conservative Movement," *Mother Jones*, February 5, 2013, www.motherjones.com/politics/2013/02/donors-trust-donor-capital-fund-dark-money-koch-bradley-devos.

42. "Title IX," Foundation for Individual Rights in Education, July 13, 2018, www.thefire.org/issues/title-ix/.

43. Jim Sleeper, "What the Campus 'Free Speech' Crusade Won't Say," *Alternet*, September 4, 2016, www.alternet.org/education/what-campus-free-speech-crusade-wont-say-0.

44. See, for example, Alan Charles Kors and Harvey A. Silverglate, *The Shadow University: The Betrayal of Liberty on America's Campuses* (New York: Free Press, 1998).

45. "Alan Charles Kors on Campus Speech Codes, Libertarianism, and the Case for the Humanities," *Reason*, September 11, 2012, at www.youtube.com/watch?v=jjPYjvOnPx4.

46. Blaine Harden, "In Virginia, Young Conservatives Learn How to Develop and Use Their Political Voices," *New York Times*, June 11, 2001, www.nytimes.com/2001/06/11/us/virginia-young-conservatives-learn-develop-use-their-political-voices.html.

47. Leadership Institute profile, Conservative Transparency database, http://conservativetransparency.org/recipient/leadership-institute/.

48. Jennifer Kabbany, "No-Whites-Allowed 'Day of Absence' Lives on Despite Last Year's Uproar at Evergreen State College, *The College Fix*, May 16, 2018, www.thecollegefix.com/no-whites-allowed-day-of-absence-lives-on-despite-last-years-uproar-at-evergreen-state-college/.

49. Paul Fain and Rick Seltzer, "Family Ties," *Inside Higher Ed*, February 7, 2017, www.insidehighered.com/news/2017/02/07/betsy-devoss-connection-college-fix-conservative-higher-education-news-site.

50. "About ISI," Intercollegiate Studies Institute (website), https://isi.org/about-us/.

51. Michael Vasquez, "Leaked Memo from Conservative Group Cautions Students to Stay Away from Turning Point USA," *Chronicle of Higher Education*, June 15, 2018, www.chronicle.com/article/Leaked-Memo-From-Conservative/243688.

52. Nick Roll, "Leaked Documents, Audio: Conservaive Turning Point USA Quietly Funding Student Government Campaigns Across the U.S.," *The Lantern*, February 28, 2017, www.thelantern.com/2017/02/leaked-documents-audio-conservative-turning-point-usa-quietly-funding-student-government-campaigns-across-us/.

53. Turning Point USA, Facebook video, August 5, 2017, https://www.facebook.com/turningpointusa/videos/trigger-warning-charlie-kirk-destroys-safe-spaces-anti-free-speech-culture-on-co/1383639458351433/; Tom McKay, "Tweets About Diapers Broke the Entire Conservative Youth Movement," Gizmodo, February 2, 2018, https://gizmodo.com/tweets-about-diapers-broke-the-entire-conservative-yout-1823345007.

54. Jane Mayer, "A Conservative Nonprofit That Seeks to Transform College Campuses Faces Allegations of Racial Bias and Illegal Campaign Activity," *The New Yorker*, December 21, 2017, www.newyorker.com/news/news-desk/a-conservative -nonprofit-that-seeks-to-transform-college-campuses-faces-allegations-of-racial -bias-and-illegal-campaign-activity#brochure.

55. Amy Binder, "There's a Well-Funded Campus Industry Behind the Ann Coulter Incident," *Washington Post*, May 1, 2017, www.washingtonpost.com/amphtml /news/monkey-cage/wp/2017/05/01/theres-a-well-funded-campus-outrage-industry -behind-the-ann-coulter-incident/.

56. David Brooks, "Understanding Student Mobbists," *New York Times*, March 8, 2018, www.nytimes.com/2018/03/08/opinion/student-mobs.html.

57. Mari Uyehara, "The Free Speech Grifters," *GQ*, March 19, 2018, www.gq.com /story/free-speech-grifting.

58. Clio Chang, "Right Wing Donors Are the Ones Threatening Campus Free Speech, You Idiots," Splinter News, March 9, 2018, https://splinternews.com /right-wing-donors-are-the-ones-threatening-campus-free-1823651572.

59. Joseph Bernstein, "Alt-White: How the Breitbart Machine Laundered Racist Hate," *BuzzFeed News*, October 5, 2017, www.buzzfeednews.com/article/joseph bernstein/heres-how-breitbart-and-milo-smuggled-white-nationalism#.inq1rVA0D.

60. Douglas Fisher, "'Dark Money' Funds Climate Change Denial Effort," *Scientific American*, December 23, 2013, https://www.scientificamerican.com/article/dark -money-funds-climate-change-denial-effort/.

61. Christopher Mele, "Professor Watchlist Is Seen as Threat to Academic Freedom," *New York Times*, November 28, 2016, www.nytimes.com/2016/11/28/us /professor-watchlist-is-seen-as-threat-to-academic-freedom.html.

62. Turning Point USA homepage, https://www.tpusa.com/.

63. Daniel Schulman, "Charles Koch's Brain," *Politico*, September/October 2014, www.politico.com/magazine/politico50/2014/charles-kochs-brain.html# .W-yXUXpKjOR.

64. Rich Fink, "The Structure of Social Change," *Liberty Guide*, October 18, 2012, at https://ia601304.us.archive.org/10/items/TheStructureOfSocialChangeLiberty GuideRichardFinkKoch/The%20Structure%20of%20Social%20Change%20_ %20Liberty%20Guide%20_%20Richard%20Fink%20_%20Koch.pdf.

65. Jane Mayer, *Dark Money: The Hidden History of the Billionaires Behind the Rise of the Radical Right* (New York: Anchor Books, 2017) 68–69.

66. Mayer, 97.

67. Mayer, 99.

68. Mayer, 106.

69. Beth Saulnier, "Getting It Straight," *Cornell Alumni Magazine*, March/April 2009, http://cornellalumnimagazine.com/getting-it-straight/.

70. Jane Mayer, "How Right-Wing Billionaires Infiltrated Higher Education," *Chronicle Review*, February 12, 2016, www.chronicle.com/article/How-Right -Wing-Billionaires/235286.

71. Mayer, *Dark Money*, 124–25.

72. Mayer, 126–28.

73. Mayer, 182–84.

74. Mayer, 286.

75. Matthew Barakat, "Documents Show Ties Between University, Conservative Donors," Associated Press, April 30, 2018, https://apnews.com/0c87e4318bcc4eb9b8e69f9f54c7b889.

76. James Paterson, "Nearly All States Slashed College Funding Over the Last Decade," *Education Dive*, October 5, 2018, www.educationdive.com/news/nearly-all-states-slashed-college-funding-over-last-decade/538941/.

77. Michael Harriot, "Millions of Students Are Quietly Being Taught the Koch Brothers' Whitewashed Version of Black History," *The Root*, March 14, 2018, www.theroot.com/millions-of-students-are-quietly-being-taught-the-koch-1823742091

78. "UnKoch My Campus," Essential Information report, www.unkochmycampus.org/los-ch5-part-2-campus-free-speech; Jim Manley, "Campus Free Speech, a Legislative Proposal," Goldwater Institute, January 30, 2017, https://goldwaterinstitute.org/article/campus-free-speech-a-legislative-proposal/; Fernanda Zamudio-Suaréz, "Wisconsin Regents Approve a 3-Strikes Policy to Deal With Students Who Disrupt Speakers," *Chronicle of Higher Education*, October 6, 2017, www.chronicle.com/blogs/ticker/u-of-wisconsin-regents-approve-a-3-strikes-policy-to-deal-with-students-who-disrupt-speakers/120499.

79. "Overview," Speech First (website), https://speechfirst.org/about/.

80. Interview with Noam Chomsky, undated, at www.youtube.com/watch?v=3MkjtXylEQE.

81. Oxfam International, "Reward Work, Not Wealth" report, January 2018, 10, www-cdn.oxfam.org/s3fs-public/file_attachments/bp-reward-work-not-wealth-220118-en.pdf.

## Chapter 7: Speech and the Streets

1. Katherine Casey-Sawicki, "Seattle WTO Protests of 1999," Encyclopedia Britannica, www.britannica.com/event/Seattle-WTO-protests-of-1999.

2. Keith Collins and Kevin Roose, "Tracing a Meme from the Internet's Fringe to a Republican Slogan," *New York Times*, November 4, 2018, www.nytimes.com/interactive/2018/11/04/technology/jobs-not-mobs.html.

3. John Bowden, "Trump Rebukes Holder, Clinton with 'Jobs not Mobs' Refrain," *The Hill*, October 19, 2018, https://thehill.com/homenews/administration/412316-trump-rebukes-holder-clinton-with-jobs-not-mobs-refrain.

4. Peter Hermann, "Meetings of Acivists Planning to Disrupt Inauguration Were Infiltrated by Conservative Group," *Washington Post*, January 25, 2017, www.washingtonpost.com/local/public-safety/meetings-of-activists-planning-to-disrupt-inauguration-were-infiltrated-by-conservative-media-group/2017/01/24/b22128fe-e19a-11e6-ba11-63c4b4fb5a63_story.html?noredirect=on&utm_term=.4cfc299dee85.

5. *USA v. Matthew Hessler, et al.*, Superior Court for the District of Columbia, June 4, 2018, at https://thinkprogress.org/wp-content/uploads/2018/05/reply-and-mot-for-add-2.pdf.

6. Natasha Lennard, "How the Government Is Turning Protesters into Felons," *Esquire*, April 12, 2017, www.esquire.com/news-politics/a54391/how-the-government-is-turning-protesters-into-felons/?visibilityoverride.

7. "Rioting or Inciting to Riot," Code of the District of Columbia, 22-1322, at https://code.dccouncil.us/dc/council/code/sections/22-1322.html.

8. Kelly Weill, "Feds Use Right-Wing Militia's Video to Prosecute Trump Protesters," *Daily Beast*, October 11, 2017, www.thedailybeast.com/feds-use-right-wing -militias-video-to-prosecute-trump-protesters?source=twitter&via=desktop.

9. "Growing Connections Between the Far-Right and J20 Prosecution," It's Going Down, December 13, 2017, https://itsgoingdown.org/growing-connections -far-right-j20-prosecution/.

10. Jim Naureckas, "J20 Judge: Informing Public May Be Criminal Conspiracy," Fairness and Accuracy in Reporting, December 16, 2017, https://fair.org /home/judge-tells-jury-informing-public-may-be-criminal-conspiracy/?utm_campaign =shareaholic&utm_medium=twitter&utm_source=socialnetwork.

11. Defend J20 Resistance, "Federal Prosecutor in First Inauguration Day Trial Tries to Use Alt-Right Video as Evidence of Conspiracy," press release, November 30, 2017, http://defendj20resistance.org/2017/11/30/Federal-Prosecutor-Uses-Alt-Right -Video-As-Evidence-of-Conspiracy.html. This website has since been taken down.

12. Alan Pyke, "Judge: No, Wearing All Black Isn't 'Inciting Riot,'" Think Progress, December 14, 2017, https://thinkprogress.org/judge-strikes-felony-charge-j20 -bc4904dcc9d7/.

13. "US Drops Charges Against All J20 Anti-Trump Defendants," Al Jazeera, July 7, 2018, www.aljazeera.com/news/2018/07/drops-charges-j20-anti-trump-defendants -180707081836772.html.

14. Keith Alexander, "Inauguration Day Rioter Is Sentenced to Four Months in Jail," *Washington Post*, July 8, 2017, www.washingtonpost.com/local/public-safety /rioter-in-jan-20-inauguration-protests-sentenced-to-four-months-in-jail-for-rioting -assault-on-police-officer/2017/07/07/8c5b368c-6336-11e7-a4f7-af34fc1d9d39_story .html?utm_term=.5c877b3df3ea.

15. Ellen Bresler Rockmore, "How Texas Teaches History," *New York Times*, October 21, 2015, www.nytimes.com/2015/10/22/opinion/how-texas-teaches-history.html.

16. Harry Truman to Dean Acheson, March 31, 1950, Gilder Lehrman Collection, www.gilderlehrman.org/content/harry-s-truman-responds-mccarthy-1950.

17. Maggie Rosen, "A Feminist Perspective on the History of Women as Witches," *Dissenting Voices* 6, no. 1 (September 2017), https://digitalcommons.brockport.edu/cgi /viewcontent.cgi?article=1062&context=dissentingvoices.

18. Alex Kingsbury, "How the Red Scare Destroyed a Small-Town Teacher," *Boston Globe*, February 4, 2016, www.bostonglobe.com/magazine/2016/02/04/how-red-scare -destroyed-small-town-teacher/OyzaMTrsxMsx54liP1YX9I/story.html.

19. Ellen Schrecker, *Many Are the Crimes: McCarthyism in America* (New York: Little, Brown, 1998), 15.

20. Schrecker, XIII.

21. Schrecker, 369.

22. Schrecker, 13.

23. "Spanish Civil War," The Abraham Lincoln Brigade Archives, www.alba-valb .org/history/spanish-civil-war.

24. Schrecker, 47–48.

25. Schrecker, 62–63.

26. Schrecker, 63.

27. Schrecker, 66.

28. Associated Press, "Anti-Communist Oaths Persist Despite Court Ruling," *USA Today*, February 23, 2013, www.usatoday.com/story/news/nation/2013/02/23/anti-communist-oaths-persist-despite-court-rulings/1940865/.

29. Schrecker, 67.

30. Schrecker, 68.

31. Schrecker, 90–92.

32. Alden Whitman, "Earl Browder, Ex-Communist Leader, Dies at 82," *New York Times*, June 28, 1973, www.nytimes.com/1973/06/28/archives/earl-browder-excommunist-leader-dies-at-82-doctrine-invalidated.html.

33. Schrecker, 106.

34. Schrecker, 107.

35. Michael Steven Smith, "About the Smith Act Trials," in *Encyclopedia of the American Left*, Mari Jo Buhle, Paul Buhle, Dan Georgakas, eds. (New York: Oxford University Press, 1998); *Dennis v. United States*, 341 US 494 (1951), https://supreme.justia.com/cases/federal/us/341/494/.

36. Gilbert King, "What Paul Robeson Said," *Smithsonian Magazine* online, September 13, 2011, www.smithsonianmag.com/history/what-paul-robeson-said-77742433/.

37. Lee Sustar, "McCarthyism and the Civil Rights Movement," *Socialist Worker*, August 17, 2012, https://socialistworker.org/2012/08/17/mccarthyism-and-civil-rights.

38. Schrecker, *Many Are the Crimes*, 190.

39. Josh Jones, "The Red Menace: A Striking Gallery of Anti-Communist Posters, Ads, Comic Books, Magazines and Films, Open Culture, November 18, 2014, www.openculture.com/2014/11/the-red-menace-a-striking-gallery-of-anti-communist-propaganda.html.

40. Schrecker, *Many Are the Crimes*, 154.

41. Schrecker, 241.

42. Schrecker, 280.

43. Lorraine Boissoneault, "The Senator Who Stood Up to Joseph McCarthy When No One Else Would," *Smithsonian Magazine* online, September 13, 2018, www.smithsonianmag.com/history/senator-who-stood-joseph-mccarthy-when-no-one-else-would-180970279/.

## Chapter 8: Whose Speech Matters?

1. Alice George, "The 1968 Kerner Commission Got It Right, But Nobody Listened," *Smithsonian Magazine* online, March 1, 2018, www.smithsonianmag.com/smithsonian-institution/1968-kerner-commission-got-it-right-nobody-listened-180968318/.

2. Emily Chertoff, "Occupy Wounded Knee: A 71-Day Siege and a Forgotten Civil Rights Movement," *The Atlantic* online, October 23, 2012, www.theatlantic.com/national/archive/2012/10/occupy-wounded-knee-a-71-day-siege-and-a-forgotten-civil-rights-movement/263998/.

3. Georgianne Nienaber, "Sacred Burial Grounds Sold to Dakota Access Pipeline," *Huffington Post*, September 23, 2016, www.huffingtonpost.com/georgianne-nienaber/sacred-burial-grounds-sol_b_12152790.html.

4. "Guards Accused of Unleashing Dogs, Pepper-Spraying Oil Pipeline Protesters," CBS News, September 5, 2016, www.cbsnews.com/news/dakota-access -pipeline-protest-turns-violent-in-north-dakota/.

5. Rafi Schwartz, "Shocking Footage Shows Police Hitting #NoDAPL Protesters with Water Cannons in Freezing Weather," Splinter News, November 21, 2016, https:// splinternews.com/shocking-footage-shows-police-hitting-nodapl-protester-17938 63893#_ga=2.190576553.323724040.1544208153-627112021.1544208152.

6. Alleen Brown, Will Parrish, and Alice Speri, "Police Used Private Security Aircraft for Surveillance in Standing Rock No-Fly Zone," The Intercept, September 29, 2017, https://theintercept.com/2017/09/29/standing-rock-dakota-access-pipeline -dapl-no-fly-zone-drones-tigerswan/.

7. Will Parrish, "An Activist Stands Accused of Firing a Gun at Standing Rock. It Belonged to Her Lover—An FBI Informant," The Intercept, December 11, 2017, https://theintercept.com/2017/12/11/standing-rock-dakota-access-pipeline -fbi-informant-red-fawn-fallis/.

8. Parrish, "An Activist Stands Accused."

9. Will Parrish, "The Federal Government Is Trying to Imprison These Six Water Protectors," Shadowproof, May 18, 2017, https://shadowproof.com/2017/05 /18/federal-government-trying-imprison-six-water-protectors/.

10. US Department of Homeland Security, Field Analysis Report, May 2, 2017, at https://theintercept.com/document/2017/12/11/may-2017-field-analysis-report/.

11. Antonia Juhasz, "Paramilitary Security Tracked and Targeted DAPL Opponents as 'Jihadists,' Docs Show," Grist, June 1, 2017, https://grist.org/justice/para military-security-tracked-and-targeted-nodapl-activists-as-jihadists-docs-show/; Alleen Brown, Will Parrish, and Alice Speri, "Dakota Access Pipeline Company Paid Mercenaries to Build Conspiracy Lawsuit Against Environmentalists," The Intercept, November 15, 2017, https://theintercept.com/2017/11/15/dakota-access-pipeline-dapl -tigerswan-energy-transfer-partners-rico-lawsuit/; Earth Rights, "Court Dismisses Frivolous and 'Dangerously Broad' Lawsuit Against NGO BankTrack for Opposing Dakota Access Pipeline," press release, July 25, 2018, https://earthrights.org/media /court-dismisses-lawsuit-against-banktrack/.

12. Julia Carrie Wong, "Police Remove Last Standing Rock Protesters in Military-Style Takeover," Guardian, February 23, 2017, www.theguardian.com/us-news/2017 /feb/23/dakota-access-pipeline-camp-cleared-standing-rock.

13. Steve Horn, "Poison PR Campaign Has Biased Jury Pool, Say Dakota Access Protester's Lawyers," Desmog (blog), August 24, 2017, www.desmogblog.com/2017/08/24 /dakota-access-red-fawn-fallis-biased-jury-pool-pr-campaign.

14. Clara Chaisson, "A Statue at Standing Rock Sends a Powerful Message of Resistance," OnEarth (blog), Natural Resources Defense Council, November 23, 2016, www .nrdc.org/onearth/statue-standing-rock-sends-powerful-message-resistance.

15. Ted Gregory, "The Black Panther Raid and the Death of Fred Hampton," Chicago Tribune, December 19, 2007, www.chicagotribune.com/news/nationworld/politics/ chi-chicagodays-pantherraid-story-story.html.

16. "Community Survival Programs," online content for A Huey P. Newton Story (PBS, 2002), www.pbs.org/hueypnewton/actions/actions_survival.html.

17. Brian Glick, War at Home (Cambridge, MA: South End Press, 1989), 78.

18. Jeff Gottlieb and Jeff Cohen, "Was Fred Hampton Executed?" *The Nation*, December 25, 1976, www.thenation.com/article/was-fred-hampton-executed/.

19. A. Peter Bailey, "Dr. King Targeted by J. Edgar Hoover," *Pittsburgh Courier*, April 4, 2018, https://newpittsburghcourieronline.com/2018/04/04/dr-king-targeted-by-j-edgar-hoovers-fbi/.

20. Margaret Talbot, "Opened Files," *The New Yorker*, January 20, 2014, www.newyorker.com/magazine/2014/01/20/opened-files.

21. Paul Wolf, "COINTELPRO, FBI Counterintelligence, Covert Operations, Black Bag Jobs, Church Committee," Freedom Archives, September 3, 2001, 306, www.freedomarchives.org/Documents/Finder/Black%20Liberation%20Disk/Black%20Power!/SugahData/Government/COINTELPRO.S.pdf.

22. Robert Justin Goldstein, *Political Repression in Modern America from 1870 to 1976* (Chicago: University of Illinois Press, 2001), 407.

23. Wolf, "COINTELPRO," 306–07.

24. "Student Nonviolent Coordinating Committee (SNCC)," King Encyclopedia entry, Martin Luther King, Jr. Research and Education Institute, Stanford University, https://kinginstitute.stanford.edu/encyclopedia/student-nonviolent-coordinating-committee-sncc.

25. Branko Marcetic, "The FBI's Secret War," *Jacobin*, August 2016, www.jacobinmag.com/2016/08/fbi-cointelpro-new-left-panthers-muslim-surveillance; Editorial, "FBI's Deadly Games," *New York Times*, May 12, 1976, www.nytimes.com/1976/05/12/archives/fbis-deadly-games.html; Ward Churchill, *Disrupt, Discredit and Destroy* (New York: Routledge, 2010), 5.

26. Duncan Campbell, "How the FBI Used a Gossip Columnist to Smear a Movie Star," *Guardian*, April 22, 2002, www.theguardian.com/media/2002/apr/22/mondaymediasection.filmnews.

27. Marcetic, "Secret War."

28. Beverly Gage, "What an Uncensored Letter to MLK Reveals," *New York Times*, November 11, 2014, www.nytimes.com/2014/11/16/magazine/what-an-uncensored-letter-to-mlk-reveals.html; Michael Eric Dyson, *I May Not Get There With You: The True Martin Luther King Jr. Story* (New York: Free Press, 2000), 217.

29. Wolf, "COINTELPRO," 558.

30. Editorial, "Beating a Dead Horse," *Jacobin*, August 2016, www.jacobinmag.com/2016/08/fbi-cointelpro-communist-party/.

31. Elaine Brown, *A Taste of Power: A Black Woman's Story* (New York: Anchor Books, 1992), excerpted on Libcom, http://libcom.org/history/reflections-jean-seberg-black-panther-party-elaine-brown.

32. Marcetic, "Secret War"; Wolf, "COINTELPRO," 472, 547, 585.

33. "Findings on Martin Luther King, Jr. Assassination," National Archives report, 371, www.archives.gov/research/jfk/select-committee-report/part-2b.html#conclusion.

34. Nelson Blackstock, *Cointelpro: The FBI's Secret War on Political Freedom* (New York: Pathfinder Press), 121.

35. Zaheer Ali, "What Really Happened to Malcolm X?" CNN, February 17, 2015, https://edition.cnn.com/2015/02/17/opinion/ali-malcolm-x-assassination-anniversary/index.html.

36. Timothy Williams, "New Inquiry of Deaths on Reservation in the 1970s," *New York Times*, June 12, 2012, www.nytimes.com/2012/06/20/us/new-inquiry-of-deaths -on-reservation-in-the-1970s.html.

37. Blackstock, *Cointelpro*, 12.

38. "The Liberal Myth of Free Speech," It's Going Down, August 25, 2017, https:// itsgoingdown.org/liberal-myth-free-speech/.

39. Unmasking Antifa Act of 2018, H.R. 6054, 115th Congress, www.congress .gov/bill/115th-congress/house-bill/6054/text?format=txt; House Bill 4618, West Virginia Legislature, introduced February 13, 2018, www.wvlegislature.gov/Bill_ Status/bills_text.cfm?billdoc=hb4618%20intr.htm&yr=2018&sesstype=RS&i=4618; Simon Davis-Cohen and Sarah Lazare, "Law Enforcement Has Quietly Backed Anti-Protest Bills in at Least 8 States Since Trump's Election," *In These Times*, April 16, 2018, http://inthesetimes.com/features/police_anti-protest_laws_trump.html; "US Protest Law Tracker," International Center for Not-for-Profit Law, www.icnl.org/usprotest lawtracker/?location=&status=enacted&issue=&date=&type=legislative; "Texas Backs School that Expelled Girl Over Pledge of Allegiance," BBC News, September 26, 2018, www.bbc.com/news/world-us-canada-45656149; Meagan Flynn, "Georgia Police Invoke Law Made for KKK to Arrest Anti-Racism Protesters," *Washington Post*, April 23, 2018, www.washingtonpost.com/news/morning-mix/wp/2018/04/23/georgia -police-invoke-anti-mask-law-made-for-kkk-to-arrest-racism-protesters/?nore direct=on&utm_term=.9f0db2d92660; Ed Pilkington, "Crystal Mason Begins Prison Sentence in Texas for Crime of Voting," *Guardian*, September 28, 2018, www.theguardian .com/us-news/2018/sep/28/crystal-mason-begins-prison-sentence-in-texas-for-of -voting; Martin de Bourmont, "Is a Court Case in Texas the First Prosecution of a 'Black Identity Extremist'?" *Foreign Policy*, January 30, 2018, https://foreignpolicy.com/2018 /01/30/is-a-court-case-in-texas-the-first-prosecution-of-a-black-identity-extremist/#.

40. Cora Currier, "FBI Pressed Detained Anti-ICE Activist for Information on Protests, Offering Immigration Help," *The Intercept*, August 7, 2018, https://theintercept .com/2018/08/07/fbi-pressed-detained-anti-ice-activist-for-information-on-protests -offering-immigration-help/.

## Chapter 9: Free Speech in the Panopticon

1. Dave Maass, "Facebook Warns Memphis Police: No More Fake 'Bob Smith' Accounts," Electronic Frontier Foundation, September 24, 2018, www.eff.org/deep links/2018/09/facebook-warns-memphis-police-no-more-fake-bob-smith-accounts.

2. Maya Smith, "Police Official Says Bob Smith Account Friended Over 200 Activists," *Memphis Flyer*, August 21, 2018, www.memphisflyer.com/NewsBlog/archives/2018/08/20 /police-official-says-bob-smith-account-friended-over-200-activists.

3. George Joseph and Murtaza Hussain, "FBI Tracked an Activist Involved with Black Lives Matter as They Travelled Across the U.S., Documents Show," *The Intercept*, March 19, 2018, https://theintercept.com/2018/03/19/black-lives-matter-fbi-surveillance /; Mark Morales and Laura Ly, "Released NYPD Emails Show Extensive Surveillance of Black Lives Matter Protesters," CNN, January 18, 2019, www.cnn.com/2019/01/18/us /nypd-black-lives-matter-surveillance/index.html.

4. Tod Seelie, "Inside an Abandoned Panopticon Prison in Cuba," Atlas Obscura, June 19, 2017, www.atlasobscura.com/articles/panopticon-prison-cuba.

5. Jeremy Bentham, *The Panopticon Writings* (London: Verso, 1995) 29–95, at www.ics.uci.edu/~djp3/classes/2012_01_INF241/papers/PANOPTICON.pdf.

6. David Alm, "Somebody's Watching You: Ai Weiwei's New York Installation Explores Surveillance in 2017," *Forbes*, June 15, 2017, www.forbes.com/sites/davidalm/2017/06/15/somebodys-watching-you-ai-weiweis-new-york-installation-explores-surveillance-in-2017/#6428b4ea4d0a; Timothy Williams, "Can 30,000 Cameras Help Solve Chicago's Crime Problem?" *New York Times*, May 26, 2018, www.nytimes.com/2018/05/26/us/chicago-police-surveillance.html; Ian Evans, "London No Safer for All Its CCTV Cameras," ABC News, February 25, 2012, https://abcnews.go.com/International/report-london-safer-cctv-cameras/story?id=15776976; P. E. Moskowitz, "This Is What It Will Be Like to Protest in 2020, When the State Is Watching Your Every Move," *Splinter News*, October 27, 2016, https://splinternews.com/this-is-what-it-will-be-like-to-protest-in-2020-when-t-1793863216.

7. "Face Recognition Technology," ACLU (website), www.aclu.org/issues/privacy-technology/surveillance-technologies/face-recognition-technology.

8. Micah Sifry, "Did Facebook Bring Down Mubarak?" CNN, February 11, 2011, www.cnn.com/2011/OPINION/02/11/sifry.egypt.technology/index.html.

9. Jared Keller, "Evaluating Iran's Twitter Revolution," *The Atlantic*, June 18, 2010, www.theatlantic.com/technology/archive/2010/06/evaluating-irans-twitter-revolution/58337/.

10. David Blumenthal and William Galeota, "Band Invades, Violently Disrupts Center for International Affairs," *Harvard Crimson*, September 26, 1969, www.thecrimson.com/article/1969/9/26/band-invades-violently-disrupts-center-for/.

11. Yasha Levine, *Surveillance Valley: The Secret Military History of the Internet* (New York: PublicAffairs, 2018), 62–63.

12. Levine, 22.

13. Levine, 27.

14. Levine, 30.

15. Levine, 44.

16. Levine, 44–46.

17. Levine, 71.

18. Noam Chomsky, "Chomsky on War Research at MIT," University College London, February 25, 2017, transcript at https://libcom.org/history/chomsky-war-research-mit.

19. Levine, *Surveillance Valley*, 86.

20. Levine, 128.

21. Levine, 129.

22. Levine, 110.

23. Levine, 136.

24. Levine, 143.

25. Levine, 147.

26. Matt Novak, "Google Was Originally Called BackRub," Gizmodo, July 15, 2014, https://gizmodo.com/the-evolution-of-googles-iconic-logo-1582297667/1605435217.

27. Daniel Kurtz-Phelan, "Big Fruit," *New York Times Sunday Book Review*, March 2, 2008, www.nytimes.com/2008/03/02/books/review/Kurtz-Phelan-t.html.

28. Nitasha Tiku, "Google's Diversity Stats Are Still Very Dismal," *Wired*, June 14, 2018, www.wired.com/story/googles-employee-diversity-numbers-havent-really-improved/.

29. Safiya Umoja Noble, *Algorithms of Oppression: How Search Engines Reinforce Racism* (New York: New York University Press, 2018), 2.

30. Sandra Harding, *Feminism and Methodology: Social Science Issues* (Bloomington, IN: Indiana University Press, 1987), 7.

31. David Levesley, "Why Princess Diana Is an Enduring Queer Icon," *them*, May 19, 2018, www.them.us/story/princess-diana-queer-icon.

32. "Google and Facebook Tighten Grip on U.S. Digital Ad Market," eMarketer (website), September 21, 2017, www.emarketer.com/Article/Google-Facebook-Tighten-Grip-on-US-Digital-Ad-Market/1016494.

33. Anthony Cuthbertson, "Who Controls the Internet? Facebook and Google Dominance Could Cause the 'Death of the Web,'" *Newsweek*, November 2, 2017, www.newsweek.com/facebook-google-internet-traffic-net-neutrality-monopoly-699286.

34. Levine, *Surveillance Valley*, 173.

35. Levine, 167.

36. Levine, 179; Natasha Singer, "How Google Took Over the Classroom," *New York Times*, May 13, 2017, www.nytimes.com/2017/05/13/technology/google-education-chromebooks-schools.html.

37. Levine, *Surveillance Valley*, 183.

38. David Post, "A Bit of Internet History, or How Two Members of Congress Helped Create a Trillion or So Dollars of Value," *Washington Post*, August 27, 2015, www.washingtonpost.com/news/volokh-conspiracy/wp/2015/08/27/a-bit-of-internet-history-or-how-two-members-of-congress-helped-create-a-trillion-or-so-dollars-of-value/?utm_term=.dcf6768d079e/.

39. Aja Romano, "A New Law Intended to Curb Sex Trafficking Threatens the Future of the Internet as We Know It," *Vox*, July 2, 2018, www.vox.com/culture/2018/4/13/17172762/fosta-sesta-backpage-230-internet-freedom.

40. Samantha Cole, "Pimps Are Preying on Sex Workers Pushed Off the Web Because of FOSTA-SESTA," Motherboard, April 30, 2018, https://motherboard.vice.com/en_us/article/bjpqvz/fosta-sesta-sex-work-and-trafficking.

41. Glenn Greenwald, "Facebook Says It Is Deleting Accounts at the Direction of the U.S. and Israeli Governments," *The Intercept*, December 30, 2017, https://theintercept.com/2017/12/30/facebook-says-it-is-deleting-accounts-at-the-direction-of-the-u-s-and-israeli-governments/.

42. Hannah Gais, Twitter post, November 8, 2018, https://twitter.com/hannahgais/status/1060417376930463744.

43. Justin Ling, "Eric Schmidt Says Google News Will 'Engineer' Russian Propaganda Out of the Feed," Motherboard, November 20, 2017, https://motherboard.vice.com/en_us/article/pa39vv/eric-schmidt-says-google-news-will-delist-rt-sputnik-russia-fake-news.

44. Russell Brandom, "Using the Internet Without the Amazon Cloud," *The*

*Verge*, July 28, 2018, www.theverge.com/2018/7/28/17622792/plugin-use-the-internet-without-the-amazon-cloud.

45. Russell Brandom, "Amazon Pitched Its Facial Recognition System to ICE," *The Verge*, October 23, 2018, www.theverge.com/2018/10/23/18013376/amazon-ice-facial-recognition-aws-rekognition.

## Conclusion: Toward a Smarter Definition of Free Speech

1. Martin Gilens and Benjamin Page, "Testing Theories of American Politics: Elites, Interest Groups, and Average Citizens," *Perspectives on Politics* 12, no. 3 (September 2014), www.cambridge.org/core/journals/perspectives-on-politics/article/testing-theories-of-american-politics-elites-interest-groups-and-average-citizens/62327F513959D0A304D4893B382B992B/core-reader.

2. Philip Bump, "By 2040, Two-Thirds of Americans Will be Represented by 30 Percent of the Senate," *Washington Post*, November 28, 2017, www.washingtonpost.com/news/politics/wp/2017/11/28/by-2040-two-thirds-of-americans-will-be-represented-by-30-percent-of-the-senate/?utm_term=.87cdddd831a0.

3. Alex Carey, *Taking the Risk Out of Democracy* (Chicago: University of Illinois Press, 1996), 18.

4. Carey, 80.

5. Carey, 81.

6. Carey, 83.

7. Kathryn Vasel, "Six in Ten Americans Don't Have $500 in Savings," CNN, January 12, 2017, https://money.cnn.com/2017/01/12/pf/americans-lack-of-savings/index.html.

# INDEX

**P. E. Moskowitz** is the author of *How to Kill a City* and a freelance journalist who has covered a wide variety of issues, from environmental disasters to the vestiges of racist urban planning. A former staff writer for *Al Jazeera America*, they have written for the *Guardian*, the *New York Times*, NewYorker.com, *The New Republic*, *Wired*, *Slate*, *Buzzfeed*, *Splinter*, *VICE*, and many others. A graduate of Hampshire College and the CUNY Graduate School of Journalism, they live in New Orleans.